Lots of
Things will
hopefully remind
you of the Red River finns!!

enjoy!

Margaret Webster 9/17/09

A FUNNY THING HAPPENED ON THE WAY TO THE CEMETERY

BY MARGARET OLSON WEBSTER

A FUNNY THING HAPPENED ON THE WAY TO THE CEMETERY

BLUEPEARL BOOKS
10008 422 Street
Tamarack, Minnesota, 55707

FUNNY THING HAPPENED ON THE WAY TO THE CEMETERY
by Margaret Olson Webster

Printed and bound in the United States of America
by Bang Printing, Brainerd, Minnesota.
Book layout and design
by Kollath Graphic Design, Duluth, Minnesota

ISBN

Cover: Blue Pearl, or Swedish Granite is a favored stone in Lakeside Cemetery, notwithstanding the fact that it now is imported from Norway. The rose design is also very commonly used in Lakeside, and other local cemeteries, from the early nineteen-hundreds until today. Flat, low stones are favored by cemetery boards for ease in mowing around them.

TABLE OF CONTENTS

Acknowledgments

THE DANCE OF LIFE: Experiences in life and death are as universal and timeless as they are unique and new.

*H*usband Dan, your patience in seeing manuscript pages scattered in our living area, a preoccupied wife who quite often bounces ideas, often in paragraph form, is so much appreciated. Son Paul, you have taught me so much, have spent so much time reading and discussing passages and helping, as only a top notch English instructor could. Kaija, your insight into the psyche of your generation, and your pertinent comments are so on target. I couldn't have written this book without your gentle encouragement to update my equipment. Perry, what a project you were willing to take on—scanning photos employed both a great amount of time and your great talent. Andrew, speaking of talent, thank you for employing your artistic excellence as a photographer for the project. I knew I was blessed with an exceptional family, but you have certainly all reconfirmed that fact. Thank you.

Karin, Bryan McGinnis, Pastor Bob Kleinke, Esther Sanfelippo—thank you for your input early on. Your encouragement kept me thinking that this was a possible project.

Jasper Beseman, Toini Aho, Sulo and Delores Walli, and many other friends and relatives, you have given precious life stories and experiences. Your willingness to share memories with me has been invaluable. There would not have been a book without you.

Thank you, Karen and Bob Aikins from Northland funeral home, for your technical help on the cover and other things. Kelly Studio, thank you for use of photos.

Rick Kollath, thank you and your staff, especially Bonnie Wenborg, for believing in the project, professionally whipping the manuscript into shape.

I am humbled as I think of all of you, who are the essence of this book. "Thank you" seems inadequate, but know that appreciation is deeply felt.

Margaret Webster
Tamarack, Minnesota

Foreword

Death registered!

A Funny Thing Happened on the Way to the Cemetery

This book title might seem incongruous to some—what's "funny" about a cemetery? In answer I remember a waggish saying of long ago: "Don't take life too seriously, you'll never get out of it alive anyway!" I do not intend to be flip about losing the company of a dear friend or relative. Death is a profound and life altering experience... the closer one is to it, the more intense the impact on a person. I have, however, faith that human experience on this earth is a preparation for another experience which will be eternally joyful, peaceful, and wonderful beyond our current understanding. The relationship and transition between life and death are often difficult for us to perceive and traverse, yet so interrelated they are impossible to separate.

When my children were going through the throes of dealing with playground bullies, bad hair days, unkind contemporaries, and other difficult situations, I often advised them that humor is a sound way to defuse some problems. I have observed this truth employed by many people, and have used it to good advantage myself. When our dear mother died, we siblings gathered, and in a very good and natural way had a cathartic session of remembering the wonderfully humorous, crazy experiences we had shared as a family. We remembered some touching and challenging times too, but the humor got us through the very difficult time and left us feeling that life is indeed a balance that we are capable of maintaining.

But let us look at this "funny" word: FUNNY. The dictionary definition obviously mentions humor, but furthermore it mentions "strange coincidence," "strange to say," "puzzling" or "comic." FUNNY BONE: "Part of the humerus over which the sensitive ulnar nerve passes at the elbow. When knocked it causes an odd, rather painful, tingling sensation." I think this could describe the contents of this book. Life (and death) is a mixture of humorous, sensitive, odd, painful, exciting sensations, as are these collected words. Some of the most sensitive persons I know have the wonderful ability to see things with a good amount of humor, a quality which probably helps them to keep their sanity. My children for some odd reason refer to me as "the funny lady" and to our home farm as "the funny farm." I have no idea how far this will go; last week our daughter, Kaija, hooked us up on e-mail—giving us the address "Thefunnies@."

4367—7-31-37—10M

MINNESOTA DEPARTMENT OF HEALTH
DIVISION OF VITAL STATISTICS

DEATH RECORDS

Why the Living Need Accurate Records of the Dead

Human life is sacred. When a human being passes out from our life it is important that an immediate record be made of all the essential details of the event—an immediate record, because it is well established by years of experience that an accurate record in all cases can not or will not be made unless the law requires it to be made at once. Such a record should include the facts relating to the exact time and place of death, the full name, age, sex, color, civil condition, occupation, place of birth, and other details relating to the individual, and also, a very important requirement, a statement by the attending physician, or by the health officer or coroner, of cause of death. These facts may be of the greatest legal and social importance.

(1) Certificates of death, or certified copies are constantly required in courts and elsewhere to establish necessary facts;

(2) Pensions or life insurance may depend on proper evidence of the fact and of cause of death;

(3) Titles and rights to inheritance may be jeopardized by the failure of records;

(4) Deaths should be registered that public health agencies—National, State and Municipal—may know the cause of death and act promptly to prevent epidemics;

(5) Deaths should be registered promptly that the success or failure of all measures attempted in the prevention of disease may be accurately determined;

(6) Deaths should be registered that individual cities and localities may learn their own health conditions by comparison with the health conditions of other communities and determine thereby the wise course of public health activity;

(7) Deaths should be registered that homeseekers and immigrants may be guided in the selecting of safe and healthful homes.

3

Humor and fear are often played against or parallel with the other emotion, both in real life and in our dramatic or other art forms. A laugh often releases tension built from fear/tension. In visual art it is the use of light against dark, and so it is in life. If we see our experiences as only dark or light, we may have a problem getting a true picture of our existence. I have known persons who see life as a dark "thing" they must get through. Conversely some individuals seem to feel that if they ignore problems they will go away.

Son Andrew used fear— played against humor very successfully in his portrayal of Fagen in a play based on Charles Dickens' Oliver Twist. He was seventeen at the time, but entered the soul/spirit of the somewhat demented man and had the audience gasping and laughing at nearly the same moment. Death of a comparative innocent did occur in the play, but hope and humor prevented it from being a tragic saga. MUCH LIKE LIFE

The sudden death of hundreds of people on September eleventh, 2001 in the World Trade Center and the Pentagon caused commentators, humorists and social scientists to discuss the importance of humor in dealing with death in the United States. The other important factor became the importance of spirituality. These two major strains have been evident since the first draft of this manuscript.

"The source of all humor is not laughter—but sorrow."
—Mark Twain

CEMETERY is defined as a place to bury the dead, but also as a "sleeping place." I think of it as a forum, on either side of death. One could interpret the title of this book as an account of things that I experience until I rest in such a burying place, or that happen between my daily times of sleep. I also have made many trips over to the local cemetery to work there, and have shared trips there (both temporary and permanent) with many other people. I would say that the book is a mixture, a montage of all the above.

The material for the book has been collected over many years, unfortunately it is not possible for me to list all of the people who have contributed to this book. The most obvious are my husband Dan, children: Paul, Kaija, Perry, and Andrew. Some names have been changed, for obvious reasons, and some stories set in other locations. I hope my neighbors understand that this is a story about human nature in general, not an account of individuals living or dead, although all of the material here is inspired by real life. These words construct a painting, rather than a photograph.

LIFE IS STRANGER THAN FICTION

Then there is the question... "What do a forum and a cemetery have in common?"

Because live people in our community often stop to discuss important topics when they catch me in the cemetery, or persons lingered long for discussion after a funeral, I have no difficulty in accepting cemetery turf as a prime forum location for the living. Then, sometimes as I visualize the forum depicted in Wilder's OUR TOWN I can almost hear persons buried in this spot discussing many topics, as characters in that play did. Do we have good communication in this world or a next? Is it like the comedic forum in Gelbart and Shevelove's "A FUNNY THING HAPPENED ON THE WAY TO THE FORUM?" I can't answer, I can only ask.

Ghost Forums

1

The Dance of Life

THE MOON RISES FOREVER

A timeless quality of this photo addresses the interdependence of life—person to person, child to parent, humans to the universe. It is almost spiritual in it's serenity, yet sharp black and white contrasts introduce tension to the peaceful scene. The circle of adults and children represent the generationally cyclic nature of life, while light and shadow effect may indicate dark and light time experienced in a lifetime. The early part of the century was still a time when recreation wasn't found in the media or a faraway place, inspiration for life was found in connecting to each other and to the earth.

Why the cemetery?

"I've been at the cemetery again, checkin' things out," I said, in answer to daughter Kaija's phone question, "What's up?"

"Well then, I guess you've been talking' to people you haven't seen for a while!"

She's right…I've heard, do hear, many voices in the century old resting place. Voices of dear family members, friends, local legends. If not those no longer "here," then those very much alive who find my presence in the cemetery a good opportunity to tell a story, share a remembrance.

After years of work on location and research I became accustomed to "live ones" dropping by to ask about the work, or to make specific comments over specific graves:

"He was a gutsy son of a biscuit!"

"You could tell it was Kajander from a mile away, with that huge bushy red beard."

"Liniment was the drink for Bentti!"

"Isak (English: Isaac or Isaak) Walli was the first settler in the township."

"She lost two children and her young husband to summer complaint."

"He killed a bear, rode on it's back for a while first."

"She wore one large gold earing, he wore the other. They ate off of the same plate."

"Her husband wouldn't even buy her a spool of thread. No wonder she went crazy!"

"He was the best (horseman, woodsman, talker, heavy lifter, builder, farmer) around."

"She was the best (cook, gardener, dairy manager, school teacher, singer, healer) around."

"_____ did not get along with _____ at all!"

"They might have had an 'eye for each other'" (especially interesting if not a couple).

"Grandma came on the train when she moved here, followed tree slashes to the farm."

"Quiet work here, huh?" or "Nice quiet neighborhood."

"This is quite an undertaking."

"Bet you feel good, working above so many people?"

"Must be a great place—people are dying to get in!"

"Lose your heel, but not your soul!"

Another specialty was short stories:

"I remember when old Antti here first lost his wife. He was having so much trouble with his eyesight. He couldn't even see to read the creamery slip till one of his kids noticed that he was wearing his departed wife's glasses. They must

have buried her with his eye wear. Bet she's down there laughing yet!"

"Sukie had quite a time thawing the ground enough to dig those winter graves. He'd burn tires, coal, or anything he could get his hands on to thaw the ground enough to dig. Well, one time he got hold of a mattress to burn. It wasn't burning fast enough, so he tossed on some dynamite to get the job done. It sure was hard for people to stay serious at that funeral, with that cotton batting hanging all over the trees!"

Another time he was digging with a helper. They got tired, so he said to the other guy, "Let's go home, finish this tomorrow." Well then, he went back and dug it all out, propped up a big board somewhat level with the place where they had left off, spread a light layer of sand over that. When his helper came in the morning and jumped in to start digging again he came out in a big hurry! Never came to help dig a grave again. Never.

YA GOTTA LAUGH OR YOU'D CRY

Life is such a full menu, such a montage of experiences, emotions and enlightenments. I have come to believe the adage which speaks to the fact that life is to a degree, (more or less) what you make of it.

Once during an official learning experience, I took a

Board minutes, written in Finnish until 1963, might seem taciturn, cryptic to readers of the present time, however, they do outline the business of Lakeside. Sons and grandsons of early board members relive the serious occasion of a Board meeting. Eino (Matt) Latvala, Sulo (Isak & Jacob) Walli, Roland (Hiskias Johnson) Olson and Rodney (John) Walli enjoy a retrospective time in a reminiscent setting.

test to determine whether I was a person who enjoyed the "journey" or the "destination." That is to say, "do experiences on the way to life's goals seem most important, or is the ultimate in importance getting to the place you want to be?" I could have saved the test effort on that question. The journey of life is such a roller-coaster ride. On any given day one might experience something surprising, shocking, touching, frustrating, satisfying, puzzling, inspirational or profound. Each day is an adventure. Then, too, I would have difficulty establishing that ultimate life goal, because at twenty I would never have been able to imagine in my wildest dreams what life has brought me. My eternal goal has remained the same, but in this life our destination is universal—death.

"Why are you so hung up on cemeteries?"

People hang out in cemeteries—and people, no matter where you encounter them, or what you learn about them, are the most fascinating of all of what life has to offer. I have had the luxury of being the third generation of family concerned with our local LAKESIDE CEMETERY. It is relatively natural to know much of the fabric of life of those buried there. When I began spending so much work time in the cemetery many people would stop, park the car and share some memories and comments on the life of those buried there, or other places. So many stories were humorous, eerie, profound, or touching that I began jotting them

down. All of the stories told in this volume are true, some names and situations have been changed slightly. One of the great things about painting a portrait is that the artist can give an impression, an essence of the subject. That is also the great thing about telling a story, we can sift and choose emphasis so that in the end we give a truer picture than a strictly historic account might have given.

"Doesn't being in a cemetery 'spook' you? I have no fear of spiritual messages. I believe that I have received many of them, but most of my para-normal communication has come in other locations. If one believes there is a spirituality in life and in death, (which I do) it follows that this spirituality is not centered in a cemetery. However, spending time meditating in a cemetery or any other location will put one more in touch with this aspect of life and death. I feel that if there is a negative unseen force it probably would not impose itself in a cemetery, although this seems not to be an entirely unknown occurrence. There are plenty of other places, especially in today's world, for evil to exhibit and communicate. I fear more: today's media, people who exhibit cruel behaviors and an all too common insensitivity. Spirituality, to me, has always been a positive thing, part of life and death.

I FEAR THE MORTAL, NOT THE IMMORTAL

DEAD BODIES

It seems strange for a culture which routinely dispatches humans violently in many of it's "entertainment" forms is so unnerved by dead bodies. When one stops to think about it we are not much more than primal when it comes to placing value on each human being. Primitive also is a common state of mind when dealing with the physical remains of a person. Our emotions often range from morbid curiosity to a fear/aversion reaction. I know many who will not attend funerals, be caught live at a cemetery or even visit the home of someone who has recently passed away. But lacking human physical immortality, we creatures of dust or ashes must deal with the remains. It could take an entire book to discuss the historic, social, and psychological aspect of this universal task I will only discuss here what I have observed, and have discussed with my generation and the preceding generations of my acquaintance.

In this area of northern Minnesota some early inhabitants placed their dead in a bier, raised by four poles. Some of the necessities of life were left with the body to provide comfort in the next realm. It was well understood that the remains would be used to nourish the earth and it's living

If we see it as alive it must be living. This might be true of flowers, as well as humans.

creatures and plants in various ways. The cycle of life, death, life was a natural, continuous process. Life, in general, for these people, had been lived in a way that was spiritually at one with nature, and so in death that same unity continued in a natural way. Mounds, or small groups of mound graves are also found in the area, probably the first form of burial. One such group of mounds is now a Catholic cemetery in Wright.

Some of the first non-native people to sojourn in our area were the voyageurs. They could be looked upon as the first teamsters, or as lowly beasts of burden. They were the young (usually), misfits (usually) hired by the fur companies to bring out from the area the valuable pelts of the beaver, muskrats and mink. They were required to carry one and one half times their weight plus needs for personal daily sustenance as they crossed the land masses (portages) between the canoe routes. Economic and political competition existed between French and English investors, with the French laying the earliest ground work, and later the English making more connections in the area. My computer, obviously biased toward the English, redlines my French spelling of the word voyager (voyageur). At any rate, these men were usually devout Catholics if they had come from France. They had, at their

last opportunity, made what meager offering they could to the patron saint of voyageurs, St. Anne[1]. Missionary Father Baraga did not say Catholic mass in the area until 1835, a time when the English were more influential. Following the war of 1812 British influence waned as American interests took over. The life of a voyageur might sound romantic in our historic literature, but it was quite dangerous. The line between life and death was very fine for several reasons: The fur companies, in an effort to protect their investment, felt that if a paddler could not swim he would be much more likely to keep the canoe, with it's valuable cargo, upright. So it is said that many of the voyagers who paddled through the rocks and rapids could not swim. They were also the first to intrude upon indigenous inhabitants of the wilderness. One must recognize that there were risks to that situation. Sometimes provisions, scant to begin with, ran out with no time to find food. Then there was the matter of carrying that exorbitant weight year after year. Although they wore bands on belly and knee they often fell victim to hernias, often fatal. So how were these remains handled? Most Catholics would have preferred burial in "Holy Ground." These cemeteries were few and far between, so as conditions dictated simple wooden crosses often marked burial locations near the point of death, especially at the dangerous white waterfalls. Sometimes the mortally ill were left with a jug of cheap alcohol to help to alleviate the pain of death. Then they were abandoned to the forces of the natural world. No worry about disposal of a body. Some drowning victims became part of the flow of life in another manner.

The lumber industry dominated the area for the next hundred years. Early on the "Jacks" lived without many of life's creature comforts and died, were buried and forgotten without much notice. We have one such unmarked grave in our town, I'm sure the lone grave is not unique, as many times close family continued to live in another country, far removed.

The point of all of this discussion is to say that organized cemeteries as we know them today probably did not exist until the area was settled by families of people in the late1800s or early1900s. Lakeside cemetery was founded in 1907, the land donated by a local family seeing a need.[2] A stillborn uncle, of whom I had never heard, was one of the first occupants. One did not talk about some aspects of the

We all need beauty and color in our lives, and maybe even in death, but it is sometimes difficult to provide a real, living display. So we may take a route to brightening our cemetery which might vary from the tradition of live flowers in another place, but here again, we do what we can.

harshness of life on this frontier area. But be assured a cemetery became a necessity all too soon. The ceremony and proper proceedings connected with death could now be observed in this bit of the world. Some of the fear of the body could now be alleviated by following these prescribed procedures. Then, too, it became possible for curious peo-

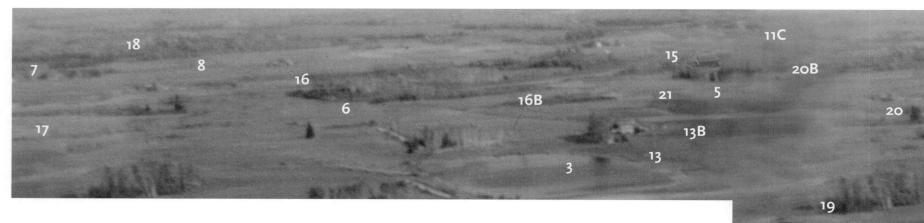

AIR VIEW—NINETEEN-SIXTY-TWO

Early Finnish homesteaders chose to settle this area because of the abundance of lakes, rivers, bogs and low places. Most of them built homes and saunas on the shore of a wooded lake, which thereafter bore their name. Forest had been largely burned from the area,1918 fire, when this photo was taken from the air in 1962. This three-square-mile area is the origin and setting for most of the stories in this book, and innumerable others if truth be known.

KEY TO LAKES AND HOMESTEADS OF THE LAKESIDE AREA

Lake	Homestead/chapters located
1 Long Lake	**11** Long Lake Farm 2, 4, 6, 7, 11, 14
	11B Uncle Uno's Oak 1
2 Bakka Lake.	**12** Bakka Homestead
	12B Latvala Homestead
3 Luoma Lake	**13** Luoma Homestead
	13B Author's family
4 Oja Lake	**14** Oja Homestead 7
5 Schoolhouse Lake	**15** Lakeside Schoolhouse, Clubhouse
6 Walli Lake	**16** Isaac Walli Homestead
	16B Lakeside Cemetery
7 Cole Lake	**17** Olson farm 4, 6, 13
8 Mattila Lake	**18** Mattila Homestead
9 Cranberry or Maa Lake	**19** Maa Farm
10 Leander Oja Lake (Vallijarvi).	**20** Leander Oja Homestead
	20B Hunuri Ghost House 9
11 West Branch/Kettle River	**21** John Walli Homestead 4

Lakeside Schoolhouse—the Clubhouse.

ple in the next generations to spend time in this place of bodies in an attempt to learn more about the people who had previously populated this place.

CHICKEN OSCAR

A friend told the story of his grandfather "Chicken Oscar," so called because he was one of the earliest area poultry farmers. Chicken Oscar and his wife had carved out a place to raise a family and secondly to earn a living from the rocky, timbered land in more northern Minnesota. They experienced many of the hardships which plagued those early families. One heartache was the birth of a still-born. The only thing to do with the body was to bury it in a pleasant location on their property, and move on with the things that had to be done. Somehow, this was not good enough for a neighbor, who might have had a dispute, or power problem. At any rate, the county officials were soon out to the farm, threatening to "dig up those remains and move them to a proper burial site." Upset, but not to be outfoxed, the family donated the grave site and surrounding property to the township "for a proper cemetery."

Years later my friend was there, visiting his wife's grave when a cemetery caretaker approached.

"Are you visiting a grave here?"

"Yes I am."

"Oh, is it this one? We wondered who this person is related to?"

"This is my wife's grave, and I am the grandson of Chicken Oscar."

"Uno, Uno! Come here. This guy is the grandson of Chicken Oscar!"

"No lie! Well, well. He donated this land, you know. Do you know the story?"

"Yes, I know the story."

"Well, well. Isn't this something! The grandson of Chicken Oscar!"

Though there were often rules enforced to promote burials in "proper cemeteries" there are many "family plots" on private land. Then there were some bodies which were denied entry to the "proper burial site." My uncle Uno died of diphtheria at eleven years of age in 1905.[3] The legend is that he was denied burial in a cemetery, so his grieving family buried him on their highest hill and planted an oak tree on the grave. My uncle Ted claimed that the tree would never grow to full height, but rather remained an immature oak. Son Paul says that the tree began to grow only when Uncle Ted died. One could speculate on the spiritual ramifications of this phenomenon, but it probably is best left as one of life's mysteries which will never be fully understood. It is certain that diphtheria was rightfully feared by the settler families. Other communicable diseases which were sometimes considered too dangerous to bring into the cemetery were typhoid, tuberculosis, and influenza. Until 1963 some Catholic cemeteries would exclude women who were "Unclean"[4] (died in childbirth, menses or having given birth out of wedlock). Protestant churches have been known to inflict the same pain, but not often. I wonder where all the bodies would be buried if the regard of the same "chaste" standard were imposed on the other gender, or if breaking the other commandments was cause to be banned from cemetery proper. "We can't bury that man, he

has ripped someone off in business." There is a cemetery in our area in which, tradition has it, the "unbelievers" were buried outside of the cemetery proper. It seems that if a road, fence or other barrier separates the mavericks from those who ran a more acceptable course, the pure will not be tarnished or punished for fraternizing with the enemy.

A variety of "sinners" were denied burial in community or church plots. Usually these outcasts were women or those who struggled with economics. Everyone was poor, but then there were the shamefully poor. The "baby trap" often helped society set a double standard for men and women in matters of morality. Sometimes the exclusion was based on nationality or religion.

Suicide was often considered a reason to deny burial in the "cemetery proper." We have, however, at least five persons in our cemetery who ended their own existence in this world. Friend Jasper Beseman mentioned that he has counted fifty-three suicides among people he has personally known.

SACRED (OR SCARED) FOREVER

Once a piece of land had been consecrated as a cemetery that sacredness was well respected by the general populace, even the donor. One of Lakeside's donor's daughters (now in her eighties) told me recently about the strict warnings concerning berry picking in the cemetery. She remembers noting that the blueberries "were always huge and lush" in the forbidden, fenced-in, sacred ground.

"Raspberries, blackberries, Juneberries, and gooseberries too," chimed in her seventy-five-year-old brother.

"I tried to sneak through the barbed wire one time, and got a very bad tear in my leg. I still have a scar," she said, still carrying the guilt of that escapade in more than one way. "Mother put salt pork on it and wrapped it with a rag." That treatment must have intensified the pain. I wondered if that might be part of the lesson taught, the feeling that one must not tread on "God's ground" in an unauthorized way. She must have recalled reading the Biblical quote: "Vengeance is mine, says the Lord."

On the other hand, some young people played on the reputation of the place to play fright games there. One of the most common was for a couple of young men to take the young women of their choice "parking" in or near the cemetery. The young men would excuse themselves with some pretense or errand. Soon strange and frightening things began to happen. The car would shake, apparitions appear, disturbing noises could be heard. "Those girls were really scared, screaming and ducking down in the seat," laughed the storyteller.

"Or were they just playing their part of the game?" I asked, with some insight into the importance of roles and expectations in our gender relationships.

"Well, yes, I guess so," he laughed, probably remembering that a dose of fear is a good excuse to snuggle protectively for a time. "It's us against the other world."

At times the gender doing the spooking might be female. One night in the thirties a group of guys was celebrating the life of a just departed friend. Drinking it up in an abandoned house, which was used as a granary, the only one in the area with an eight-foot-wide fireplace. The women, who were in the house having a more proper gathering, got the inspiration to throw a heavy hunk or two of wood unto the granary roof. Though they would not admit it, the guys were indeed spooked, and the party broke up quite abruptly.

At times fear may be feigned, but fear of cemeteries is deeply ingrained in our culture. Drama, art, including paintings, comic books and photos all depict strange, frightening, dramatic events happening in burial places. "Why?" we may ask. Death itself is frightening. Often pain or suffering is related to our imagination of final moments on earth. Some who have experienced near death time have, in most cases, said that they no longer fear death. From the time we are tiny babies one of our worst fears is separation from those we love most. That fear never leaves us. Then, there is the fear of the Post Death Unknown. Many of us have faith in existence after this life, but no detailed certainties are in the picture for many people. Then, do the spirits or souls of the dead separate from the bodies? Or are they lingering for a time, if so, how long? We also are certain to be more intensely aware of our limitations of time on earth as we stand in a cemetery. So we are SCARED by cemeteries. About how much fear do we want in our balance? How much fear do we want to attempt to instill in the next generation?

Compared to proceeding generations it seems much more difficult for my generation to accept and understand that something may be SACRED, and it may be even more

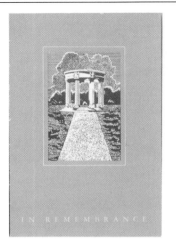

In Remembrance Cards.
Top—1950s, 1960s, 1970s.
Bottom—1980s, 1990s, 2000s

difficult for succeeding generations. To hold something SACRED we hold it in respect which exceeds normal. I tell stories in this book which my parents might think of as irreverent, not reflecting proper respect. My children might make jokes which make me a little uneasy. I believe that one of the most negative forces which will be at work in the next generation might be that it is difficult for them to respect. (Or even appear to respect, and I do not mean that they should respect to the point of fear.) It is difficult for young people to respect institutions, leaders, systems, and

individuals when they have become so aware of shortcomings. They see a low standard of concern for honor, truth and justice. Many of the fears which we had held have been explained. It takes better special effects now to scare us. Also, few things have real mystery now. If my children have any questions about something, they will look it up on the web. Even most of the mystery is gone from romance, engagement and/or marriage (if you still believe in such). Reverence is closely tied with the word sacred. Respect and a little of a certain kind of fear are also connected to our

UNCLE UNO'S OAK—Born in colorful September, Uno had just celebrated his eleventh birthday when cold December came, and with it dreaded diphtheria. He lost his struggle for life, and was denied burial in Lakeside Cemetery for fear of contagion. They placed his grave on the highest hill, on the end of Long Lake. When summer came again a small oak tree was lovingly placed on his grave.

"The tree never grew to full size," said his brother, known to me as Uncle Ted.

Ted lived for nearly eighty productive years, before leaving us with an empty space which can't be filled. The long stunted tree now seems free to grow. Still small for one hundred years of growth, the oak still stands in silent tribute to a boy who never had a chance to grow to full height feeling that something is extra-ordinary. Those are feelings that we have traditionally had about cemeteries, though those attitudes are changing. I won't venture to say whether that change is positive or negative. It is probably a matter of degree, and of our attitude toward human life itself. As in many other life issues a balance seems to be the most prudent of goals, but rarely is a balance achieved in any issue, either by individual or entire culture. In this case fear may paralyze us, yet lack of ultimate respect (fear) for something, anything can roll back civilization as we know it. If all brakes are removed, a free, uninhibited movement will result in total degradation.

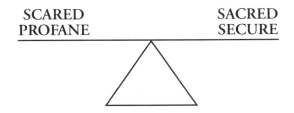

SCARED   SACRED
PROFANE   SECURE

WHERE IS THE BALANCE?

HALLOWEEN—A CELEBRATION OF SCARY THINGS

People have been doing scary things in this area for as long as humans have inhabited it, I am sure of that. Many of the scary things deal with death, others with spirits, others with scary animals, (bats, snakes, spiders) and other unknown or legendary spooky things. I imagine that celebrating spooky things in the fall may have been revived by those who observed All Hallows Eve (before All Saints Day), finding it a good day to give someone a real scare and blame it on the restless spirits. In this area the day began as a day observed in many Christian faiths to remember those saints who had left this world. As one pastor put it, "the day before when all those that don't go to heaven raise hell." The eve evolved into a time when all those unholy entities were restless and made themselves known. Gradually it became a day to simply pull pranks, and later for the producers of candy to sell a good percentage of their product. At the turn of the century a prank in this area might have been to put a wagon on a barn roof, or tip an outhouse (toilet) over (preferably with someone in it). In the fifties it involved

putting a teacher's small car on the roof of the school, or toilet papering a yard tree, house, or other handy place. Scaring someone with weird noises has always been "good," while seeing a good scary movie is a start, if one is too old for the traditional trick-or-treat activity. Son Paul speaks of a "two-generation prank" or a "three-generation prank" as he refers to the number of generations which will hear about the joke and possibly retell the story. That is directly related to the unique and humorous impact the joke has on individuals who hear about it or are lucky enough to witness it. We spoke of the amount of effort that went into some of these elaborate hoaxes. "A good three-generation prank is worth a lot of effort," he smilingly commented.

I had heard that a wagon had been set on our farm's thirty-five-foot-high barn roof one Halloween night early in the 1900s. I could not visualize this being done, especially by a group of kids. The barn roof is, as I mentioned, high and steep. I received confirmation that this prank was and is, indeed, a third-generation legend. A group of sixty and seventy-year-old men were talking about old times when the topic of pranks came up. Sure enough, they recounted the prank, and even knew how it had been done! It seems that the wagon had been taken apart and hoisted to the peak of the roof with a rope—indeed a sizeable effort—but then, it is still being celebrated by the third generation!

It must have taken a great effort to lift a V.W. Beetle to the roof of Cromwell High School, but here again, it must have been worth the effort, as it is already at least a two-generation prank, so far. The worst part of that story is that the young men involved were obligated to lift the car down again. The best part, school officials were not sued as a result of the punitive requirement.

From Jennie Hanson's WRIGHT NEWS in county newspapers *"Lakeside Community Club will sponsor a Halloween Dance, Sat., Oct. 23 at the clubhouse, 8–11 p.m. Music is by Richard Olson. Costume judging is at 9:30."*

In attempting to connect the costuming tradition with the origins of Halloween I got a clue to contemporary thinking from Barb Walli, when she made the comment, "I've just always thought it was a really fun time to feel free to act like someone else, and forget about expected behavior."

Surveys have shown that there is one thing that more people fear more than death itself. That is the fear of public

FEAR IN MANY FORMS AVAILABLE ON ONE DAY—This montage of ads is from the Duluth News Tribune *from October 23, 1999. Granted it is close to Halloween, yet any newspaper, on any date would have some form or forms of entertainment listed which contained one or more scary portions. We need a little fear in our lives.*

speaking. Tie that fear into the fear of "what do people think of me?" and we have very good motivation for dressing up like someone, or something else and feeling free to act in an outrageous way. We can look and act as scary, silly, or abnormal as we need to. For at least sixty years now Lakeside Clubhouse has held a Halloween dance.

Neighbors have taken great pleasure in attempting to be so changed that they are not recognized. The dance is a good natured time of six-foot cats chasing five-foot mice, of male ballerinas twirling on the dance floor in tutu. A wolf might try to make time with a 'floozy,' while a pirate interferes. A giant frog hops about the floor, obviously enjoying the music pulsing from an ancient accordion. These people are not worried tonight about who they are, or even who "people" think they are. They are purely having fun! Movies, books, videos, theater, all forms of our "entertainment" make use of the fact that most of us like to be somewhat frightened at times.

Uninhibited, unrestrained activity on Halloween may relate to the stem words in Latin:

Mortal: Ending only in death (Frankenstein, devils, skeletons, ghosts, angels, etc.)

Morbid: Not natural or healthy, ending in death (same as above)

Mortician: One who deals with bodies (caskets, wrappings, death masks)

Mortify: Subdue the body; to humiliate (clowns, silly characters, gender bending). We let go of our fear of admitting that when all is said and done

We are only human, we will die, we might as well have a little fun with that fact, and throw to the winds any fear of embarrassment or self-consciousness. We can celebrate being as human or non-human as we want to be on this one day.

Talk about scared! Another cemetery keeper/grave digger told of the time he was removing brush from a part of the cemetery which was on the lowest side of a steep embankment. As luck, or Murphy's Law, would have it, several school children were walking along a nearby path just as Roger clambered up to the top of the rise. Roger laughingly surmises that it must have looked to the children as if someone was rising from the grave and coming toward them at a good pace. "Well, anyway, those kids started off running in the other direction; didn't stop till they had gone about two-hundred feet. Then one of them panted, 'What are we running for?'" They continued walking fast and Roger didn't see any of them look back.

Children are recognized as the future, in almost any community in this country. In 1908 Eric Nelson was dele-gated to be in charge of constructing a thirty- by forty-foot log building to serve as a school. The site, as you would expect in a Finnish community, overlooks a lake, appropriately renamed School Lake. The school was built on another important community institution, no longer in use, the logging camp. Fifteen students attended the first school. A small house called "the teacherage" was also built on the site. One Halloween unknown pranksters wrapped slat and wire snow fence around the building, making exit of the teachers impossible. In 1929 a second room was added, as another community school closed, sending students to Lakeside, so that the number of students totaled ninety, in grades one through eight. This seems like a high number, looking at the community today, but it was not unusual for a family to have eight or thirteen children. Like every school system in the nation the system moved to larger and larger central schools when transportation permitted it. Classes were last held at Lakeside in 1940, with sixteen students then transferring to Wright School. The school had always been used for dances, parties, Sunday School classes, funerals, weddings and other meetings and festivities. It seemed only natural that in 1948 a Lakeside Community Club was formed, and is still functioning, to serve many of the same activities. It stands, well kept, only a quarter of a mile from Lakeside cemetery. Its beautiful hardwood floors still gleam, its picture of George Washington still looks down on visitors. A metal hand pump still provides very good water for the building and a few community people who still carry water from it.

The school stands about one-fourth of a mile from the cemetery, which is located between two Walli homesteads.

Both Rod Walli and his cousin Sulo lived near the cemetery, and both of them say it was customary to walk on the road past the cemetery, until one came up even with it. At that time it was imperative to run, run as fast as one could go, until the other end of the cemetery was safely behind the young runner. It is doubtful that any young child ever walked calmly by that stretch of road, especially at night. Roger also told another "Sukie" story (see page one). Sukie had convinced another man, Ole, who "did not like cemeteries" to come and help him dig a grave. The reluctant man had also been the butt of many of Sukie's practical jokes, wasn't anxious to be the patsy for another one. But he consented, finally, when a promise was given that no more jokes would be forthcoming. They had dug at least four feet down when they encountered a huge rock. They hoisted the boulder out of the hole, leaving a large secondary hole. While Ole was still busy dispatching the rock, Sukie furtively put his arm down in the hole, quickly covered his arm with sand, leaving only his hand sticking up.

"Look Ole, Lena is wearing a wedding band!"

Ole needed only one quick glance down at the seemingly unearthed hand to propel him at top speed out of the grave, out of the cemetery, and out of doing any more favors for Sukie.

Coincidently, Sukie tore down a house on that farm, leaving a small 20' x 15' house which our kids called the "ghost house." They had heard stories of a man who hung himself in one of the buildings.

Roger's son Craig digs almost all of the graves in Lakeside now, but he almost quit the work when he was quite young. He was helping his father dig in another local cemetery. Young Craig was in the hole when they heard a loud crack. Craig had started to fall through the tell-tale yielding earth when he managed to scramble out.

"D-D-Don't dig. N-N-No digging any more dad," he managed to stammer, clambering out of the potentially disturbing cave in.

It is our good fortune that he had the fortitude to continue working in local cemeteries. He is a good, conscientious digger.

I sometimes wonder who dug Sukie's grave, and if they pulled any pranks while digging it.

"LIFE IS WHAT HAPPENS TO YOU WHEN YOU'RE MAKING OTHER PLANS"
John Lennon

2

Not In This Cemetery

It is said that serving in the United States military is a great equalizer. This may be true in some ways, but was not in others. We do know that this huge Fort Snelling Cemetery in St.Paul Minnesota does not discriminate in some of the same ways that some smaller burial places might. No one has been turned away for nationality, economic, marital, "moral" status or cause of death. Serving in the Army, earned Grandfather Webster the right to be buried here, along with his spouse. At times race, gender, health, or sexual orientation have been criteria for acceptance into the military, thus burial at this military cemetery.

Bias Dies Hard

Adults give children a feeling for their heritage without even realizing it. Customs, food, words, stories all contribute. Dan and I had decided to make a conscious effort, however, to help our children connect with a part of their Norwegian history, we would visit great Aunt Blanch on her North Dakota prairie farm. Our arrival at 2:00 A.M. was marked with a wonderful Smorgasbord: pickled herring, deviled eggs, thick slices of home baked bread, and much more food which was effectively carried to the table by the sturdy no-nonsense woman who still had a twinkle in her eye. After a sound sleep under hand stitched quilts and a huge breakfast ("you only fix your husband ONE egg??!"), we set out for the tiny township church and surrounding cemetery. Our children were quite young, but they enjoyed seeing the old country church, listing to the ancient organ, then touring the neatly kept church cemetery.

My grandparents and many other relatives were buried in neat rows of well kept graves, stones standing straight and tall, flowers marking the fact that someone still honored these prairie settlers. Then I saw, in a far corner of the cemetery, tall grass, disheveled leaning stones, and an absence of flowers.

"What's that over there in the corner, Aunt Blanche?" I asked, pointing to a small area.

"Oh," she said matter-of-factly, "Those are the Swedes."

We finished the guided tour of that cemetery, and it was only later that my Swedish husband wryly commented, "Well, at least they buried them inside the fence.

This was not always the case with nationality conflicts. Minorities, whatever their nationality, were not always treated with kindness, even in death. Although there are some other nationalities represented in Lakeside the cemetery is known as THE FINN CEMETERY.

A look at the cemetery stones will bear this out. We became much more aware of an ethnic variation in names after an excursion into another ethnic area close to our home

WHAT'S IN A NAME?

One Sunday we took a ride with our (adult) son Paul in search of metal for his blacksmith business. We drove through Finnish farmland, dotted with both rocks and saunas. We made several field stops, one to see the Automba park, with its native granite memorial stone dedicated to the memory of what once had been a thriving home to three

hundred and fifty residents! The stone also memorialized the Native Americans, who had met at this place. The name AUTOMBA is a Native American word which means "the meeting place." A bustling hub of activity is hard to imagine now, as all that remains is one house and an old deserted church a mile down the road. Finnish survivors, however, did not forget those who lost their lives in the great fire of 1918, some five hundred and fifty people in all. A small park stands in the midst of the now deserted pasture land. The short, sturdy, functional, whole log picnic tables reflect the nature of their creators in an unintentional sort of way. Very practical, making use of natural materials from close at hand, humble and straight forward, inviting interaction on their own terms, they wait quietly as the world rushes by, They are ready with strong support should they be called upon.

A second stop put us into a retrospective frame of mind as we looked at the remains of an old farmstead. From a distance only a row of trees indicated that the land was a home site. Upon closer inspection, all that remained recognizable was a greying, collapsed barn roof and some cement footings. No trace of a sauna was found, indicating that we were now into Polish territory. Ground hogs, grey squirrels, and gophers, surprised by our visit ,scurried to hide 'till peace and privacy returned. We noticed a difference in terrain as we drove into the Polish ("Polock") community: Larger, flatter fields, bigger barns, and a lack of the ever present and numerous rocks, trees, and lakes which dominate "Finn country." The well constructed, well maintained farmsteads lay unused now: a monument to a people who worked hard to produce dairy products and other crops. They were squeezed out of production because of policies which have virtually phased out the family farm in the United States.

We proceeded to the farm home of the iron sellers. The older couple who operated the remarkably well stocked iron yard did so as a way to survive, and to try to keep title to the land which had been in their family for at least one previous generation. While Paul looked at the metal Mrs. Milczarek showed me a little about how the farm had operated. She spoke of times of flood and drought, and of four children who lead productive lives in far-away cities. As we drove out I commented on the evidence of a lot of hard work reflected by the farm.

"Yes," mused Paul. "And on the bodies of the Milczareks, too."

I had noticed, also, that sheer determination seemed to be what kept the couple physically able to function at the level needed to maintain the business. The Finns would call it Sisu. Paul also had observed Mrs. Milczarek's painful gait as she mounted the three wheeler and zipped off to the shed which stood in the outermost reaches of the yard (to alert Mr. Milczarek of our presence). He needed both a cane and

a three-wheeler to facilitate his mobility. I guessed them to be in their late seventies or early eighties.

On our return trip Dan and Paul indulged my strong desire to visit the cemetery of St. Joseph's church. Cut and polished into stone were names like: Kretzschmar, Gresczyk, Kopf, Adamczak, Tomczac, Zgono, Skyivseth, Gjessing, Chmielewski, Durtsche and Jusczac.

"They certainly don't use any extra vowels in those

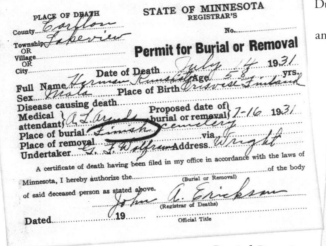

Burial Permits

names," I commented, as we attempted to pronounce the more unfamiliar monikers I thought of all the Finnish names on Finnish stones: Maa, Eero, Aili, Haapoja, Laajala, Haare, Luusua, Aho, Saari, Tiili, Fiina, Waananen, Vuohelainen, Piirainen, and Siiri. Not satisfied with a liberal use of vowels the Finns often double them, dot them, the sounds rolling out in a rather soft, musical way.

Paul had located a two-foot metallic urn in the far corner of the cemetery. A puckish grin established that he had made a humorous discovery.

"YES… YES… I bet THIS is where they store all their unwanted vowels. YES… Then on dark nights the Finns steal over and claim the unused vowels to use in their names. Kind of a vowel movement! Enough vowel language used in a cemetery!"

Our children's paternal grandfather, (and later his spouse, grandmother) was buried in the national military cemetery, FORT SNELLING, located in St. Paul, Minnesota. It is impressive, if not mind boggling to view rows and rows of simple white stones, stretching for what seems like miles, and to realize the scope of service to country represented here. We found grandpa's grave, and were allowed to decorate it with flowers which would be left there for one day.

One thing to think about was that dozens of nationalities all rested under this sod, without regard to country of origin. These men, and now women, had fought, and in some cases, died for America. They were all Americans.

Our children all remember seeing grandfather's grave, and have attained a deeper feeling for family history, their own past and for their country. It would be productive if all youth could have meaningful experiences to give them a feeling for their past, as it relates to their future.

DEATH KNOWS NO FAVORITES

3

The Nuts and Bolts
of the Grave Yard

OOPS—A COWSLIP

Lakeside Cemetery is a pastoral place, it does border a cow pasture. Cows do not have all of the same feelings humans do. One variance might be to consider the cemetery a sacred place (or not). On the other hand, the bovines might feel that they have just as much right to be here as anyone. "Cow pies" bear silent (if not tidy), witness to that attitude. This cow has apparently dropped in to see what was happening, as the excavation was a point of interest. Cows are curious. It seems that my father made a ramp with his backhoe as an escape route for the hapless cow.

Without a Hitch

It may be the permanence of a cemetery, or the respect inherent in the location of graves, or the desire to know that death has its own certainties, but mistakes are not a part of the public image of cemeteries. Yet every sextant, grave digger or funeral director can tell you at least one story of human error in connection with cemetery experience. These people have learned to bury their mistakes, and maybe to have a chuckle over them at their own expense. If one accepts the rituals of death in the same light as some other of life's rituals one must also accept that slip-ups, goofs, or "Acts of God" should well be taken with some humor. Even small mistakes are not supposed to happen at funerals, so if one can rise above the embarrassment they cause, they are rather funny! Pallbearers who carried the casket of a comparatively large woman down a rather steep church stair stumbled at an inopportune time. One told me he will never forget the sound and motion of the large body being shifted to the front of the casket, and the struggle to maintain decorum for the rest of the trip to the hearse. I'm sure congregation members in another church will not forget the free rolling trip a casket made down the inclined

aisle, coming to a sudden and abrupt stop at the altar. A massive exhaling sound was heard when if became apparent that the casket would stay upright and closed!

Take the case of the "too neat" gravedigger. Lakeside Cemetery lies along a less traveled tar road, extending only about sixty feet back from it. It is usually easy to see any activity which has taken place there. That visibility is often how one is apprised of a death. A staked or newly dug grave is rarely overlooked. One of the local undertakers was counting on that fact when he, with appropriate dignity, led the fairly long procession of headlighted cars past Lakeside. Wait a minute… Past? Yes, the hearse proceeded slowly along the entire length of the cemetery, with the driver hoping to see the tell-tale mound of sand, or some disturbance in the earth. It was with some panic that he realized that he was at the end of the cemetery, with thirty cars behind him, and no visible open grave! The bereaved were distraught, mourners confused.

"It's the first time I ever did a "U" turn with a funeral coach in a procession! We'll just have to tell that gravedigger not to be so neat!"

People enjoy rules, tradition and conformity when it comes to cemeteries. Heads must always be to the west, so we have two or three to the east. Husbands must always be to the right-hand side of the couple, so we have several on

the left. One husband told me, however, "The missus is going to be on the left of me, cuz that's where she always slept." Graves must always be marked, so we have a couple that we could not locate, even with extensive research. The funeral must be a solemn recount of the departed one's faith or accomplishments here on earth. On occasion it has not been.

Some parts of South Dakota are very flat, with visibility from highways sometimes stretching for miles. It seems incredible, then, to think of a funeral procession being lost for two and one half hours! Thirty cars, lights glowing, persistently traversed the long lonely roads for that amazing amount of time, looking for a "lost" cemetery. One can only imagine what the drivers, passengers, officials and small town observers were thinking as the procession made it's long journey. Kathy Haugse, Tamarack, is the only participant that I have spoken with, and she, being Kathy, saw the humor of it all. She saw the humor, too, when her sister reported having attended the "wrong" funeral. She had entered the Funeral Home, dropped her card into the box and gone into the congregation which had gathered for the reviewal. It was then and there that she realized that no one seemed familiar, not even the deceased. She excused her exit, retrieved her card from the repository and proceeded to look for the "right" funeral. This is probably not an isolated experience in light of the multi-funeral homes now serving even smaller towns. I have heard of people entering the wrong church, only to leave suddenly.

Room for errors might have been greater around the turn of the century, especially in remote areas where funerals were held from homes (hence "parlors"), and different attitudes prevailed.

Grandma of a local family died in a sitting position. So in spite of precautions: blocks, straps and other efforts to keep the body flat, she suddenly sat up during services.

Another family had a local undertaker out to the house. He had neatly laid out the body on Friday night, only to return for Saturday services to find the same corpse in a far different condition. Hair mussed, tie askew, shirt torn ,the body showed some signs of unscheduled activity. "We wanted one more picture with uncle Harvey" was the only explanation. Please don't let your imagination run with this one, especially if you are attempting to sit in a solemn funeral congregation.

Kathy also remembered some nurses coming into her Tamarack store, still discussing a "lost body" situation in a larger Duluth hospital. It seems to have been lost for about three hours, in and out of elevators, code blues, hallways and other areas of the hospital, with a variety of personnel involved (maybe trying to be uninvolved). We can only speculate who else might have been conducting a futile search for that missing body during those same hours.

Kathy's husband's grandfather had been a local "undertaker" during the infamous 1918 flu epidemic. Haste in disposition of bodies was important for the prevention of further contagion. He and his helper had taken an early morning trek to the cemetery with the team and hearse wagon. Tired from the non-stop schedule of burials resulting from the high death rate, the exhausted undertaker took opportunity on the way back to town to rest in the bed of the hearse wagon.

"ARE WE THERE YET?" was the startling question townspeople heard loudly coming from the funeral conveyance. More than one of them woke in a hurry from morning complacency.

A QUIET NEIGHBORHOOD

One of the primary decisions upon death is to locate a proper place for the remains. Lakeside has been providing a family type resting place for nearly one hundred years now. Few people realize, however, how confusing it has been in past times to identify or maintain an orderly way of placing graves.

"I hate hitting boxes."

Dad made every effort to know where he should or should not open a grave in the local cemetery. He had unearthed unpleasant evidence that a family was mistaken when they assured him that it was safe to dig in a certain location. He went to great lengths to avoid scooping out the wrong location with his backhoe. I had seen him "witching" for disturbed earth, walking back and forth in a pattern, each giant hand grasping one end of a reshaped wire coat hanger, waiting for the wires to cross, and dip down on their own (a process used in our area to locate underground water). The old cemetery keeper had died, and with him any knowledge which might have helped to solve some mysteries. Often the graves were stepped off without benefit of any other, more accurate measurements. The corner markers, if there ever were any, were long gone. Early records of Cemetery Board meetings were written in Finnish. Semi-circles replaced straight rows in some cases. The only existing map was one hand-written copy of a placement of twenty-three large (16-grave) lots assigned to families. It showed a row of smaller (8-grave) lots across the front, near the road. It also showed a bank of three large lots where the actual property dropped down a steep embankment to a level at least ten feet lower than the useable level. The map was probably drawn by an engineer from his office in St. Paul. Many graves were unmarked, many uneven and impossible to identify after the bulldozing done in mid-century. Hay growing over graves made location even more of a game of chance. It was my father's nature to take things in stride, but he made it clear that it was not fun to dig where distraught relatives pointed, only to find disturbing evidence that it was a mistake. Images macabre sometimes found way into my overactive teenage imagination. The problem did not become mine, though, until years later.

Dad's heart stopped one early spring morning and the responsibility of preparing the grave passed to us. We could not operate the digging machine. My cousin shoveled the grave by hand, a labor of love, an unusual one at that. So, the dead buried, we needed to see to the care of the living—

Mother. It seemed that of the four siblings, my family was the only one able to make the move back home, just down the road a bit from Lakeside cemetery.

"That cemetery is a mess," stormed friend and neighbor Lenny Carlson. "I panic every time I'm supposed to locate a grave."

Lenny was not easily daunted. She had moved out from Chicago to become a farmer. It was a great leap from the previous type of life she gave occasional hints of having led. I don't say "lady farmer" either, because she was soon accepted by even the most hardened chauvinist as a hard working, no nonsense manager who could chew the fat, take or dish out a ribbing with the rest of 'um.

She served on the township board for decades, and was well accepted as a community leader. It is a credit that she, a non-Finnish female was elected to the cemetery board. I can not remember another challenge that she had trouble coping with (including her last difficult illness). But "That Cemetery" was another matter.

"I almost lose sleep every time someone asks me to mark a grave," said the cemetery official who was used to doing things up right.

KNOW THE LANGUAGE

In 1978 she and I began measuring, marking and researching. As I crawled through the tall grass mapping out the existing markers I was struck by an unfamiliar sounding name. Hmmm, I really don't remember ever hearing the name "Syntyny," and yet here it was written in stone. Just then John Oja's pickup rattled to a stop. He greeted me as he strode over to see what was new. After the appropriate small talk I took my opportunity to find out about the strange family name.

"John, who were the SYNTYNYS?" I asked, expecting to hear a list of names and an account of life's highlights for this unheard of family. John was the kind of man who smiled a lot, but I had never heard him laugh out loud. So it was a real surprise to hear the rolling laughter come rumbling out! When he had regained his composure enough to speak he solved the mystery for me.

"Syntyny means born," he said, wiping a tear of laughter from his eye. That did make perfect sense, for when I cleaned out the accumulated sod and moss from the lower part of the stone it read:

Maria J.
Syntyny 1866 (Born)
Kuollut 1919 (Died)

Walli,

It was, again, a time when I wanted very much to have learned the Finnish language. Oh, well! Many questions were asked, questions to elder neighbors, questions to visitors to the cemetery, questions researched in documents.

"Who might this widow have married? Is she buried here?"

"I remember this man... Is he buried at Lakeside?"

"Are there any living relatives? Where can I contact them?"

"Is this person really buried in a walkway?"

It might have surprised someone driving by Lakeside on one dark night to see Dan, lying down at the foot of a stake, looking up at the stars. It was his way of helping us to establish true north. We borrowed some even more sophisticated equipment and began surveying to establish true north, to put in corner markers, and establish walkways. We knew we were on the right track when we found several old corner markers buried deep in the ground as we began to dig the new markers in. We try to make sure that what we do is correctly done.

"The Maki family is ordering the headstone today," the funeral director continued at his end of the phone line. "Do we put Joe on the left, Mary on the right?"

"Well, I don't really know," I said. "That grave for Mary was not dug where I staked it." The memory of measuring and marking Mary's grave according to the six closest corner markers was still fresh in my mind, having done it only days before. I also remembered that the grave digger had "put it a couple of feet over to match the others so Joe could be on the left."

"Our grave digger thought he should put it so that there

Maria Walli's stone

would be room to bury Joe on the left. I had staked it where Joe had asked me to, 'just north of mother's grave,'" I explained. The digger thought that tradition was more important than family requests. "Is there a hard-fast rule about men being buried on the left?"

"A couple of cemeteries in Duluth have the entire plan of men on the right," he said. "Family preference should be more important than 'tradition' in this case. So then I should put Joe's name on the left of the stone?"

"It's not that simple." I searched for words to explain the problem. "The graves in the lot are all a couple of feet to the north of where they should be, I had marked the grave to correct the error. When I explained that to the digger he said he could squeeze Joe's grave in on the left. I told him that doing that "would be his problem." I wondered how this might be recorded on the cemetery map. "He will probably be the one who will attempt to fit Joe's grave in without unearthing either of the other two graves."

"Well, that could really be a problem," commiserated the director. He paused, then continued, "Joe is really a skinny guy, we could just put him in handy wrap and fit him in there!"

That was many decades ago, it worked out well enough without skimping on Joe's grave.

THE PLOT THICKENS

It was a confusing call from the funeral home. "How many babies are buried in the eight-grave lot of the Rengo's? How many adults? How many graves are left unfilled? How shall we fit all remaining folks into which remaining lots? The family is here asking."

I quickly checked the map. "My records show three remaining graves on the south end of the lot. Five are marked and recorded."

"Good, that totals eight."

It was then that I discovered the two babies who were recorded as buried in the lot in another list." I can go over to the cemetery right now and check this out," I volunteered. What better to do on a sunny summer day?

I wonder what internal forces continually pull the cement corner markers down—down, until they become lost in a heavy layer of sod. It renders them challenging, if not impossible, to find. Probably the same force that pushes rocks and fence posts up in the fields so that a new crop of stones may be harvested each spring. This time I was in luck! I located four corner markers of the Rengo lot quickly.

"Yes, the map was correct: five marked graves are on the lot, leaving three remaining open on the south end," I said on my return call to the funeral director.

"Well then, we have no problem," said George from his office in the funeral home. "We can put two cremations in the northern most grave."

"Wait, we've never voted to put two cremations in one grave. Far be it for me to give the go-ahead for that policy. I'll have to poll board members and get back to you."

"Well, you would be the only cemetery not doing it—but I can understand the politics of it all, making that decision." George had worked with cemeteries before.

"Yes," I quipped." I don't want to step on any live toes!"

"Oh, and, by the way, Silvia wondered if you know about the strange man buried in their lot?"

"Strange man?"

"Yes, supposedly there is a 'strange' man buried somewhere in their lot."

"Where—who?" I asked with excited interest. (Remember, I had been searching and researching for information for nearly two decades.)

"I don't know, but I can find out for you—maybe she knows."

"We'll probably hit him when we bury Samuel."

"Just our luck to do that," mused George.

"We've made an attempt over the last twenty years to mark all the graves with homemade cement markers if there are no known survivors willing or able to do it," I explained.

"Looks like this might just be one of those cases."

"I can see myself making the stone-carving out the letters in concrete: STRANGE MAN 19?? TO 19??"

George chuckled, "I can see the same people putting the same mark on my stone: 'STRANGE MAN!'"

"Amen," I laughed. "Very likely words for my eternal I.D. also...STRANGE WOMAN." What can I expect, when my own children call me the 'funny lady.'

Some of the weird things that happen are a result of interaction between people who deal with death procedures every day. Such a story was told to me by a local, happened in Minneapolis, Minnesota.

A product supplier continued to pull small pranks, tease, and otherwise hassle the secretary at a funeral home there. She took that "fun" in stride for a number of years. Then one day, after a particularly bad joke, she decided to take action.

When the salesman visited the funeral home that Monday he was surprised to see the staff in a sad state. Grief stricken, disoriented faces, heads shaking, silent workers were so unusual, he had to ask: "What's wrong here? What's going on?"

"Oh, you wouldn't believe what's happened here over the weekend," lamented the director, with a nod toward a sheet covered form on a slab.

Feeling quite at "home" the jokester ambled over to the sheeted form and curiously flipped over the sheet heading, revealing the stiff, prone form of the secretary. His jaw dropped in startled disbelief. Just then the form began to move; sat bolt upright!

"GOTCHA!" shouted the now laughing secretary.

I don't know whether this falls into the area of oops, or is deeper in the layers of events which are beyond our understanding. Charles Sedlander, Cromwell classmate, recounts the story which occurred near there at the turn of the century. As was the custom, a funeral procession had formed to take the body from the church to the cemetery. The pastor rode with the coffin on the horse drawn wagon, while the mourners walked behind. When the snaps which secured the reins to the bridle came loose, they were quickly reconnected, but not without causing wonderment as to how it could have happened. The spring operated snaps were not designed to come loose, and did not commonly do so. The procession began to move again. Again the rein snaps mysteriously unhooked, leaving the hearse wagon at the mercy of the team. Should the team decide to bolt, or diverge from the trail there would be no way to control them. The situation did not present very positive specula-

tion for either the living or the dead.

One can imagine that at this point some concern about why this unusual thing had happened not only once, but twice, seemed natural. The snaps were checked, rings examined, harness replaced. Everything seemed in order, so the procession moved toward the cemetery once more. It shall never be known what that pastor was thinking when the reins came loose for a third time, but he jumped from the wagon and silently walked the rest of the way to the cemetery.

In our cemetery, if the funeral was conducted from Lakeside Clubhouse such mishaps were avoided by requiring the pallbearers to carry the casket the quarter mile to the cemetery. It must have been a real labor of love to walk that distance while supporting the weight of a body and casket. It is still done that way occasionally, but more often the role of Pallbearer is simply ritualistic or honorary.

"NOBODY GETS OUT OF LIFE ALIVE"

Children View Death

SYMBOLIC NEW LIFE

The butterfly is not too far out of the cocoon. Fragile in appearance, yet lovely, it trusts. Christian faith employs it as a symbol of life forever. So it is with the child. A child's life seems to stretch ahead forever. The child, stronger in many ways than appearances would indicate, is innately trusting and optimistic. A bond may exist between the child and the butterfly, as children are close to nature, if allowed to be. Often the death of a pet or other creature will provide the child's first experience with death. This child and butterfly co-exist, with no thought of death.

Deeply Universal

One can learn much about life, the world, human nature from children. I am always amazed that if a person is willing to be carefully intent in a relationship with a child, even an infant, one can learn so much! I believe that this observation is one of the most legitimate ways to study the nature of humans, as the child functions more on the dictates of innate instincts, rather than learned behavior (although it always amazes me to see how quickly a child picks up on and mimics attitudes and behavior). The reason I mention this human quality is that it seems that the urge to put ceremonial closure on death is deeply and universally ingrained in even the youngest humans. This instinct most often manifests at about the same time that the child begins to grasp the complicated, nebulous concept of death.

Death, for many children, is often experienced first in an animal (sometimes a pet). Many of us can draw into conscious memory a reaction to that experience. We remember having a funeral for a field mouse, a favorite cat or dog, or other creature. Many of us have assisted a child in making a casket or in some other aspect of this humanizing activity. We will have shared our cultural and personal attitudes

toward death at this time. It may have been easier to handle at this occasion than it would be at the death of a human. On occasion a child will already have experienced a human death and "acts out" what has been observed at that time.

Our three young sons were definitely interested in and attracted to snakes. They built habitats (however rudimentary) for the garden snakes found around our home. They seemed to find many snakes, maybe this was due to close proximity to the earth both in stature and in spirit. They were still "low to

MR. SNAKE'S FUNERAL
Andrew, Perry Webster and Junior Nelson mourn some reptile friends.

the ground" and they had spent most of their time outdoors. The snakes were considered pets, so I was surprised one day when I saw them carrying a snake that had obviously come to some form of violence.

I soon saw that their destination was a grove of trees on a hill, not too far from our yard. There was already one long, narrow grave. They had collected quite a few of the artificial flowers which had once graced Lakeside, but that had been removed during spring cleanup. I could see that the ceremony was going to be a somber, dignified event, and I was not to be invited. I did ask one question before I left. "What did Mr. Snake die of?" "Loss of blood."

I believe that a survey of my generation or the previous one would reveal that a large percentage of families had held death ceremonies for either a dog or cat. It stands to reason that these animals were often accepted as family members, because of time spent with the animal, and the bond which often developed, especially with the children, (or child), of the family. It follows, then, that when a pet died it was essential that the death be marked with a funeral.

THE GRIEF OF LOSING A PET:

On 1/6/2002 TODAY, (NBC) a segment on the death of a pet was featured, as a reaction to the accidental loss of former president Clinton's dog "Buddy." Clinton had once referred to the dog as "my one loyal friend in Washington." Comment was made about the joy brought by animals, even to presidents, crossing economic, lifestyle or other differences. Dr. Phyllis Cohen, Psychiatrist, gave some reasons for this: Animals don't judge us, Nurturing is good for us, We take better care of ourselves when we have a pet, and they fill a slightly different niche in our lives. She listed ways to deal with the loss of a pet:

Allow yourself to take the loss seriously

Take care of yourself

Talk to someone, (even if it is the checkout person)

Tell the story

Find a support group

Expect to feel guilty

Follow your own grieving path (Leave reminders out or put them away, as you desire)

Follow your own heart (Don't replace just because someone says it will help you)

Do these suggestions sound familiar? Are they strangely applicable to human losses?

Many humans have observed animals in mourning—either at the loss of a well loved human, or another animal. That may be why some animals are now listed in human obituaries, and sometimes animals are afforded their own obits. I have heard specific, verifiable stories of cats, dogs,

FRIENDS FOR GENERATIONS

Long Lake Farm, 1925
Author, 1944
Andrew, 1976
Teddy, 2002

cows, goats, horses, geese, elephants, and others acting out grief at the loss of a mate, master, or special friend. They may refuse to leave the last place they saw the living, or a favored spot to be together, or even the grave. They may refuse food, other usual needs or activities. They may howl, yowl or make other intense and upsetting noises. It has been documented that an animal grieving animal may even will it's own death successfully. Item from Jennie Hanson's WRIGHT NEWS, published in county newspapers: *"Our sympathy to the David and Sharon Lake family on the recent death of their hamster, Bart, a family member for three years. He is buried in the family pet cemetery."*

FAMILY MEMBERS:

Pets on our farm have demonstrated on too many occasions to recount that they deserve a decent burial. Here are a few:

Dauber Dog—Grandson Teddy and I were out on the

snowy ice making snow angels. Dauber rolled out on his back and made his own version. This activity pleased him better than seeing us slide down the hill. I don't know whether he barked frantically during that activity because he was concerned for our safety, or because he was not included.

Dandy Lion The Cat—Personified his namesake when he came swimming with us. After spending the time swimming around, yet not diving, he would exit the lake with his wet, white body hair all waterlogged and slicked down while the yellow/orange head and neck fur was all fluffed out.

Coffee Bean The Cat—Could tell who was wearing skates, and jumped on that person's shoulders to enjoy a spin around the lake. She opened her present on Christmas eve, led the UPS man in at slow motion (only him) and taught us much about raising children (tough love).

Balushy The Goat—Would call Akalroid, the pig, in to their shed when he had escaped through the fence and it was time to be inside.

Peace the Cat—liked to engage the family in a lively game of tag, naming the top step of the basement stairs her goal, where no one could touch her.

Honest to God—as I write this Dauber Dog is out on the step crying loudly because our son Andrew and two dog friends have visited and have just left.

Close relationships with pets seems to transcend generations. Four generations spanning over seventy-five years is undoubtedly just a surface look at this quality.

THE EXECUTION

This story is disturbing in several ways. It speaks to the integrity of children, and how we as adults might force them to compromise this integrity. It is offensive to those of us who love animals, and it is almost unbelievable (a friend's father recounted this story first person, as did an uncle, independently living in another state).

A horse became blind in old age and began to suffer with this infirmity. The man who owned the horse could not bear to dispose of the horse himself, as he respected (or even "loved it") after years of close association. Such an admission did not come easily for a man in the early 1920s. But, swallowing his pride, he approached his closest neighbor.

"I have had that horse so long I just can't shoot him myself, and he can't live with that blindness any longer. Would you take care of that for me? I will pay you to dig the grave and kill my old horse."

The neighbor, being a typical stern father who placed difficult demands on his children, assigned his two early teen aged sons the task. The boys knew how to dig the grave, using a large scoop to remove the soil. The horse, hitched to the scoop, literally was forced to dig it's own grave. The boys then loaded the gun and put a halter on the horse. One of them held the halter, and bid the other "SHOOT."

"I can't do it," said his brother. "This horse has been a friend for too long. I just can't shoot him!"

What to do? They were not ready to face father's wrath for not accomplishing the assigned task. Somehow, they came to an unfortunate decision on an alternative method of killing their friend. They knew that another neighbor stored dynamite in his shed, so they requisitioned a stick, and securely tied it to the horses neck. They lit the fuse. Then things took a really bad turn. The horse, although

blind, could smell the sulphur, or hear the fuse sizzling.

He took off on a run, and having been blind for a time, easily found his home barn. He ran into the barn, and the boys watched in horror as the barn exploded. Windows flew out, and doors were blown off their hinges. The killing was accomplished.

The aftermath included a whipping for each boy, and the difficult, mind numbing task of dissecting what little remained of the horse to bring it to the grave. Cleaning the

mess was difficult in so many ways, but the brothers knew that alternatives were more intolerable. They were only trying to follow directions while maintaining their own personal sense of what was right in their own value system. How often do we adults violate this innate sense of right or wrong, or bother to discuss it with our children? What happens when we model violence or need for power and control?

THE BIG BANG

Funerals for animals or humans seldom seem to completely alleviate confusion and misunderstandings about death ceremonies. Karen Atkins, from Northland Funeral Home told me of an incident which happened to her when she worked as a funeral director in another town. The funeral was for a man who had served in the military. When time came for the military honors, including the gun salute, mourners were warned to prepare for that ceremony. The group of military "Brass" assembled at the grave site was ready for the noise of firearms, but the deceased's daughter was not. She tried to muffle a startled, gasping, scream which escaped from her throat. Her small son, who stood

holding her hand, heard the reaction and put two and two together.

"OH, MY GOD—THEY SHOT GRANDPA!" at which not anyone remained stoic.

Children have been fascinated by burial ceremonies. Toini Aho recalls the teachers at Lakeside school "made us quit having funerals." It was a big, regular part of recess activity for a time. Frogs—bugs— mice—what ever could be found dead, became a regular object of the children's death ceremonies. She tells of a group of friends walking by Godfrey Wolfrom's "Mortuary," not knowing what it was, and breaking into a mad run when they saw a casket—and even more scary the cover opened, and a body sat up. Speculation later seemed to tie the event in with the fact that Mr. Wolfrom would let one of the town's most frequent imbibers sleep off the effects of over consumption in the caskets he reserved for more permanent sleepers.

Toini also recalls being forced by a neighbor to touch a body which was laid out in the granary on her farm. She doesn't recall being upset, but her mother was. And she did remember it for over seventy years.

A LESSON IN BURIAL

Children born before the depression learned early that items such as oranges, and store bought clothing were rare treats, so it followed that all items which were simply to be enjoyed were out of the question. It was not "good" to even wish for them. This did not seem to be a burden, as we had the freedom of the great outdoors, and did not mind eating flour pudding, especially if it had our home made maple syrup on it. The depression was over for our family friends in the city long before it was a thing of the past for us on the farm (I wonder if it ever was). My mother managed to feed and sleep those friends who enjoyed visiting the farm, while my father often put them to work.

I was about four years old, just beginning to understand that if you put something into the ground it would grow bigger, or even multiply! It was an exciting concept for me. The entire family was out in the garden one beautiful spring day, taking the first steps necessary for this miracle to happen, when "company" from the great metropolis of Duluth drove in. Hugs and handshakes taken care of, one of the women handed my oldest brother a strange looking white cardboard box with a wire handle on it.

"Open the top flaps," said the lady, with some mysterious excitement in her voice.

We crowded around, as Bud opened the special box. It was filled with water! Then we all saw it. "Oh. Wow." There was the most beautiful, golden fish swimming gracefully around in the box. We had never seen anything like it. This was a treat, totally non-functional—given only to bring joy to us. We spent time taking turns watching the fish, offering ideas for a permanent place to keep this wonderful gift. My parents and older siblings soon moved to the kitchen for a long "coffee time."

With others so involved I decided to take action on a wonderful idea. 'If one goldfish was marvelous, how much better it would be to have more.' Even many. I knew how to make that happen—Plant the Goldfish. I carefully carried the white box out to the garden, and using a hoe, opened a hole in the soil. I tenderly laid the fish in it, and just as tenderly covered it up. When I had finished I sat in the shade of a tree and imagined how wonderful it would be to have all those goldfish! Soon my mother passed by, on her way to the barn for chores.

"Are you still studying that Goldfish?... Where is the box?...YOU WHAT!?"

My mother was consistently mellow, and I couldn't even remember more than one time when I had displeased her. This anger and disappointment on her part really shook me to the core. I couldn't understand why everyone seemed so angry at me. It was an earthshaking time, and for a long time afterward I felt the sting of disapproval from my entire family.

DOESN'T SOMETHING ALWAYS GROW AGAIN WHEN IT IS BURIED?

LOGIC

A neighbor who had not heard that story told the following: Joey's gold fish died, and he had persuaded his mother to help him hold a ceremony and bury it. When it came time to dig the grave she presumed it would be an easy, tiny hole to dig.

"No, No," cried the boy. "It needs to be this big!" He indicated a two-foot by one-hole size. "But why would the grave need to be that big for one small fish?" questioned the mom.

"Well, it's inside the cat!"

DEATH IS UNPREDICTABLE—OR IS IT?

Panda was the lead cow in our herd of about 25. She was intelligent, and had the personality for management, but the fact that she had been allowed to keep her horns was a big factor in establishing her leadership. Skinny, conversely, was at the lowest end of the order. She was an old cow, hornless, so short that her 'bag' (udder) dragged in the mud. She walked with her head down, trying hard not to be singled out for attention, an acknowledgment of her low status. I could tell you of the personalities of most of the cows which fell into an established social order between these

COWBOYS may be played without other children, or horses for that matter. Cows were often children's pets. Fine company, but in some situations became difficult, for instance when cows were used as beef. Most children learned to accept this as a fact of life, or learned to put it out of mind.

two: Gussie the fence breaker; her daughters Gussielena and Gussielum; Lena the Guernsey; Babe the beauty. I remember these cows as I would remember childhood friends, as in a way they were among my best playmates. I taught their calves to drink from pails, I helped to put up the hay that would be their winter food, I rode on their backs and called them home with my E flat Alto Horn.

One summer day my dad came in from the barn to announce: "Crazy is dead."

The proclamation was the beginning of a nightmare from which the family probably never totally recovered. In

the 1930s the deadly poison arsenic was given to farmers, mixed with sawdust and sometimes a sweetener, as a way to control the invasion of grasshoppers. Our neighbors, from whom we rented pasture land, had stored some in an old open barn. Our best cows ingested the most, but heifers got an amount of it too. The few cows not dead within five days aborted their calves, or were useless for breeding (thus producing milk). Babe, my brother Bud's beautiful 4H Jersey, who looked like a deer, died with her head on his lap. I remember looking down from my upstairs bedroom to see the rendering trucks rumble by to remove the bodies of my friends. I was about seven years old, old enough to realize that our survival on the farm, thereafter, was touch and go. Our neighbors collected enough funding to replace several cows, and we did build up a herd again.

My parents were too busy "making a go of it" to worry about my socialization. This was probably not uncommon in that time period. The difference was that we were rather isolated from other families with children. I found my playmates where I could. Some of my best friends turned out to be cats. When I was very young I dressed them in doll clothes, gave them rides in my doll buggy and invited them to tea parties. From the time that I was about seven years old I slept in the hay mow, (second story of the barn) from the time the snow was gone to the time when it snowed again. The cats were my constant companions. It was such a comfort to have a gentle purr in your ear, a soft, warm friend to snuggle and an alert guard to keep the snakes and mice away. I really loved those cats.

It was hard for me to leave home to attend college. One of the difficult factors was leaving the cats at home. I was able to come home for week end visits. It was nice to see mom and dad, and Slatey Grey cat. She was soft grey, a very loving friend and a wide ranging hunter. One Sunday night as I said my goodbyes I looked down at Slatey. I "saw" her lying lifeless, with matted wet fur, sunken/shrunken eyes, a grimace on her face. She was in a state of decomposition.

The next time I came home I found her out in a field, just that way

It was the first of my death premonitions. Others, dealing with humans, came later.

CHILDREN SEE MORE THAN WE PRESUME THEY DO

Children or adolescents seem to be more in touch with extra-sensory communications than adults. Son Andrew seemed to know at age nine that his grandmother would pass from this world quite soon. He warned me to spend more time visiting her. Niece Wanda remembers that at age twelve she was discussing her grandfather (my father) with her siblings, when suddenly she started to cry. She had received a very concrete message that he had died.

Now they had not received any more normal indications, as he died out in the field doing his spring work they had not received word of any terminal illness. My brother Bud, an adult, also had an extra sensory perception of that death, and had warned my mother, who was in St. Peter Minnesota attending to my first baby and me, that there was trouble at home, and that "Dad won't be there to meet you." She asked him many times how he knew (either as an adult or child), but what can one say? I have had several early death notices, but as an adult I did not want to believe them. I know I saw the pictures in my mind, felt the chill without reason. One time I walked into a crowded baby shower, saw one of the guests as a corpse, months earlier than it became reality.

DEATH—A HEADLINE IN THE LONG LAKE WEEKLY

When Mother was young, (age 13–23) she and her siblings published a "newspaper" entitled THE LONG LAKE WEEKLY. Printed on their father's leftover brown bakery

Dog and cat illustration, October 20, 1920

paper, it was a chronicle of events, situations, humor and creativity on the farm overlooking "Long Lake." (It was really Douglas Lake, but that was not a popular name for the lake in either the family or community) I treasure sixty five copies of the hand written paper. dated from 1915–25. The October 8th, 1921 issue contains a reflection of how death of a pet was received by young people during that time.

LONG LAKE WEEKLY
Oct. 8, 1921   Vol XV1 No 30
EXTRA

A cold blooded murder was committed on Main Street on the 6th of October, at 12 0 clock. The victim was Mrs. Paddy Ryan, wife of the prominent business man Mr. Patrick Jesiah Ryan. She was immediately taken to the Mercy Hospital, but died on the way. The murderer, Mr. Geo. E Peterson was released on bail. His trial will be held. Mrs. Ryan left a large circle of friends to mourn her untimely death, besides her husband and two kids, Snowball, Lavender, aged 5 years and James Whitcome, aged six. Mr. Ryan is at Dakota, working in the harvest fields, and therefore unaware of the cat-a-strophe, but will be summoned home immediately to look after his children. It is reported that after Mrs. Ryan's illness last summer when she turned to thieving as a means of living, which in probability was the cause of her death. A picture of the Ryan family is printed on the back page of this paper. Mrs. Ryan's maiden name was Miss Plupu.

Mr. Ryan's birth announcement had been printed in a previous issue of the LONG LAKE WEEKLY:

"We announce that the smallest kitten has been named Paddy Ryan." All animal deaths were equated with human. A pig caught escaping from the fence once too many times was to be *"executed at sunrise."* We don't know how the rooster died, but Mr. Buster, (the dog) dealt with the situation. *"Mr. Buster proved his extra-ordinary 'intelligents' by standing guard over a dead rooster, so that the cats could not molest it. Mr. Buster is getting very prominent in Society Circles.*(Plupie was the offending cat.)

DIED!!!!! LONG LAKE WEEKLY
July 28, 1923 No_____ Vol_____Page 3

"Miss Geraldine Hortensen, a tadpole, protege of Miss Ruth, died here at 9 minutes after 10 on Tuesday, the 24th day of July, 1923.

After a consultation it was decided that the cause of her death was due to heartbreak on account of her guardian leaving her for other duties more urgent than taking care of the tadpole.

She was buried in the Garden Cemetery on Thursday. The professor (ten-year-old brother, Ted) officiated as parson at the funeral. One of our reporters was pallbearer. A beautiful song entitled "Just a Little Blue For You" was rendered by the choir. We offer our deepest condolences to Miss Ruth and all of Geraldine's friends who are left to mourn her untimely death."

The death of animals seems the only way in which death could be discussed. In all the sixty five copies of THE LONG LAKE WEEKLY there is only one human death or funeral recorded. That one was so close to the children it could not be ignored and is told later in the chapter. Maria, much beloved mother of the Peterson-Johnson family, died on December 24th 1919, yet in the next issue which exist, January 8, 1920, there is no mention of that death, or the grief the children must have been experiencing. The following poem appears nearly one year later:

> *Hundreds of stars in the pretty sky,*
> *Hundreds of shells on the shore together;*
> *Hundreds of birds that go singing by,*
> *Hundreds of bees in the sunny weather.*
>
> *Hundreds of dewdrops to greet the dawn,*
> *Hundreds of lambs in the purple clover,*
> *Hundreds of butterflies out on the lawn,*
> *But only one Mother, the wide world over.*

An older sister, Emma Peterson Putnam seemed to have been living at home at the time or shortly after Maria's death in 1919 died only three years later, yet there is no surviving mention of that death either. Many weddings and other events are discussed, but only one human death, that of a peer.

Maria's husband, Mr. Pa, left the family some time after her death, but that major loss of the family father is never mentioned either, even in a diary which I have read from those years. A diary reads: "Mr. Pa visited school today, gave Teddy and me a chocolate bar and a five dollar bill each." (Martha Johnson diary) My grandfather became one of

those persons who chose to die to his family. He lived the rest of his separated life in a religious commune in far away Ohio. People there were not aware of his family in Tamarack until his physical death in 1932, when they went through his effects. Outright death would have been easier for the family, though his stepsons reportedly encouraged his departure.

LONG LAKE WEEKLY

December 24th 1927

Claude Rhodman—November 24–1924

Shortly after seven on an extremely dark night the three Rhodman boys left home for Johnson's to enjoy an evening of skating. Claude seemed more anxious to get started, after partaking of a cup of coffee, he hurried off: Cecil and Vernon following with the lantern. When Cecil and Vernon got by big island the foremost fell into the lake, his brother pulled him out. They thot they heard someone calling but they hurried on home, telling their folks they thot Claude was drown. Mr. Rhodman left immediately for Lungen's where he got some assistance. The Aho girls and Jacob had also come here to skate, Later Norton and Kai (Kelly) arrived. Kai stayed in the house for a few minutes, then she started for the lake. She heard Mr. Rhodman yelling about Claude. She came back and told us, at once Vic (Peterson) went to the island where they searched for him. They found the lantern which Cecil and Verna had used, but no traces of Claude. For the three following days people from all the community dragged and dynamited the lake.

Shortly after five on Thanksgiving a few men dragged the lake with an extra large net, in which he was caught not far from where he had fallen in evidently.

On Sunday the funeral was held at the Presbyterian Church, Mr. Canner officiating. Richard, Willis, (Latvala?) Eino (Marsyla?) Jacob (Bakka?), Teddy (Johnson) and Waino (Marsyla?) acted as pallbearers. His brother, sister, niece, aunt and cousins came from Nebraska.

Recently a cousin who was seven when this drowning took place gave her account of the tragedy: "They couldn't find the body, so they put a plank between two sleds, Vic (oldest of the Peterson boys) sat on it and two guys pushed the sleds over the ice, while Vic broke the ice. He was the one that found the body." I can only think of how much courage it must have taken to break the thin ice, with only a plank between you and the freezing water, searching for a

macabre reminder of the danger and power of that lake. Meditating, serious, my cousin continued: "That night none of us could sleep—that lake kept groaning and moaning—OOOeew… 00ooooOOOOOOgh… GroooOOOooooooooo! It is impossible to describe the sound she made during the account, but it raised the hair on the back of my neck. "Must have wanted that body—that lake made those unearthly sounds all night!"

I was sharing the story with brother Bud when he suddenly grew serious. "Vic was taking me ice fishing with a team of horses and sleigh. We were pretty near Little Island (where the drowning had taken place) I was sitting on the back of the sleigh when I heard the whip crack—Vic never whipped the horses—then I looked down to see that there was water almost up to my knees, and the ice kept cracking as the horses struggled to pull the sleigh out."

"Did you jump?"

"No, Vic got that sleigh out, and we wasted no time in getting off the lake ice." He shook his head, still not believing the fact that they had escaped drowning.

"You know, to my knowledge, Vic never again went fishing—winter or summer." I know that both men were thinking of the skating fatality at the time of the near miss, and that Bud was thinking of it now, as he recalled his dangerous encounter with the ice near Little Island on Long Lake. He is one of the many, many, who remember the death event vividly as we move into the twenty first century, and individuals from the third generation could probably retell the story. It represents the dark, lurking ironies of death, and the untimely aspect also.

PEOPLE STILL SKATE ON THIN ICE

A POIGNANT ACCOUNT

Alma Siiro Lunden published a comprehensive history of the area about ten miles west of Lakeside, CORDUROY ROADS[5]. Alma, born in 1906, discusses the struggle and rewards of settlement of neighboring Rice River. Much of her life narrative parallel my mother's experience, including the loss of mother when she was still very young. She prefaces the account by saying: *"Mother had always been a contented homebody and seldom went anywhere unless someone needed help in some way, but the summer when I was eight she and I took a long trip by foot and visited many houses—a real walking tour."* (Nine families are detailed.) Here is an excerpt from her account:

"I remember the beautiful Sunday that warm fall—Mother and I were visiting the Andersons. It was either Halloween or near it because Nestor (brother) who was also there, and Arvid and Jack were making plans to walk to the village for some mischief. 'Tricks or Treats' was not in style then—it was tricks only—nothing worse than pushing over a few outhouses. The boys were working over their strategy and noting that with no snow on the ground their tracks would not show.

Mother suggested that we walk home by way of the barn gate. We always used the shortcut, but we crossed what we called a stone bridge—it was just a long low place filled with rocks from the fields to make a loose foundation for the driveway. About three-fourths way across the bridge Mother stopped and told me, "I will make a monument"—monument is too big a word for what she called it. She selected a large flat rock, then placed a somewhat smaller one on top of it, then looked around until she found a large chunk of white quartz and set that on top of the other two. It was on the south side of the drive.

I often had toothaches in those days and had stayed home because of one that Friday, early in November, but it let up toward evening and Mother and I went to visit the Korventaustas after supper while Mother's bread dough was rising. She often baked bread or sweet rolls late in the evening when everyone else was in bed. Our coffee grinder was out of order and Mother wanted to grind coffee for morning with theirs. On the way back from Korventausta's she again wanted to take the long way by the gate—the house gate this time, which was hardly ever used.

Later my toothache returned and Ida and Manda (sisters) took me to bed in the other house. Mother and Father still had their bed in the summer house and father went to bed. Nestor was at Anderson's. Mother was baking her bread but she had come to check on me and asked the girls how I had been. She went back into the summer kitchen, took the last loaves out of the oven, and then her work was done.

CHAPTER 18: A SAD TIME

What woke me was the long ri-ip, rip of cloth in the other room, but at first I was aware only of something strange going on. I sat up in bed as by a spring in my back when I noticed Ida and Manda sitting on the edge of the bed in the dark room, crying quietly, and saw at the same time that the lamp was lit in the big room. Alarmed, I asked what was wrong. Manda asked Ida, "Should we tell her?" and Ida answered, "I guess we'll have to." and then she told me Mother had died.

I cried, "Oh, no! No!" and ran into the other room where Mother had been placed on the couch. Father, Frank, and Nestor were there, and Cousin Mary, who was a nurse for Dr. Walters in Moose Lake, but happened to be home that Friday night, November 5, 1915. She was tearing strips off a white sheet to bind Mother's chin into shape.

I later learned that Father had woke up about eleven to the chill of the night after the fire had died down, and found the lamp still burning on the table with the loaves of fresh bread all out of the oven, the door wide open and Mother not in bed, nor even in the cabin. He dashed out to look for her and found her just outside where she had fallen face down when reaching to shut the door. He then went to wake Frank, Nestor, Ida and Manda, telling them, "Something has happened to Mother!" Someone ran to Anderson's—very likely it was Frank, and Mary came to help. Andersons had no telephone yet so a little later—in the middle of the night—Father and Frank walked the two and a half miles to tell the Haltonens and Grandma who was living with them about Mother. Uncle Haltonen took over from there, calling the coroner in Aitkin the first thing so that he could catch the early train to McGregor.

It happened that Hilja was "Central," as the telephone exchange person was called, and Uncle had to wake her up in the early morning hour with the shocking news in order to put the call through to the coroner. The telephone exchange for the area was in Lawler, and the office with its switchboard was located in the front part of the Weimer Hotel. Central was on duty twenty-four hours a day, so the was a double bed in a curtained partition of the room and Hilja slept there. At that time Hilda, too, was in Lawler, doing dressmaking, at the hotel. It happened that Hilda was spending the night at the house where she was sewing that week, and Hilja did not want to wake her. Hilja tells how awful the rest of the night was—alone. She did call the Jarvis to ask Tillie to come in the morning and take over her job for a while. Mrs. Jarvi had waked (sic) Tillie with, "Central's Ma Died!"

Nick Toumi, who was working for the Haltonens, got Hilda and Hilja from Lawler with the Haltonen's horse and buggy, and later he brought Aunt Ida and the coroner to my home. the corner pronounced the cause of death to have been cerebral hemorrhage. Later, when the coffin had been made and the paint dry, Aunt Ida came again to fix the interior of the box

CHILDREN OF LOSS?

Is it sadness, anger, or insecurity which is written on the faces of these unidentified children of early in the twentieth century? Or is it just a reflection of the adult social standard of a slightly earlier time that "only clowns and prostitutes smile for photos?" Were they spooked when the photographer covered his head with a black cloth? (Toini Aho says she was.) Have they experienced the loss of a mother, not unusual enough in the time period? Or is it just that life was hard, even for children, at the beginning of the twentieth century (or much later)?

and the body into it. Matt Bottila, from the north end of the township, was the person who made coffins in the neighborhood when needed, although factory made ones were available at Moose Lake. Haltonen had bought one for Grampa nine years earlie, but they were expensive, and Mother would have insisted on a plain pine box, no question about that—nothing TURHA (Finnish for overly fancy—mw) for her.

I can remember so well the warm sunny day—although it was November—I was standing near the steps watching Mr. Bottila a little to the south, toward the elm, his back toward me, one knee on the ground, sawing, planing and fitting the coffin together. Father was facing him on the other side of the work area, his hands behind his back, talking with Mr. Pringle on his left. Mr. Pringle had walked over that Saturday to offer his condolences. As Father watched and talked he spat on the ground a few times in a gesture I interpreted as a substitute for tears, and I recall how sorry I felt for him. For myself I remember only a heavy feeling inside. I do not recall thinking of myself. I knew I would get along, then too, I was too young to think, "If only I had—" or "Poor Mother." But, whatever I may or may not have felt at the time, for sixty years I could not smell turpentine without the scene flashing into my mind—of Matt Bottila painting the coffin with black paint mixed with turpentine. When I took up oil painting at UWS (University of Wisconsin-Superior—mw) as a "Senior Citizen," I began associating turpentine with art and got over that.

The day of the funeral, which was Tuesday, was still warm and sunny. Haltonens and Grandma came first, driving the team of black broncos and the black two-seater buggy up from the seldom used house gate which Mother and I had just used returning from the neighbors the night Mother died. I was standing on the east side of the path between the house and the summer kitchen and I watched as Uncle tied the horses to the Maple. He then helped Grandma climb down from the buggy, holding to his hand with one of hers and gathering her full black cashmere skirt with the other. She looked straight ahead as she walked into the house where the body was laid out—the coffin resting across two sawhorses.

Soon the Beckmans arrived. Uncle Beckman, being the lay minister, read the prayer and led in a hymn before the body was taken from the house. I was still standing by the path alone, when I saw Jack, the youngest of the Beckman cousins walking down the path dressed in a wide collared white blouse with a bow at the neck, and knickers and knee socks—the style for boys at the time. He was always cute but not always so dressed up,

with his light hair carefully parted on the side. He was eating a big apple and I remember thinking "How can he be eating an apple as though nothing had happened! Then before anyone else arrived Aunt Ida came out of the house and took my hand saying, "Lets go see your mother now." Mother was dressed in a navy wool serge two piece outfit and white cotton stockings. There were no flowers.

A lunch was served to everyone in the summer kitchen, then the little service by the coffin, and the long procession started for the cemetery.. The procession was not long in length, although there were several wagons, slowly klunking along the rough roads—also a few buggies pulled by horses which had to be held back—but it was long in time. We had to go north, then west, north again and then east, and finally the last sad turn south to the lonely little cemetery in the very center of the township. There were only a few graves, including Grampa's and little Cousin Axel's then.

Someone had climbed to the Sunnyside belfry and as the procession passed, he tolled the bell by hand so that it tolled only, dong-pause, dong-pause." A half century later I heard that same sound while attending services at the beautiful old Kannus (Finland—mw) church of which Mother often spoke. As something at the head of the casket. Hilda, Hilja, Ida and Manda were nearest to me—two on each side. Ida was on my right and Hilda on my left, and I remember Mother had explained, announcements are read there each Sunday of births, engagements, weddings, deaths and as the deaths are read the bell tolls in the bell tower in the front churchyard—the tower that Grandma's brother Jacob Jarvja designed and built. Listening, I remembered the sad day fifty years ago.

By the grave side that November, 1915, people dressed in black stood all around, but I have a clear picture in my memory of only the four girls by me. We stood at the east end of the grave, and Uncle Beckman was reading thinking, "If only they would stop crying." There was nothing I could do to comfort them.

As we stood there a cold wind suddenly came from the north bringing some flakes of snow. A few dry leaves from the tree close to our right flew past along with the snowflakes and dropped onto the coffin and into the grave. I could feel my toothache again and as we turned to go I wrapped my heavy white woolen scarf around my face.

That was the last time I saw Mother except in a dream the following summer—the only time I have ever seen her in a dream. It was so plain—I dreamed I saw her coming down the path toward the house and I ran out to the steps to meet her. She was wearing the navy serge dress and I was surprised that the white stockings were not soiled at all from her long walk home from the cemetery. I was excited about showing her all the new things since she had been gone—the flowers, the garden, new calves—but as I reached for her hand THE DREAM VANISHED, AS DREAMS DO."

It is amazing to become aware of the details processed by an eight- or nine-year-old girl. It is incredible that Alma was able to capture the spirit of "The Sad Time." Extended family was so important in so many supportive ways, then she in turn, at her young age, was concerned about how she could be supportive to them. All relative titles are capitalized in her story, a very revealing mark of respect. Suffering from physical problems, emotional anguish and mental concerns were a part of life, and a common way to deal with them in both adults and children was to sublimate them. The toothache probably eventually ached its way out, as did the ache of a warm, loving Mother's death. She also gives a touching picture of the never-ending work of the pioneers, especially the women, who didn't even "waste" walking time: they knitted.

Children took much responsibility for understanding, respecting and working. It was expected at an early age. I wonder sometimes if our cultural pendulum has swung too far, with our young being indulged, disrespectful and often not expected to work. Then, in thinking about it, I realize that we have some wonderful, insightful, hard working children in the next generation, and I am proud of them. I ache for those who dwell in parts of the world in which death is an all too common and awful fact of life. So many children live where there is not the means to put closure to it in the form of ceremony, where they need to wonder "who is next?"

The human spirit, though, is capable of the resiliency of hope, no matter how negative the surrounding conditions may be.

A Closer Look At Death

DID YOU HEAR?

Lines of communication just as apparent as telephone lines existed in our small community. Death was communicated quickly, and the support network was incredible. Stories of certain deaths have been widely related to second and third generation individuals. In the early part of the twentieth century, (or even later) medical help was not always easy or quick to access, thus many area deaths seem unnecessary to us now, as we look back on those times.

We Do What We Can

Day in and day out it was expected, following settlement of the area at the turn of the nineteenth century, that neighbors assumed many roles in each other's lives. They became, as need demanded: barber, shoemaker, baker, councilor, doctor, hired hand, nurse, chauffeur, teacher, preacher, banker or midwife. They filled immediate needs with varying degrees of qualifications to back their earnest desire to help. The words icy and stormy describe the day that mother and dad were called to the Luoma home to fill some neighborly roles as a result of Mr. Nickoli Luoma's sudden death. They would serve to council, and to assist the undertaker. The facts that Mr. Luoma was a large man (some estimate "well over six-feet" tall) and that harsh Minnesota winter weather was not making activity of any kind easy, made the mission of mercy more urgent. As mother prepared the obligatory food she and dad decided that the weather might not permit them to make it back home. It might disconnect phone communication, might make life too complicated for a nine year old home alone, and so I obediently accompanied them to the

Luoma farm. I was assigned to a round back chair near the outside door. For the next three hours I was "seen and not heard."

Only a few flashes of memory remain... One recalls Mrs. Luoma at the large round kitchen table, silently rolling out pie crust. I wondered how she could do the ordinary work so mundanely, as if nothing had happened. I remember the neighbor women visiting in the parlor, occasionally coming to the kitchen to hover over Sanna, in case she might "weaken" and admit to some emotional need.

I remember studying the big "central office" that took up a corner of the kitchen. The switchboard looked complicated to me, with it's wires and plugs in many rows. I knew it was the hub of much community activity, and that Sanna was very capable of using the system to expedite many community needs, routine and urgent. She knew that someone at Bakka's would answer their large wooden box phone if she cranked "two longs and a short," while Ojas would respond to "long, short, long," and almost everyone would want to listen to everyone else's phone conversations if they were in the house to hear the ring—"rubbernecks!" She knew how to connect with other "lines" and even cities and to systems farther away. Such a call brought the old Finnish coroner from Cloquet Minnesota to make an official

proclamation concerning Mr. Luoma's death (heart attack in the woodshed). The weather was not the kind in which one would make a fifty mile trip of one's own volition. Neither were the deeply drifting snowfall or the wind polished patches of bare ice making his job easier here on the farm.

Some things can not be translated from one language to another without losing some color or inflection, and I'm told that this was the case with the words which exploded from Dr. Jummala's mouth as he slipped and fell on the ice near the door. "THIS IS A HELL OF A PLACE TO DIE!"

"Just where would one want to expire?" a nine-year-old thought to inquire.

"Hell" or not, it seems ironic that it was in that very house that husband Dan and I lived as we built our own house on the Luoma farm, and in that house I operated a clothing factory for a number of years. Our son Paul and his wife Kris rejuvenated the house into nice living quarters for a time. We have owned the Luoma farm for over thirty years, or it has owned us.

At Nikkoli's death Sanna Luoma was forced to re-pattern her life in a drastic way. In that time period the roles which

TWO EARLY GENERATIONS OF PARTNERS
Below: *Isak (Isaac) Walli (1854–1918) came to*
America from Finland, becoming a U.S. citizen in
1900. Maria (1845–1919) followed later with five
of their six children. They had wed in 1875, and
can be considered a Patriarch and Matriarch of the
area, as it has been called by some "Walliville."
Suhonens, Loupas, John, Nels and Jacob Walli, are
descendants. Isak died in the 1918 fire, just four
days after his sixty-third birthday. He and Maria
had donated the land for Lakeside Cemetery, but
he was expediently buried in a mass grave in
Moose Lake, in the massive effort to protect the
living by burying fire victims as soon as possible.

Above: Jacob Walli (1888–1959) was eight
when he came with his mother to the area to
join father, Isak. He met and wed Serafija
(1889–1969) in 1912. She had immigrated
independently from Finland at age eighteen.
They parented twelve children, most of whom
stayed in the area along with great, great (in
number and generation) many grandchildren.

men and women played, especially as a team, were rigid and comparatively uncompromising. This adherence to traditional gender roles was often unfortunate in life, but often became tragic in death. The male dominant role included doing most out of home, or off farm activities, controlling the financial decisions, heavy disciplining of the children, doing the work that required the most strength, driving vehicles, doing "business." They met people outside of the home and were not expected to show much soft emotion. Women cooked all food, washed clothing, prepared it for wear (often sewing or knitting it), harvested wild food, gardened, preserved food, bore and attended to the children. They often operated the farm in terms of daily milking, haying. The weaker sex "kept house" on the side, and worked with the children's education and dealt with the family's emotional needs. Maybe we should say that both of them "kept farm."

Death of a spouse made dealing with life very difficult—when half, more or less, of ones survival skills suddenly were missing. The respectable waiting period before remarriage was understandably short because of the inter-dependency. Some marriages of such urgency were predictably ill-advised. The fact that Sanna had no small children gave her more options. She did remarry. She did sell the farm. Her new name had the typical ring of a good Finnish name—Sanna Linna. They both rest now, beneath the sod. He no longer must speak to community about the dangers of alcohol, and she no longer must worry about things over which she has no control.

Ole and Leena jokes have been told to cover most of the situations common to life as it is lived in this area, and most of them deal with the relationship of marriage. One such story deals with the Scandinavian self reflection on the death of a spouse: "Ole had been seriously ill for some time, might even say he was on his death bed. Well, all out of the blue he smells lefse baking. He thought he was either in heaven or hallucinating, but then he thinks it might be coming from the kitchen downstairs. He painfully hoists his body out of bed, and eases downstairs. There is Leena—rolling out that wonderful potato treat. He reached for the stack with a trembling hand. SMACK...Down came the lefse turner on the outstretched hand... 'NO no Ole....that's for the funeral!"

TOGETHER FOREVER

YOU DIDN'T SEE A DOCTOR ABOUT THINGS LIKE THAT IN THOSE DAYS

We have said that many of the settlers died early; some of their death stories are tragic, some poignant, some uncalled for.

"Three neighbors had decided to kill a cat." recounted Toini Aho. She has a remarkable memory for previous times. "Well, they were all shooting at the cat—I don't know why it should take three of them? Well anyway, somehow, Mr. Ranta was shot! Blood poisoning set in and he died."

WHEN IS DEATH NORMAL?

"Never talk on the phone during a thunderstorm," my mother always cautioned. "A neighbor did, and a bolt came right in the house and killed him."

"Be very sure the ice is thick enough where you skate, a boy drowned—went right through the thin ice at a skating party on Long Lake."

"A tree which has been cut, but gets hung up on another tree so it doesn't fall is called a 'widowmaker' in this country."

"What are the odds of living through ten or thirteen home deliveries?"

"If you are going to drink yourself into a stupor, do not lay out in the sun—you can die from a bad sunburn! A neighbor did, and died."

"An area man froze to death in his cellar."

"The little six-year-old was frightened to death by the large farm bull, even though the bull was behind a fence."

"He was shot in a random shooting in Chicago."

"A family decided to go back to Karelia, the part of Finland taken by Russia. They were thrown into concentration camps, starved and killed. Maybe one survives."

"Remember, lightning is nothing to fool around with, don't try to fix telephone lines during a storm, both you and the phone will end up dead!"

"Horses are dangerous: One man's heart stopped as a result of a kick to the chest, another from a deadly hoof to the belly."

Death seemed to have been, and still seems, normal if it comes in old age, if the cause might be expected, (illness, natural causes, or as a result of poor judgement, and unfortunately now violence). An unanswerable oft discussed question asks: Is death more or less acceptable if it comes suddenly, shockingly, or slowly, painfully expected? We humans probably will never accept death with much grace or ease, especially if we do not live with faith.

FAITH, HOPE, AND LOVE

"Faith, hope and love...the greatest of these is love." Cor.13:13 The Bible

The depth of love is often the determining factor of grief, the depth of faith is the determining factor in dealing with grief, the depth of hope the determining factor of faith. To me, these defining words could be thought of as flowing in a never ending cycle. Husband Dan's great grandmother, Gesina Bahnen came to the united states from Germany in 1852. She was working in Cincinnati when she received the following letter from her mother Anna Margareta Bahnen. The second page was not available:

Spahn, September 10, 1855

To Gesina Bahnen, born in Spahn.

My dear child, we see that you have not forgotten the fourth commandment, namely: Honor your father and your mother that you may be well and have a long life here on earth.

When is love most perfect? It is when we give. When is love most pure? It is when we forget ourselves. When is love deepest? It is when we are unselfish. Now, what is love? Two souls and one thought, two hearts and one will.

So, my dear child, you have sent a present to your parents. First, for your father a silky shawl. Second, for your mother also new clothes. Third, for your grandfather a new book and for your brother a new book, and for each of your sisters a new dress and a wonderful picture.

My dear child, great joy was in our home when we opened your package the afternoon of September 9 at 2 o'clock; when we saw the wonderful clothes and books and pictures. The whole house was full of joy; not only the whole house, but the whole neighborhood; even from the village they came to see the presents, and everybody said that you have done very well, and you were praised by everybody for what you have done so nicely. Your grandfather was saying a long time that he needed a pair of glasses, but now you have sent him such a nice and suitable book that there is no need for glasses; he was so glad and thankful, and he will not forget you, as I know, in his prayers.

ANTTI'S FUNERAL

A community group gathers at the farmstead of the Pitkanens for the funeral of Mr. Antti Pitkanen in 1919. He died young, leaving his wife Maria to care for two young children. Most of the names of the settlers, whose faces reflect a very real struggle with life and death, as well as a rugged individuality are still familiar in this community: Suhonen, Walli, Johnson, Peterson, Luoma, Oja, Kari, and Karkie. The death occurred the year after the great fire and flu epidemic when Antti was only forty-four years old. His wife, survived for more than thirty years, his grandson a high school classmate.

In 1919 neighbors had gathered in Pyrinto hall for an undetermined social event. A young farmer decided to forgo the event in order to capture a couple of spirited horses to begin plowing. It is suggested that a rabbit or something else startled one horse. At any rate, the certainty is that Antti received a powerful kick to his belly. He was found lying in the field. A bell on nearby Lakeside school was rung, alerting the people gathered at Pyrinto Hall. He was taken to Wright via horse and wagon, then to a Duluth hospital by train. Doctors of the era were unable to treat the peritonitis, and Antti's return trip on the train was in a coffin. So a happy social event turned, in a matter of days, into a very sad funeral for a young husband and father.

So, My dear child, you have sent us books, pictures and clothes. It makes us happy. But with amazement we were looking upon the small, strange parcel that looked like a book, and when we opened it, we found two persons with big eyes. We were looking and found Anna Gesina Bahnen there, and we recognized you at once. Everybody was wondering and glad to see your face, for your pictures are really nice; they brought us so much happiness. We said we would not give away these pictures for 10 thaler.

So, dear child, we have seen your picture; we would like to speak with your picture, but it didn't want to speak. But in your letter we could learn that you are doing well. Also, through our writing we want to tell you that we are in good health; this is the best… (Remainder of letter missing)

The next letter certainly is in a different tone. It is three years later, and Gesina is a married woman.

Spahn, December 19, 1858

My dear daughter;

A very heavy blow happened here. Namely, your father died on December 16, 1858. Unfortunately, he died by accident. He went into the well of Bernard Dietter. Since we are having a dry time the wells are also dry, and people tried to make other holes and to deepen the wells from inside. As they did so there came unfortunately a rock from above; there were two men in the well, John Dietter and your father. The rock hit your father right on the forehead and caused a big hole. Immediately his senses were lost and he died after a quarter of an hour in the well. John Jahne brought him out. It happened on December 16 at 11 o'clock in the morning.

Dear daughter, be consoled. On December 12 he went to confession, what according to our Christian faith is the best for him. For we have a jubilee in our parish for one month, and the last day will be December 25.

Dear daughter, be consoled. We all have to die, and we don't know what kind of death we will have. Some died here a sudden death. Your father died with honor; here a few died with shame, because they caused their own deaths.

Dear daughter, what can we do now but pray? Let us pray for him. It is advisable to pray three Our Fathers for him after meals. Dear daughter, where shall we begin? The children are small. Good help and advice is a good deed. Your brother is 11 years old, and your two sisters are still too young to earn bread

and money.

Dear daughter, on November 13 we sent our last letter to you. Did you receive it or not? We don't know. We hope to get an answer from you soon. There is not much courage here, so I will close.

Mother Anna Margareta Bahnen

Writer John Bernard Hulsmann

Death of loved ones in the "old country" must have been one of the most difficult aspects of immigration, no matter what the home country.

WAKE UP AND SMELL THE COFFEE, OR, IF YOU NEED IT, MAKE IT

"OH oh… I knew I'd forget to mark that grave," I thought, as Toivo Walli's white Corvette circled the driveway. Toivo had talked to me earlier about marking the location for his wife Esther's grave.

Esther had been married to Toivo's brother until he was killed on his job. Toivo had been Esther's husband for almost fifty years now, and stepfather to his brother's girls. Standing in the cemetery with her ashes in a dilapidated cardboard box he seemed to have no clear direction of what was to proceed from here. As relatives from the large Walli clan gathered at Lakeside clubhouse to witness the burial, I eyed the cardboard shipping box, it did not seem to be an acceptable mode for sending "ashes to ashes, dust to dust." Toivo absently returned the box to his trunk.

"I'll see if I can find something to put those ashes into," I said, thinking of some of the larger vessels I had thrown on the potter's wheel. "Can I see those ashes again, so I know how big it needs to be?"

"Sure," Toivo said, as he threw open the trunk and took out the tattered box again.

"Hilda Nivala might have something big enough." It was clear, then, that none of my hand-thrown clay containers would work.

"This number-three coffee can should do," said Hilda, after a hurried search of her premises she brought her collection of previously used wrap and ribbon to the table. Gayly decorated wishes for many occasions were sorted out to reveal, at last, a single piece of silver wrap.

"That's just about big enough to cover the can." And so

we covered the gap with an appropriate looking gold on gold ribbon bow, after pressing the storage wrinkles out of it. A simple bouquet of wild flowers completed a makeshift urn.

As Hilda checked the coffee can urn for one last time she remembered the left over coffee in the bottom of it. "You know, Esther used to get up every morning at four A.M., fix the coffee for the two of them and then go back to sleep. We'll just leave these few coffee grounds in the can. Then when she wakes up—she can smell the coffee! She really loved her morning coffee!"

"Makes sense to me." I chuckled all the way to Lakeside clubhouse.

Many years later Kaija recalled me telling her the story and ending with the admonition: "I don't care if you bury me in a cardboard box, or what. But it better be decorated."

COFFEE'S BREWING—I'LL BE WAITING
Grave of Dick Anderson, Round Lake Cemetery

A LAWMAN VIEWS DEATH

The music seemed to me, a chaperone, loud enough to cause a headache. As I sat on a folding chair in the high school gym I was amazed and entertained by the uninhibited, sometimes graceful sometimes discordant movements of students. Now, in the semi-darkness, a tall, more mature figure approached me. I soon recognized the town constable. It was, I realized, time for him to check with me on any suspicious activity; use of alcohol or drugs, violence, underage admission to the dance. He sat down in the vacant chair next to me, and we covered the required information, then turned our conversation to small talk.

"Yes, I've had a busy time today too. Had to mark a grave, and meet with a family who had a death to deal with." His intense, perceptive gaze focused on my face.

"I wonder if it was the same death I investigated on Thursday?" he asked, quizzically.

I named the family, and the member who had died.

"Bingo." He shook his head, as if trying to refute his recent experience. "I was called to his house to investigate a death. It was very obvious, very soon, that the body had been dead for a time… days… a week? The man had no person who seemed to care whether he lived or died. Guess that's the way he lived his life. Well, anyway, more and more of his children came rushing into the house while I was there. It was a pathetic scene. The grimy, dark rooms of the small shack were bare of any real possessions, but as his kids came in they scurried around, digging here and there, trying to find something to glom onto. It was like watching a bunch of rats! They showed no feeling of sorrow, or loss—only attempted to compete for what little was left of the meager, last affects of the pitiful man. It reminded me of a bunch of rats, scrounging an empty grain bin." It was a long time, if ever, until I got that very vivid image out of my mind. We leave a legacy for our children in so many ways.

Words used to describe death, euphemisms, can often indicate a culture's deepest feelings concerning a topic. Many locals avoid the straightforward "died," choosing instead a substitute which they feel will be softer, or even more casual.

BOUGHT THE FARM, or simply BOUGHT IT. Banks extending farm loans often required borrowers to take out insurance, so that the farm would be covered in the event of a man's (almost always) death. When the "head of a household" died before the loan was completely paid off he essentially "bought the farm" for his family.

HAS GONE ON TO HER (HIS) REWARD, GONE TO HEAVEN, GOD HAS TAKEN, all, of course, are a result of the strong Christian faith in this area. It may not have been reflected much in life, but provides much comfort and "closure" at death. Fortunately the converse statement, GONE TO HELL, is nearly always reserved for situations or objects.

KICKED THE BUCKET, or simply KICKED OFF. We most often think of ourselves as "Midwesterners, but it has been said that the mentality in the late eighteen hundreds, early nineteen hundreds smacked of the "wild west." Frankly, I think there are too many Scandinavians and Finns here for that to be true. We wonder though, if the origin of this term might be a reference to the procedure of hanging someone to death.

SLEPT AWAY, EXPIRED, CHECKED OUT, CASHED IN are all used in varying degrees of frequency, are meant to soften the difficulty of death, put a positive connotation on it. PASSED AWAY is by far the most popular of this type of term.

BIT THE DUST could refer to burial in soil, or be a more theological reference to "Dust thou art, to dust you shall return."

LOOKING DEATH IN THE EYE

It is Sunday afternoon, October, 2001. Two people whom I haven't met await me at the cemetery (15 minutes early). The fact that they are farmers would explain their obviously dire financial circumstances. I silently curse again government farm policy. I show them lots near the trees and pasture, they are happy. He has cancer, everywhere in his body, is at peace with the fact that his time here is very limited. We joke, talk of many things. I tell them that I am writing a book. "Please send one to us as soon as possible, we will want to buy one!" We talk of death, attitudes and circumstances.

"Death is a happy time, I want them to drink a bottle of beer to celebrate mine!"

"Yes, and I will put a six-pack in your grave," she teased.

"Well, don't drink one first," he continued the banter.

IT WAS A PROFOUND DISCUSSION.

Water, a Matter of Life and Death

Persons probably did not settle in this area to get rich from the large, unbroken tracts of farm or forested land, not with the numerous lakes, rivers, swamps, bogs, and low places. Tiny trees shown in this scene now stand over forty feet tall. Water seems to change from moment to moment, yet eternally unchanging, and a source of peace and security. My aunt from North Dakota said, however, that building a house this close to a lake "gave a person a headache." When the children were very young not a day went by without the realization that water is a real death threat, as well as enriching life each day.

Cool, Clear Water

As we roofed our house we discovered that from that fifteen foot vantage point we could see nine lakes. Granted they might be considered "ponds," which is what our nephew from West Virginia called them, as he floated on our lake on our pontoon boat. (He had decorated it with a confederate flag.) Nevertheless, it is true that the glaciers left an abundance of "kettle" lakes in our area. I say that I grew up "in" such a lake. We would haul a load of hay, run down for a swim if Dad was feeling unpressured by storm clouds, then haul another load of hay. At very least it was the last activity of the day to cleanse one's self of the chaff and/or weariness in the twilight. It was that tradition that I was following one steamy summer day. After working a busy day in the local café until after eleven P.M. I was ready for a cool down. As I ran alone down the moonlit, winding trail I thought about how I would only cool myself in the water, I would never actually swim alone. A shadow appeared in front of me, to my right, along the trail. It wasn't where it should have been, no tree or stump was located there.

I was within arm's reach of that dark form before I realized that it was a bear. I stopped dead in my tracks, then realized that taking another step was out of the question. My knees had turned to gelatin. If "weak at the knees" is just another saying for you, you will not understand the predicament I was in. If you have ever been so frightened that you could not take another step to save your life, you will understand. Fortunately the bear turned, and not being weak at the knees, was able to amble off. I never went running down that path alone in the dark again. If one thinks about it, though, there are no deaths from wild animals buried at Lakeside. There are, however, at least three deaths by drowning.

The numerous lakes are essential to life as we know it, yet pose a real possibility of causing death also. The lakes, at one time or another, have provided water to drink, wash clothing, cook, water cattle, water garden, cool milk, build highways, make ice to cool "ice boxes." As I thought about ice, I remembered another near death experience I had near the lake. When the ice on Cole lake got over eighteen inches thick it was time to make ice... Several neighbors would band together, as this was a major operation. The theory was that if many people were attending the operation someone would be there in case something went wrong. My brother Bill probably owes his life to this wisdom. When, as a young boy, he fell into the open water that was left from removing the ice, our neighbor Anton Gustafson managed to pull him out. "They sent him up to the house so Mrs. Gustafson could take care of him before he froze solid" (Brother Bud). They had been nearer the Gustafson shore than the trail to our home.

Huge hand saws were used to saw out chunks of ice which were about eighteen by twenty four. The chunks were fished out of the water with sturdy ice hooks, or tongs, depending on a man's choice. They were loaded onto a horse drawn sleigh and hauled up the same winding trail mentioned in my bear story. The ice house had been stacked with a pile of sawdust (a nice balance, as the sawdust was a bi-product of providing fuel for heating during the cold time). The ice chunks were stacked in so that over a foot of sawdust lay between the ice and the exterior wall. The chunks were stacked as tight as possible, so that they would last through most of the summer. Black salamanders could be found easily only in the ice house, for they, too, liked the cool moist conditions. It was, indeed, a desirable place to spend time. (Note, 2000) Isak Walli's great grandson Tad and I were discussing the rarity of salamanders in the area. He said his son had some pretty authentic looking toy replicas.

"Yes," I said, "my grand daughter enjoys them, too."

"Well, I was going to pick one of the misplaced toys up one day down in our basement," commented Tad. "I reached down to pick it up and it really startled me to see the tongue come flashing out at me!" He had never seen one, nor had I for nearly forty years.

But back to my story. One winter when I was around four, I had set out, toddling down the half mile path to see what was going on (I suppose). The huge sleigh of ice, pulled by two spirited horses had just come around the bend when my brother Bud saw me on the road. He jumped off the sled and ran up to grab me out from under the squeaking, crunching runners of the sleigh. At the time I did not realize the close encounter I had experienced, but Bud shakes his head when he remembers the incident. All I remember was lying in the snow and seeing those huge metal and wooden gliders mashing the snow, inches from my legs. I am amazed now in recalling the entire ice operation, that no person in our area drowned, or was injured in that dangerous job, or from any other work around open water. I am also amazed to finally realize that this close

Major reasons for the overwhelming popularity of water may be shown here. A person can become one with the beauty and peace of nature, and at the same time challenge oneself to develop the skills needed to catch the often illusive prey. Fishing has changed from an activity involved in providing food, now it is a very popular recreational activity that it is today. Today fishing can probably be more technical, with fish locators, and depth finders, but the same instinctive fulfillment remains.

Swimming parties were held in Cole lake from the 1920s through the 1940s. It was a fun and relaxing place for social interaction. Water was, and is, quite important to life, but has and does take a life now and then, especially in recreational use.

The enjoyable waters of Cole Lake have seen death at least two times. A suicide by drowning, and a heart attack while fishing.

encounter happened in exactly the same spot on which I saw the bear.

Bud's father-in-law was a "man of quiet waters." Newman Dorman was a quiet, kind man, who never seemed to get flustered. But Bud recounts the time when Newman's team, attached to a full sleigh of ice, was spooked by an auto. The runaway resulted in a good run for some distance by the horses, a broken sleigh, and huge ice chunks strewn for a mile. Newman limped home and found his horses, with what was left of his sled. He put the horses in the barn, got into his car, drove to Duluth and bought a refrigerator. "No more of that damned ice-making."

Swamps, bogs, sloughs, rivers, and low places, as well as lakes dominate our topography. Water, although it serves many purposes, limits the land available for other uses. It must have been difficult to give up some highland for Lakeside cemetery. The sand hill is well drained, but one can see two lakes and a spruce swamp from the spot.

Deathly, deadly, dangerous creatures do not exist in our waters, as they do in some areas of the world (although pollution is approaching the point—the amount of fish eaten from our lakes must be limited because of dangerous mercury). Sharks, piranhas, crocodiles, or deadly snakes dwell

elsewhere. Brother Bud does become very serious when he recounts an episode his swimming gang experienced in Cole lake in the late thirties. The boys were lucky enough to have a diving raft and a sandy open beach on which to spend time they managed to steal away from chores. They had fun sharpening their water skills. One year, however, the specter of an aggressive black water snake haunted them for nearly all summer. The offending snake would dart out at any boy who got close to the raft. I'm sure the boys thought they were up against a deadly, deathly, lethal enemy. "It was black," says Bud, in a serious tone (age 65). "About as big around as my thumb. But it was really mean! Came at us with it's mouth open!"

"Was the snake there for a span of years?" I asked, having spent much time in the same water.

"No, the Halverson boy got it, finally, in the fall."

I can only imagine what an epic and traumatic scene that must have been. Our own farm lake was said to contain a giant pike, The Fighter, according to our young boys. He was monstrous in size, but smart enough to be exceedingly evasive. We had the little sunnies who would dart out at your ankles if you waded the beach too close to their hatching nests. Then out at our diving board swimmers would

Harvesting ice on Long Lake during the 1920s was an intense operation, under the guidance of Uncle Victor Peterson. Note the clarity of the ice, and the equipment used to bring it up in huge chunks to the Johnson/Peterson homestead in the background.

encounter the more than annoying "nipple fish." Aptly named for their habit of darting into a persons chest and tweaking attachments there, the fish were a bother, but not really life threatening. The same can be said for rashes and ear infections which sometimes plagued swimmers.

Still thinking about Bud's snake story, I contacted son Andrew to ask him if he could imagine what type of snake it might have been. My answer arrived the next day, via e-mail:

The Bud snake: the snake Bud describes is most likely the redbelly snake. The size and habitat match up, and the clincher is that largemouth bass are listed as one of it's predators. Here's an interesting excerpt:

"Redbelly Snakes have been observed creating a 'grin' by flattening their head and curling their upper lip to expose the teeth." (Amphibians and Reptiles native to Minnesota, Oldfield and Moriarty, 1994, University of Minnesota Press)

Similar to Chi-Chi, the famous Hubred dog,* this 'grin' may be perceived aggression, (or at very least, quite creepy) I can see where one would be freaked out by an aggressive snake, especially if they were in the water—an unfamiliar, even vulnerable environ.

Andrew Webster, Program Specialist
Great Lakes Aquarium
FRESH WATER, FRESH WONDER

*I must explain that Bud was babysitting one of his grand dogs whose name was Chi-Chi, but whose nick name was Smiling Jack because of his habit of curling his upper lip in a toothy smile. He escaped, jumped into a Wright man's car. The driver was half way to Wright when he looked into his rear view mirror to see the strange grimacing dog. He had some bad moments wondering if the dog was contemplating a violent attack, or grinning in friendliness.

One might be injured by a dog, but certainly not by any creature dwelling in our water.

THAT IS AS IT SHOULD BE.

DANGER

I was very aware of our water hazard as our children four, who were born within the space of five years, played outside for much of the time during their young years (well—even now as they canoe, kayak, and ice climb with regularity in some remote areas). I did not let any of them swim in our lake until the youngest was old enough to realize that he could not go into the water unsupervised. They proved their mettle, though, one day when they were in upper elementary and junior high.

They had discovered one of the heifers thrashing around, totally bogged down in a low place not too far from the house. Bogged down is not just a saying in this country. A train engine is reputed to have "just disappeared" into the bog just one mile north of the farm. Now the kids could see that the small cow had fought the mud for so long that she was exhausted, sinking deeper into the mire. They knew that she was near death, and that to contact us away from the farm was impossible. Somehow, with ropes, boards placed under her and SISU (determination, stick-to-it attitude), they had rescued her. It was truly an heroic effort, and one I was not sure I was happy they had made when I consider how dangerous the task had been, even though they had saved the heifer.

Some animal escapades into the lake were quite funny. A pig who had tired of confinement made a break for it by swimming across the lake. Pigs do not respond well to herding or chasing, and are very intelligent animals, a fact which lent an air of chaos to the previous farm owner's attempt to capture the animal.

It is amusing to watch cows swim around a fence which extends into the water to well over their normal walking range—that is if you will not be the one who must put them back into the pasture. Several dogs, a horse and some cows have drowned in the area.

A TRAGIC MYSTERY.

It is a mystery, and not easy to speak of the young father (41 years) who did not return from a local ice fishing expedition. He,

like many in the area had built and moved a simple, light weight "fish house" onto the ice on one of the local lakes. It is possible to spear fish in the darkness of such a shelter, and one could have a warming device in the shelter if desired. One could use minnows for line fishing, or to attract fish into the spearing area. The size of the hole made in the ice would vary. If one was going for crappies, the hole could be small. Northerns (pike) would require a bigger hole, especially if one were optimistic.

I do not know the details of this particular fish house, but do know for sure that the man buried in Lakeside was found in his open ice hole, his head covered in layers of frozen water which had apparently splashed up. He was a large, strong man. We will never know what happened, only that the water claimed his life that day.

An unorthodox recreational use of a fish house led to some problems for another local man. The married man was traced to the fish house, where he was involved in a recreational activity, not too fishy, yet very fishy, with a woman "friend." I don't know what the specific ramifications were, but imagine none were too positive for either the "fishy man" or his "lady friend" who had nothing to do with hooking fish.

Water, selected as a deliberate death style, or water used in recreation proved to be more dangerous than work related experiences, placing at least three bodies in Lakeside cemetery. One Lakeside person most certainly wrote a note and walked into the water of nearby lakes. One is buried in the "Swedish" cemetery in town. They chose the same death as a distraught maiden from the Finnish epic poem, THE KALEVALA.[6]

A sad marriage arrangement prompted these words:

*As in tears she rushed outdoors
to the farmyard wildly weeping,
moaning to herself aloud
in these melancholy words:
And the feelings of the blessed?
This is what their moods are like,
The happy and the fortunate,
Like the bubbling up of water,
Or ripples running down a trough.
Why is the mournful mind compared*

*To the long-tailed duck, the woe bird?
As the wailing of the woe-bird
So the grieving of the wretched,
Deep as water in a well.*

Her words cause me to wonder if those of us who live and die in these watery realms have changed so much since the bronze age. If feelings/emotions make us human, we do not seem to be such different humans in life or death than these early Northern Scandinavians.

Her prospective husband, a man who had been searching his long lifetime for a bride, was heartbroken at her drowning. He searched the water for her, caught her in the unrecognizable form of a fish. He started to prepare to consume her for his breakfast. It was only when she jumped back into the water that he spoke these words of remorse:

*Ah, a madman in my madness
Dimwit with my vaunted manhood!
Once I had some common sense,
Well-endowed with powers of thinking,
Gifted with a good heart also-
but that was once upon a time:
Now in evil days like these,
In this miserable generation,
My mind is only mediocre
And my thoughts completely worthless,
All my actions gone astray.
"Thus the one I always wanted
and awaited half a lifetime
to become my friend forever
and to be my lifelong helpmate
Found her way on to my angle
And she landed in my boat
I had not the sense to keep her,
Take her home upon my sleigh,
but I let her slip away,
Slip away beneath the billow,
Underneath the sea waves deep."
Now I do not even know
How to live or how survive,
How to live upon the earth,
Or to travel in these lands.*

These lines from the KALEVALA probably date back to the bronze age. How primitive are they? I read these lines as a comment on the practice of consuming those we love. He seemed to have a glimmer of enlightenment, as the story continues: After much additional lament, his dead mother appears, and essentially says (very poetically), "Hey, pull out of this funk, go up north, get yourself another of the beautiful girls who live there." He tries, but is never able to find and keep a wife, and at the end of the epic sails into the sunset, to the "upper worldly regions, to the lowest levels of the heavens, rested weary in his boat."

It is easy to see why the Finnish people chose this area of the United States for their new homes. Many of the runos in the KALEVALA concern water, (even the name Vainamoinen means "Man of quiet water" and his mother created the world from water. In that ancient lore the place to go upon leaving this world is TUONALA, the river of death. It is not a punitive place, the name TUONI meaning "ruler of death," and LA as a word ending which denotes that one is from somewhere. So Tuonala is an after life dwelling place, ruled by Tuoni.

So at least one of our water deaths was a suicide, that is not unusual for a Finnish Cemetery. Then we have at least one death from the recreational use of water. I am sure that as years passed the activity of fishing changed from work, (to supply food) to recreation. Then there are many other water sports, enjoyed by most people of the area: swimming, water skiing, boating, snorkeling, diving, personal water craft, ice boating, skating, and others. We have, in a wider area, lost people from every one of the water pursuits. One of the most tragic was the story of the young couple who, on their wedding night, set out on snowmobiles over a lake with thin ice. He died—she lived. Locals say "she should have tried a rescue—she might be dead, then, too."

Bud tells of a time when a cousin from Duluth decided he should swim out to the diving raft. "Can you swim well enough to do that?" asked Bud.

"Oh, sure, I know how to swim really well."

Bud saw what looked like trouble. After seeing the frantic boy go under several times Bud dove in, grabbed him by the hair and pulled him to safety. When his mother heard about the rescue she solemnly opened her purse, pulled out a fifty cent piece and said only "Here," as she placed it in Bud's hand. As an adult the cousin often joked, "Well, my life was worth fifty cents!" (More in the thirties than it seems today, but still maybe little enough to joke about.)

The third lifesaving experience for Bud near or on Cole lake happened when he was directed to help a neighbor draw water from the open ice left from harvesting. The teen warned the man not to walk in an area staked as dangerous. The man, ignoring the warning, fell into the water. Bud had the presence of mind to extend a sled to the frantic man, then pull him to safety. He was never even thanked for that effort. Darn smart kids!

As a young person I can remember wondering, more than lightly, whether I would survive one such popular, fast growing new water sport. I was probably a typical younger sister type pest when I finally persuaded my older brother and several of his friends to let me go up on water skis which they had recently acquired. I got up on the skis, and was hanging on for dear life as the fast moving boat circled around and around Cole Lake. The problem I faced was that I did not know how to exit the ride! The boys thought it was justifiably entertaining to drag me quickly around the lake, not slowing down or veering close to shore. I wondered about the specter of a watery death for some time, before I finally released my grip on the pull bar, and jetted down into the boat wake. Hanging on for dear life was more than a saying to me that day. Sometimes one must just let go. A neighbor recently told of learning that lesson on snow skis, quite painfully. I think it applies to a lot of life.

SEEING TRUTH

A water death which happened in a lake which touches our farm brings to question the matter of communication during a death/survivor experience, especially between family members.

Several friends had seen Rob out on the lake that day, enjoying the pursuit of the wily fish, casting his bait while standing in his "John Boat." The type of boat has been described as a flat, low, metal boat. "Being in the boat is like riding in a washtub." Rob wore tall, heavy, open topped fishing boots, which would fill with water quickly in a dunking. It was the last time anyone saw him alive. He was recovered from Valley Lake late that night, another drowning victim.

A junior high aged son was profoundly affected by his father's death. He became uncommunicative, almost sullen, especially when with his mother. When he reached maturity he joined the Navy, and was away for a number of years, not in touch with her. It was a heartbreaking situation, one which seemed to cloud both lives in sorrow.

It was only years later that the true source of his anger and frustration was revealed. He felt that his father had committed suicide, and that it was his mother's fault. So he had been blaming her for his father's death for these many years. The real tragedy was that he did not know one important detail regarding the death... His father had been found with a fishhook in his eye! It doesn't take much speculation to imagine the panic and reaction which might and must have occurred as a result of a cast going wrong, snapping the weighted hook back into painful and frightening contact with the caster's eye. The pain could have, and most likely did result in an instinctive action which probably cast Rob out of the unstable boat, and to a watery death.

IF ONLY COMMUNICATION HAD CLARIFIED THIS SITUATION YEARS EARLIER

Children and youth are not shielded if one tries to protect them by denying information or more complex feelings. They understand more, and think more deeply than we give them credit for.

A SPECIAL LOOK AT WATER

Much as the modern water cooler is a social center, the swimming hole was a social center for adults as well as children, especially in the thirties and forties. One such gathering was brought to mind recently, at a senior citizens meeting in Wright. Discussion had turned to suggestions for the celebration of the Carlton County Historical Society's fiftieth anniversary. Everyone at the meeting was thoughtful—what would be fun?

"I wish we could have another of those old creamery picnics," said Bud. Many people were old enough to remember the grand gatherings that had been held at and in Cole lake. The creamery picnics were among those many social events. Everyone was silently thinking over that possibility when he continued. "Old Mr. Joki decided that as long as everyone in the lake was having such a good time he should go swimming too. So he ducks into the trees, takes off his pants and shirt and trots out to wade into the water in his long Johns."

People smiled at the thought of the long legged and full armed, one piece mandatory men's winter wear. They remembered hearing stories of the underwear being washed once a winter, whether they needed it or not. People at this meeting of senior citizens chuckled softly as they recalled the functional, if not always dependable "trap door" which was a design feature planned so that a fellow could expose his behind without removing the underwear. It was a large square flap, held in place (ideally) by two or three buttons.

"Well, when old Mr. Joki splashed into the lake people on the shore began laughing and clapping. Seems he had forgotten to close his flap! Never forgot that picnic!"

Here I must digress from my water theme, so that I can tell you the rest of the story.

" Your story reminds me of Little Frank Lundgren," laughed Mrs. Peterson. He and Fanny were living near Cloquet. He worked at the mill, and she had some chickens. But she started having trouble with a fox getting into her coup. Well, one night they heard a commotion out there, so she got Frank's shotgun out for him, hurried him out there..His big black lab followed close behind. No time to put anything on over his long johns. I guess they must have been missing some buttons on his trap door. Well, anyway, he stopped suddenly and when that big black lab's cold nose hit his bare butt, he TOOK OUT TWELVE CHICKENS!"

"That certainly caused a flap," quipped Art Jauss.

We cannot discuss the importance of the abundance of topographical water to this area without mentioning it's spiritual, or inspirational impact. Most Finnish homesteads were built directly on the water for several reasons. Number one: The sauna was of primary importance, it was often the first building on the homestead. Every Finnish homestead was graced with a small building, usually near a lake. A chimney distinguishes it from other farm buildings, and facilitates a stove which is topped with a bin of three to five-inch rocks. Throwing water on these rocks is what creates steam in a "real" sauna (pronounced "sow-uu-na"). The building usually was divided into two rooms—a dressing room and the steam room. In the development of the homestead the sauna could be used immediately if a water source was near. A well might come later, but a lake insured no interruption of the cleansing, soul refreshing sessions in the Sauna. The sauna was, and is considered a sacred place to many Finnish people. It is a birthing place, and occasionally a dying place. It is carried with the Finnish soldiers as they troop to battle. I remember it as a place to have one's skin almost scrubbed off by an energetic aunt, who was obsessed with cleanliness, as were, and are many people with Finnish roots. The saying "Cleanliness is next to Godliness" is most certainly rooted in the subconscious mind of most Finnish people. It was rather common to see who could take the most heat and steam. White fingernails, passing out, and burns happened.

Number two reason for placing a farmstead close to water is that it provided a natural place for cattle to drink, and for other farm proceedings requiring water to take place sans a well, or laboriously hand pumping water before the installation of electricity to the farm.

Another reason might have been a factor, but may not have been recognized by those early settlers as important to them. That is the need for beauty. A sunrise or sunset, or a moon reflection shimmering across the water is often soul stirring, if one takes the time to enjoy it. Add to that the beauty of a white pine reflected on the water, or the call of a loon echoing across the water, intensified as it reaches your home. The lake is a constantly changing, an almost living entity, reflecting the weather, the mood of nature, the activity of birds, beasts and fish.

I have just scratched the surface of what an important part water plays in life and in death. I know though, there are many people here who are deeply passionate about defending our precious water systems (including Lake Superior).

"WATER, WATER, EVERYWHERE—
AND NOT A DROP TO DRINK!"

Living Death and Death Living

7

The dead can be brought to life in many ways. Here I bring an ancient (bronze age?) "Witch" to life through drama. Louhi, Mistress of Pohjola, is known in the Finnish epic THE KALEVALA, as a leader of the north. After years of my portrayal I began to identify more strongly with her, visited groups to speak for her, wrote a play from her viewpoint, and a novel of her life. Bringing Louhi to life not only frightened children, at times it frightened established patriarchs.

Dead, But Not Buried

Living death might be defined as a state of existing physically in this earthly realm, but not in spirit or soul. Although the body might still be functioning, the person is not connected in relationships, or any other pursuits or functions which might define one as human. Living Death has been imposed on some, but often imposed by the person on oneself.

In the year of 1943 it was wartime, a man had been trained, but decided war was not for him. He and two other young men had come home to Wright for a furlough before being sent overseas to enter the fray. Now it was time to depart for places and experiences the young soldiers didn't even want to contemplate. As the train left the station Steven had still not arrived at the depot. He had made a decision with which he lived for the next sixty years. He died to his family, to his friends, to his community and to his country. He has been dead for nearly sixty years now. One can only imagine the hell he has experienced during that time, living in the spruce swamps near home, yet so very far away. The trauma of furtively attempting to fulfill needs to keep his body alive filled his days. Surviving the

long hard Minnesota winters without most creature comforts must have been a challenge. Yet he persisted, longing to see his mother and brother more often, or other human contact, yet unable to feel comfortable in doing so. In the early decades he must have been alert at every moment for an unusual sound or sign, as he was hunted by the F.B.I.. Sometimes locals still see his "ghost," but it must be only in imagination. It even has been said that he was taken to a local nursing home, after being found comatose (for how long?). Be that as it may, the man is dead.

It is said that in this year of 2000 he is living (?) in a Duluth nursing home.

What about life for the young men who made it to the depot, who embarked on that journey to fight the war?

John Oja remained in camouflage until 1998 when he was buried at Lakeside. Now I don't mean that he wore the green and brown mottled clothing of the army—far from it! He did make every effort to mask the physical, mental and

THE UNKNOWN SOLDIER— Marker at Salo Cemetery, Aitkin County, Minnesota

emotional pain of the war which dogged him for the remainder of his days here. He carried shrapnel in his back and legs which might have put a lesser man in a wheel chair. If he ever felt the urge to speak of that constant physical pain which racked his body, (according to close family) he smiled and told a joke instead. He carried in his mind the memory of battles and blood, sweat and fear. If he felt compelled to warn others of the horrors of war he consumed alcohol until the vision and memories left his mind (thus part of his life was constantly lost—he died a little at a time). If he felt in his spirit unable to emotionally cope with the inhumanity of war he went to help a neighbor, or do community service. (One of the last contacts I remember well was his participation at eighty in a play "A SCANDINAVIAN DINNER THEATER" which I wrote and directed for presentation at Lakeside Clubhouse. It was a somewhat daunting challenge for him, but he played the part well, and remembered performing at the same old schoolhouse when he was a small child.)

Adequate compensation, or treatment for the effects of war that he suffered never seemed to be forthcoming from

CANNON FODDER
The reality of war came to visit in the personage of Victor and George Peterson. Though they are in the backwoods of Minnesota, these two soldiers are resolutely ready to do whatever they are called to do.

MOTHER AND SONS shows Maria Peterson Johnson with her sons Victor Peterson and Teddy Johnson. She had once made the comment, "I'm not raising cannon fodder." Three of her sons went to war and all came back.

the veteran's service. I am convinced that to live was a struggle for John, financially, medically and emotionally. However, he seldom, if ever, complained about those aspects of his life. I won't discuss the other men who boarded those battle-bound trains in 1943, or the dozen other veterans of war who are buried at Lakeside. Their stories could fill a book, I am sure. I know that one of my uncles became a tough, barking Sergeant in World War One. I know that another of my uncles also served in that war. The youngest uncle, Ted, served in World War Two, and made the most of his service. Clippings and stories tell of a country lad who did his job well, and made a real contribution to the effort, but most amazing, he had some fun while doing that. I know that he learned how to tie fishing flies, and locate some great fishing holes overseas. He posed for one picture in full uniform, with a pair of deer horns on his head. His lifelong interest in meeting and engaging people served him well in Europe, as did his skill in language and writing. Incidentally, when he wrote some life experiences in a small, self published book he included only a brief mention of his time in service, then only comparing damage to the countryside there to damage to this area by the fire of 1918.

All of my maternal uncles (except one buried on the homestead as a child) rest at Lakeside. A local veteran's group decorates three of four uncles graves with flags each memorial day, along with twenty other graves of our veterans. As I write this chapter a television program is naming "most important people of the last century." One person has named "The G.I.s, for because of them we have our freedom."

LIVING DEAD

Some people, in a self-centered desire to impose their understanding of humanity on others, (especially parents to children) have declared a person dead who did not measure up to their standards, or displeased them in some way. In these decades this happens when rigid, self righteous people do not understand that sexuality is something that is connected with genetic pre-disposition, and that the homosexual situation would be less damaging if we dealt with issues in humane ways, rather than abandoning people born so inclined to "living death."

Marriage outside of a race, culture, or social group is another cause of living death. I have seen these abandonments happen, and they usually hurt more deeply the one dealing, than the one being dealt the punishment.

It is interesting that people who are in a severe state of depression, who can't concentrate on living or who have lost faith are often described as dispirited. Are we saying that somehow that spirit which is in us is central to our life? Many modern churches recognize that the Holy Spirit may be in us, but do not want to talk about our individual spirit.

Getting back to the topic of living ones who have somehow died. There are substances which when inhaled, ingested or injected, allow the body to live for a time, yet rob the spirit of life. They take the mind to far-off places, let the mind lay blank and dormant for long periods of time. Those victims have also left their family, friends, community and country. They return now and then, but the pain of living is too great, so they do what they must to return to their death-like state. Is this pseudo death a comfort? It might or must be when pain, either physical or mental may cause people to choose this living death in ever greater numbers. It is a cause for a great many other problems in our culture (robbery, murder, on and on).

A young woman in her early twenties, from a neighboring town, moved to California. She, for reasons known only to her, got caught up in a drug problem there. She found that she could not withdraw far enough from life so she pulled the trigger on a gun pointed at her face. She continued to "live." Details? In a nursing home; blind, paralyzed, and very impaired mentally, obese from inactivity. In the sixteen years since that self inflicted gun shot has she been alive? Human? She died this year. The challenge is to let our children feel the value of being human—THEIR VALUE IN BEING HUMAN. What a wonderful place this world would be if ALL PEOPLE exhibited the qualities we call HUMAN, or which make us ALIVE.

A friend tells me that her father, from northern Europe, expected a great welcome home upon his return home from war, after all, he had survived! Instead, when he reached home, no one would look at him, speak to him, or give any flicker of recognition. So dead he was. He lived in relative solitude, and isolation from his family for the rest of his life. Why? The family had received word that he was dead. Well

he may have thought at times that he should have been dead. Even his own mother had shut him out of her life, as if he were, in fact, not alive. Part of this may have been due to superstition, part because of an insurance settlement which had been received.

A native of Romania, who happened to settle in our community recounted similar stories, and tied them in with tales of vampires. Some people who actually might have been in an illness or trauma-induced coma, then were for-

THAT'S MONUMENTAL—Enough said.

tunate enough to come out of it, (perhaps even during the death ritual), were actually put to death out of fear and confusion. He also tells of a person he knew who existed in a living death long after surviving a death. He lived from hand to mouth, having no work, no property, no relationships to make life a reality. Anyone caught helping him might also be considered a "friend of the devil." Superstition and fear blend with religion to form quite a frightening mix. The association of the supernatural dead to the Romanian culture is so strong that whenever I hear that neighbor speak in his heavy accent I cannot help but relate it to the midnight horror movie. Dracula is not just a figure of speech there in his mountainous homeland, but touches lives. Our media has picked up on that situation to the extent that it now is part of our culture. It blurs our perception of body and soul, to the point that some have trouble accepting transplant technology, or even the scientific definition of death. (See last story in this book.)

Son Paul teaches English and his comment to the preceding stories was to say that in the great literature of all cultures the loss of humanity through a death-like evolution is a major theme. It is frightening, and unnatural to people, because when a human loses his humanity he becomes a monster in the mind of those who have a need to believe it. Sometimes it may be true, but humans, as individuals or groups, have caused much uncalled for pain to other human beings as a result of enforced dehumanization, connected with death superstition.

Those immigrants who settled here "died" to families and friends in their country of birth when they made a decision to leave home, often believing (many times rightly so) that they would never see dear ones again. A young woman made the decision to leave Finland. Her sweetheart was devastated, but made the decision to stay in his country of birth. She married, had children, lost her husband. She again married, had children, lost her second husband. Many years later she had the opportunity to return for a visit to her homeland. While she was there her eighty two year old suitor arrived, having bicycled a great distance to see her. Again, he begged her to stay in Finland, again she left for the United States. Mrs. Kari's children and grandchildren are a big part of this area.

DEATH LIVING

Now this is a personal belief, not an official stand of my church, or maybe even most people. I believe some souls, instead of experiencing a LIVING DEATH, experience a DEATH LIVING. This state is the reverse of the Living death. The body is indeed dead, but the spirit or soul lives on. That is to say that after death they have some way of materializing into this world, and/or affecting and influencing events and individuals in this realm in positive or negative ways.

How can a person who is dead be alive? One of the most important, common ways is the strength of the person living in the mind, memory, spirit of persons who are still alive. Many endearing stories are told about this human tendency. Personal experience imprinted in memory, accounts, traditions, values, belongings, language, behavioral, genetic traits (appearance), created items, and memoirs all can contribute to the continued life of the departed.

"AGAINST THE WALL OF FISHERMAN'S CUT" is the title of the picture of Theodore (Ted) Johnson in the next World War. It is dated January 22, 1945.

In the case of a famous person, these things are shared by an entire culture, or even world. Princess Di, of England, left all of the above legacies, for example her visits to the sick, media accounts, the traditions of royalty, the values of kindness and sharing, her gowns and jewelry (which were auctioned for charity). Those things may belong to the world. In a different way these same types of things were left to her sons—on a rather different scale and in a more personal way. A trip to an entertainment park, the memory of her embrace, the stories of her childhood, birthday traditions, the value of understanding people of a different social class, words which they use which were specific to mother's language. Mannerisms and genetic traits have been given to the boys almost exclusively, will not be shared to a great degree with the world.

Most of the persons in Lakeside will have, more or less, a small circle of remembrance, with the variance coming as a result of the number of people they touched in the ways that are remembered. The memories stem from widely divergent roots. Lenny Carlson will be alive for generations because she made strides in achieving a better standard of living for the area, told some very funny stories and had a great capacity for giving to others. She is, after many decades, still very much missed in this community.

Someone who now lives in another community recently asked me, "Is Vivian Peterson buried in Lakeside?"

"Yes," I said, realizing that we were both remembering those mesmerizing morning story times, or that she made learning fun, or that she was probably the best teacher in our memory. No further words need pass between us, her presence in our memory spoke for itself. In an odd example of the flow of life, I taught her great-grandson in a church class.

I know that more than a bit of the essence of these two women is in me, and so many others in this community, where ever the children of the area have settled themselves. I probably would not have written this book, others may not have become engineers, farmers, teachers, in the best form, had it not been for one or another of these women. This impact stretches across the United States.

SO THEY LIVE, IT IS ONLY THEIR PHYSICAL REMAINS WHICH LIE IN LAKESIDE.

I have a confidence that each time I portray Louhi (an ancient character from the KALEVALA) or speak to a group as this Bronze Age shaman, I bring her to life. I know that she seems very much alive, many people have expressed that to me. "You are Louhi!"

Another way that the buried might live is in spiritual form which manifests itself in the vernacular—Ghosts. Does the very word conjure fear? Negativity? Should it, or will we understand this very common human experience some day, enough to ease our fear?

BURIED BUT NOT DEAD

Jasper trudged up the stairway to the main floor. He might have a tool in his truck which might be helpful in repairing the pump, sitting uselessly silent below him in the basement. He had answered the HELP call from the widow of his good friend Henry, who had died only recently. Now he concentrated on the intricate repair he would need to accomplish so that Mary would have water. It is not often convenient, expedient, or even possible to call an official repair man in this remote area. So she had called kind hearted and capable Jasper.

He topped the stairway, opened the door and rounded the corner into the warm kitchen.

A presence caused him to look up. There was Henry standing near the sink, studying Jasper, with a uncommitted look on his face. Jasper had been to the funeral, viewed the body laying in the casket, even helped to place the casket in it's final resting place. Then why did this seem like flesh, blood, and life standing there in front of him? A silent, motionless stare ensued, which Jasper says he knows lasted at least thirty seconds, but which seemed like eternity. Unnerved, Jasper turned and numbly walked back down the basement stairs. He thought long and hard about what he had seen, as he repaired the pump, using the tools he had at hand in the basement. It is one of many stories which all ring with similarities. The stories are told with commitment, the ghost seemed to be very normal in appearance, and they were not seeming to mean harm. Many times when unsolved issues were resolved the sightings ended.

While in college Perry, our calm, steady and perceptive son, was sitting in a friend's apartment waiting to leave the house. The house was one of the nearly century old mansions which had been divided to provide housing for students. A door opened and a person dressed as a nurse from the 1940s appeared, walked around the room as if looking for something then walked to a door, and entered.

"Hey, that's good, Janice… Maybe I should go to the costume party as a doctor!?" laughed Per.

"What are you talking about Perry?" Janice asked, emerging from the bathroom, looking quite normal, not ready for the costume ball at all.

"Then who walked through here?" quizzed a puzzled Perry.

"Come on now, you know there's no one else here—just you and I. Quit kidding around."

"No—someone came in, searched around then walked into that door," insisted Per, as he got up and looked into the door in question. It was certain that no person was in that closet. So what was that all about? What did he experience in this former nurses residence?

Our children had a "haunted house" of their own. We bought the house in Duluth when it appeared that we would have four children in college virtually at the same time, with none of them big fans of dorm life. Of course, when we bought the house it was the farthest thing from mind to consider it to be anything but a roomy late 19th century Victorian. Our plan was to rent rooms out as a way to finance our student's housing, and that is what we did. We did not expect the house to have "extra-ordinary" occupants. One of the first unusual sightings was made by a very literal, practical roomer, who was startled one night to see a strange man in his room. The man did not seem unfriendly, but only stayed a short time, then disappeared as suddenly as he had appeared. After quite a number of sightings by tenants, and Paul himself had seen an entity which was unexplainable, he placed a call to the former owner. Paul carefully couched the language of his question so that it could be answered by mentioning a number of situations: foundation faults, plumbing, other details that had required the boy's management attention.

"Sid, was there anything about the house that maybe you forgot or didn't tell us about?" There was a long silence on the other end of the line. "You mean the Ghosts?" he finally asked.

"Yes," breathed Paul. Sid then began a description which was amazing in it's parallels to what current occupants of the house had been experiencing. So this was not a case of group hysteria, Paul decided that as the entities did not

seem to menace, but rather seemed only to mind their own business, it was a situation one or ten young people living in the house could live with.

On one occasion, sometime later, many of the people living in the house had been disturbed most of the night by the sound of a dulcimer being played.. This did not surprise them, as they knew one of the roommates had such and instrument and often played it, but never all night.

"Boy, Linda, you were really jamming on your dulcimer last night!" said a roommate when next she saw the apparently inconsiderate house mate.

"I was in the cities yesterday and until the middle of the day today," she replied.

No visitors were in the house and not one of the roommates was capable of playing the instrument. Who did?

One of the entities seen quite often in the house was a grand motherly type who enjoyed looking out of the window at Lake Superior, and was often sighted doing so. One evening one of the roommates came home with rather severe injuries as a result of an auto accident. He was attempting to sleep on a first floor couch when the older women entity appeared. He had seen her previously, as had quite a few others in the house.

"Is there anything I can do for you?" she asked as she sat on the edge of the couch where he lay, in great pain. He woke several times during the night and felt her presence there, according to the injured young man. As always she was kind and concerned, never seemed to want to frighten anyone or cause problems. Her presence was a comfort. At dawn the young man jumped up and dashed up the stairs to answer a ringing phone. It was only after he had made the dash that he realized that the extent of his injuries should not have permitted him to do that run. He credits the kindly spirit with his healing.

One day nearly a year later Andrew and Paul saw two men in the back yard looking around, and went out to check on it.

"Oh, we just wanted to take another look at the old home place. We lived here for quite a while," said one of the men.

"Yes, we lived here with our grandmother. She was such a wonderful person. She sure liked to stand at that window and look out at the lake." He gestured at the second story window at which the benevolent grandmother had been

Duluthian Inspects Army Food

Food for America's soldiers gets a thorough inspection by members of the army veterinary corps before it is delivered to the fighting forces—and among the inspectors is Duluth Cpl. Theodore Johnson, 4010 West Sixth street, pictured above with three buddies looking over potatoes and onions for delivery to units in England. Left to right are Sgt. Delbert Achey, Bethlehem, Pa.; Corporal Johnson; Sgt. James A. Turner, Aberdeen, Wash., and First Lt. Joseph O. Simington, Danville, Pa., depot veterinarian. The men are stationed at a quartermaster breakdown point at a general depot in England, from which the photo was received.

Ted serves his country as he engaged in army life activity as reported by the Duluth-News Tribune.

sighted numerous times.

Paul and Andrew looked knowingly at each other, but said nothing.

Many of the roommates saw the same entities, and often would make very similar descriptions of them without having any way of knowing what someone else had seen. There was the man in the round glasses, vest and sometimes a fedora. A medium sized dog was described in corresponding terms by more than several roommates. Then there was the woman in the red dress and, of course, the benevolent grandmother.

Paul attempted to persuade the ghosts to leave, and his requests did seem some what effective, as the sightings were fewer following that communication effort.

"I just had a friendly talk, told them we would appreciate it if they would not bother us, we hold no ill will, but would like our privacy." Paul recounted his conversation with the ghost in the same calm, matter-of-fact voice he would use in discussing the history of the industrial revolution. Sightings thereafter were minimal, until the house was up for sale some twelve years later. That was the year when Perry's wife Samantha woke one night feeling that someone was in the room, watching her. She saw the man in the fedora and vest leaning over her in a concerned way. He faded away. Then she saw one of the only entities which seemed to be up to some bedevilment. He was smirking as he rose, emerging from sleeping Perry's chest. He seemed to be about fourteen years old and was wearing a baseball cap and carried a bat. Samantha, needless to say, was quite shaken. She said she saw many entities in that last year when the house was up for sale. She said she could always sense their presence before she saw them.

One sighting involved a very young boy who appeared, matured into a young man, grew gradually older until he was aged, then disappeared.

At one time a friend who was a shaman came to the house to investigate. She saw some of the same ghosts, and described them in almost the exact words used by others.

The house has been sold, I hope the permanent residents are happy with the new humans. It seems as if change upsets them. Our boys will not forget some of the extra normal experiences, nor will some of the people who shared the house (and it's ghostly occupants). Perry told of another friend who lived in a "troubled" house. One day a person who said she had extra normal sensitivity was visiting that house. "I believe that there is one troubled child in the house. I see the source of problems to be a child's possession, under the basement stairway," she told the doubtful home owner. Upon checking he found only a large pair of knee waders in said place.

"No, I don't see anything here that could belong to a child," he muttered.

"Well, move some stuff then," the spiritual person said.

There, under the fishing gear was a little corn popper toy! It was removed from the house. I, myself, have not seen individual spirits, but did one time see a crowd of people emerging from the swamp, dressed in turn of the century

clothing, all white. Men, women, children were all victoriously sweeping out of the night, toward our vehicle. Maybe sometime we will have a more specific explanation. Until then we silently wonder.

Does this card from 1911 reflect generations of oppression and war in Finland, or is it Emma's personal peace statement? Note the same Twilight Limited backdrop in the photo of J. Walli and S. Johnson.

Brother Bud came home from a two-day trip to visit family in Minneapolis. "I had a rather unsettling thing happen."

"Oh... What?" I asked.

"Well, Joan had read 'til one thirty Saturday night, then shut the light off. At three in the morning I woke up.. The light was on, and there was a woman standing by the bed. I thought it was Jo at first—but then…"

"Are you telling me that it wasn't Jo—or wasn't sleep-walking—or a dream?"

"That might be true, but this person has appeared before! To several friends of the kids, and to the previous owner of the house. I guess that's why they sold the place. Of course, they didn't tell that story until much later."

"Were any words spoken?"

"No, she just stood there—a big woman…"

I have heard too many similar stories to disbelieve this one, or think it can be explained away

Another friend tells of a time when one of her very best friends died. She placed a small windmill on his grave, "like the one over there," she said, pointing to a windmill which was turning slowly in the slight wind. "I have loved windmills, always have them on my lawn."

I made the assumption, then, that this lady is well aware of the amount of air movement it would take to move the whirling fins of the decoration.

"When I would visit the grave the windmill would start turning, no matter how still the air was. I knew my friend was there."

TRADITION

Tradition is important at the family hunting camp located in the forested glacial rills north of Wright. Generations in our family have hunted there, and a hunting shack provides comparatively primitive accommodations for those currently keeping those traditions. One well kept activity is a wild, but quite friendly came of cribbage in the evening, which might last well into the morning.

One evening the deer hunting crew had enjoyed a great beef roast, wool stockings were hung over the antique wood heater to dry and the cooler of beer was handy, in it's traditional place in the snowbank just outside the door. Friendly banter indicated that the cribbage game was in progress. Some of the players looked up to see the figure of a man move past the window, then heard the sound of their cooler being opened, and then shut. The latched outside door then opened, closed. Someone had entered. "Clarence," said my brother-in-law Bill. It was in keeping with tradition, as the nearest permanent resident neighbor, Clarence, always joined them for a good card game, and a drink of cooler beer.

The men made it a point to motor over to visit Clarence's place the next day. As they visited with his wife, mentioning the visit, she said, without hesitation, "Yep, that was Clarence, he really enjoys his traditional visits to your hunting shack."

Only one thing was different in 1999—Clarence had died in 1998.

MY SPIRIT IS RESTLESS,
WANDERS IN SEARCH OF PEACE.

SCRIPTURE SEARCH

Most pastors I have heard mention the paranormal in sermons, or have spoken personally about spiritual communication seem to feel compelled to admonish about the possible, probable evil, or non-existent nature of paranormal messages or sightings. I have, however, spoken to one quite highly placed member of the clergy who seemed open to the possibility that some things which we can not explain are not necessarily evil.

The word SPIRIT or GHOST in Greek means wind, or air. The word "spirit" is used in several ways in the Bible:

- To represent something that dwells within the body.

- To represent the manner of: "in the spirit of the prophet," soul, body.

- The Holy Spirit, which most Christians believe comes through Baptism.

- Something which produces results: "He was moved by the spirit."

- Visions and or Dreams: "Something came to me by the spirit."

- A visual sight, not flesh and blood.

It is well accepted that evil spirits (their chief being the devil) have been and continue to be around. Scripture has it that Christ removed the spirits (one time causing them to go into pigs, which then drowned themselves). Exorcisms are done today. It is also well accepted that each of us may be moved by the Holy Spirit within us. However, the line between dreams, visions, and concrete sightings seems to be quite blurred, steeped in suspicion. On two occasions Jesus was mistaken for "a ghost" (not His ghost). On one occasion when Jesus walked on water (Matt 14:26 and Mark 6:49) the disciples are said to have been very much afraid. Who does feats like that? It just isn't "human!" If it wasn't human, yet appeared very human it must have been a ghost? That is what the Bible says they thought it was! The words ghost and spirit are generally used interchangeably. Then after Christ's death on the cross his appearance to them in human form once again frightened the disciples. He had to reassure them that he was not a ghost. They obviously believed someone who was dead, yet human in appearance must be a ghost. He had to assure them that he was flesh and blood, ghosts are not, and further more that he was hungry. It was only then that they accepted the fact that he was not a ghost, because he was touchable, and ate food. Mat 14:26 and Luke 24:37–39.

Do we really know what all human experiences means in terms of our faith? Enlightenment might be one of the greatest gifts of heaven!

THE FINE LINE

It is said that scientists can now measure the slightest difference of weight between a live body and a dead one.

Uncle Vic's postcard from France.

Although we moderns have the scientific knowledge to keep a body alive, or at least a heart if not the brain or vice versa, I wonder about our ability to DEFINE the DEFINite moment of death. This definition was sometimes wrongly made in the earlier part of the century, (or even yesterday) with very unsettling results.

In the forties two neighborhood women were visiting in the home of one, both women were gifted with a suspicious amount of E.S.P. One of the women noticed another neighbor walking down the road. She thought nothing of it until later, when she heard that the women had been dead at that particular time. One of these women had dreams which often predicted the future. Early in the life of her son she saw him in a casket, surrounded with flowers. Suddenly the flowers turned to American Flags. Much later she suffered great mental anguish when her son went off to world war two. He did, indeed, have many experiences which could have resulted in his death. He told of walking behind a fellow G.I. who was shot dead. He dove into a ditch, culvert or some hiding place, with the enemy soldiers pounding the ground way too near him, searching for him with fervor to shoot him. He lived that day, but was severely wounded on another occasion. In thinking of this dream I believe it indicated that a real death danger/possibility would turn into a patriotic event (life, with sacrifice for country).

Some reported realities raise questions. The casket was to be buried in Lakeside, but for some reason was opened to reveal that the woman's body now lie face down, she had pulled out all her hair. When Sulo Walli told me this story a part of my horror was to realize that my grandmother and aunt Emma had been buried during the time period that the incident was reported by his mother to have taken place. The family is closest to the cemetery in many ways, having donated the land. At any rate, the story is very unsettling.

Dolores Walli gives this account: "The undertaker closed my grandfather's eyes, pulled a sheet over his head and went into the next room to tell the 'widow' to make plans for the funeral. To make a long story short, my grandfather lived another seven years. Grandma said, 'He was too ornery to die!'"

In more recent times several persons already given a toe tag and stored in the morgue in nearby Cloquet have come to life. When I was a child a nightmare occurred several times. I was lying in a casket when a fly buzzed around and around my face, at last landing on my nose. I could not move, or do anything to remove the pesky insect, nor do I remember any more of the dream.

"She was pronounced dead," recounted Sulo Walli. "Everyone said she was dead. Then she was brought to life! Tubes, machines, modern technology all helped to keep her breathing." One could only wonder about the definition of life, as he continued. "She is thirty today, and her body is like that of a rag doll, she can not speak, or swallow well. She is fed through a trachea tube, and is completely dependent on her parents for life's essentials. We can only guess what her mental functions are."

How precious is life? What makes one glad to be alive? We can not answer some questions as a culture, only individuals within groups know the answer for themselves.

Sulo told about a relative who was very ill, and begged for his family to help him to die. "You would not let a dog be in as much pain as I am in." Most of us know persons who have lived in constant pain before a decision to ask for release. "Take me Jesus," or "Lord, let me die" are requests which seem to be resolved soon. Some, I'm sure have lived through those times, and been glad of it! I am convinced that a person's spirit dictates to some greater or lesser degree whether that person lives or dies. I have known some persons with very strong spirits, and some persons who are very dispirited. I wonder what forces determine this quality in us. We talk of ghost stories in this book, and wonder if, or how the spirits of persons are related to the ghosts which seem to be a presence in our earthly realm. How much control do they have over good or evil? Are they related to angels? Sulo and I both acknowledged a strong spiritual force working in amazing and wondrous ways in our lives, but to define that spirit is beyond our ability, except to say we believe it is from God.

COINCIDENCE?

A two hour break in the schedule of a church convention brought me to the large lobby of the Duluth Entertainment Convention Center (DECC). A person who was a very casual acquaintance came up to begin a casual conversation. After a brief exchange of small talk I, with no direct plan or reason to do so, asked her a very spiritual question. We sat down, and for two hours we exchanged stories and experiences which were very deep in a spiritual sense, and dealt with the paranormal experiences which had shaped our lives, and faith. The woman, without hesitation began relating some intimate life experiences, and I did the same. Several days after the conference I received the following manuscript:

WAS IT SUPERNATURAL PHENOMENON?

By Marcia K Sarvela, February 17, 1993

What do you think of when you hear of supernatural events, telepathy, intuition and fate? How can you explain something that defies explanation? We normally look at super-natural events with skepticism, associating them with charlatans or witchcraft. We deny the existence of telepathy. The following account actually happened. Only you can decide if it is a super-natural or telepathic event.

Melvin and I married on September 23, 1968 in Superior, Wisconsin. As we were leaving the church after the ceremony, I intuitively knew that we would renew our marriage vows on our tenth wedding anniversary.

Time passed and we separated and divorced. I married Leonard on September 19, 1975. Sometimes Leonard's Jewish ideas and rituals seemed strange to me. He often told me of Uncle Sam. Sam always wanted to attend his grandson's Bar Mitzvah, but he died several years before the young man had taken Hebrew instruction. The Bar Mitzvah took place eventually, and during the prayer for the dead, Aunt Bertha, Sam's widow, dropped her prayer book, which landed opened to the prayer for the dead. At that moment, the family noticed a black butterfly circling above the boy's head. After saying the prayer for the dead, the family noticed the black butterfly had vanished. With all the doors and windows closed, no one knew how it got in or out. Leonard always felt that this was Uncle Sam attending the Bar Mitzvah.. Was this an example of the supernatural in action: Was this wishful thinking on the part of the family or just a coincidence?

One day, about a year after our marriage, I intuitively knew my marriage to Leonard would last less than two years. At the time, I thought perhaps we would divorce because of my difficulty in accepting some of Leonard's ideas.

In 1976 my father suffered a heart attack. We went to Illinois to visit him, following his return home from the hospital. While there, Leonard complained of pain in his leg after walking uphill. We thought, then, that the long car trip had caused the leg cramps.

Shortly after our return home the pain was so severe he went to the hospital emergency room and was diagnosed with a blood clot in his leg. The day after he was discharged from the hospital I received word of my father's death. Leonard's doctor gave me a prescription for pain medication which allowed Leonard to travel to Illinois. The doctor instructed me to contact my father's doctor on arrival Illinois and have blood tests done on Leonard. The trip was painful for Leonard, but as we stopped for dinner he noticed a man behind me having a problem. I assessed the situation quickly and began CPR, which I continued until an ambulance arrived and took him to the hospital.

On arrival at Illinois the next day I contacted my father's doctor, who did the recommended blood tests. He recommended that we return home as soon as possible and that Leonard be hospitalized. Over the next few months Leonard was in and out of the hospital several times. I started having dreams of doing CPR on the man in the hospital. The dreams continued, but changed so that I was doing CPR on my husband, while home alone.

Leonard was in pain, and according to his doctor, "a living time bomb." I began to pray: "Dear Father, please relieve Leonard of his pain. If you must take him from me, give me the strength to accept your decision. Thank you, Father. Amen"

In July, Leonard entered the hospital, this time with chest pain. On Thursday, July 14, I felt a need to be closer to God and his people for strength. I attended an evening service of the Jehovah Witnesses, the only service available that night, and felt more at peace after the service. On Friday morning I visit-

ed several friends. Later they said, "You appeared so strong and relaxed that Friday." That night as I visited with Leonard he became much worse and was transferred to the Intensive Care Unit about 8 P.M. He died about 10 P.M. When I called my sister in Seattle, Washington She said: "at 6 P.M. I became very weak and had to lie down. I couldn't even do my supper dishes, but about 8 P.M. I felt normal again and finished my dishes." There is a two-hour time difference between Superior, Wisconsin and Seattle, Washington. Did I draw all of her strength during those two hours before Leonard died? Is this another example of the supernatural?

When I called mother in Illinois she said she had been expecting my call. She and my son had prepared for bed, but in an unusual move she had taken the phone into her bedroom. She felt she needed to be near the phone. She also left her heavy support stockings on, feeling that she would need to get dressed in a hurry the next morning (she did need to catch an early morning flight). How did she know that I would call? When the phone rang my son rushed into her bedroom. How did he know the phone call meant bad news? Was it intuition, telepathy or coincidence?

Leonard died on Friday, the Jewish Sabbath. The Jews do not embalm the dead. They prohibit burial on the Sabbath, so his funeral was on Sunday. At the cemetery, as they lowered the casket into the grave, I saw a black butterfly circling above the casket. I remembered the story of Uncle Sam and wondered if this was Uncle Sam, taking Leonard to be with him?

Following the Jewish custom I burned a special candle for seven days after Leonard's death. As I went into the living room about 3 A.M. Monday morning, the burning candle cast a warm, pink glow on everything. I felt an indescribable peace. I could feel God's presence as he helped me to accept his decision. The next night I again woke about 3 A.M. and went into the living room, but no warm pink glow engulfed me. The room appeared unchanged.

Melvin and I remarried on September 28, 1978, on what would have been our tenth anniversary. Was this also a coincidence? Were supernatural forces present? I will never know, but only believe that it was not a total coincidence.

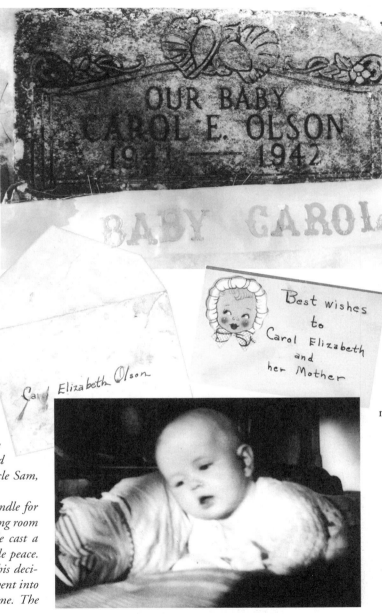

Death is difficult at any age—but so cute… So much potential.

Marcia had written the story as part of a creative writing class in which the subject matter was to be experiences in life which we could not explain. One of the students made the flat statement that she did not believe in paranormal experiences, and that she saw no sense in the assignment.

"All right," said the instructor, "we'll do an experiment. Pick a number, any number."

"Fifty-seven" said the doubting student.

The class was dismissed. The woman came back the next day and recounted the following story: "My husband was driving the family car last night. We had our children with us. My husband said, with great concern, 'I've got to have this car checked right now, every time it reaches fifty-seven miles-per-hour it starts to shimmy.'" (It wasn't fifty-five or sixty, it was fifty-seven.) A mechanical check revealed a problem which could have resulted in a crash. The woman lost a good deal of skepticism that night. Marcia and I agree that it is good to be thoughtful in evaluating life experiences, not to be anxious to jump to unusual conclusions. We also agreed that many situations had occurred in our lives that were unexplainable in human terms, with "natural" conclusions. Neither one of us lives in fear of super human intervention.

It would be interesting to have a journal of the amazing messages I have received. Here are some I recall:

- During a terrific wind storm I am driving by Lakeside cemetery on my way to a prayer meeting. I think, "What if that poplar tree would blow down on my car?" That very tree was across the road when I returned, and it would have dealt damage or death.

- My son is applying for his first job out of High School. While waiting for him in another location, I strike up a conversation with a total stranger (in Duluth, no small town) and find that the person Paul is interviewing with is a convicted molester.

- We set out to find Paul housing. Inner voice says that it will be a green house on 4th and 15th. We do a traditional housing search all day, on our way home (defeated) I tell Dan to turn up on 15th as we travel on 4th toward the freeway. Paul discovers the green house in which he will live.

- I go to bed fully dressed (a very rare occurrence at that time) and need to out run out quickly, as high schoolers Perry and Andrew have a car fire at the end of the driveway.

- I have no idea why I pick up a piece of squashed rope in a distant parking lot. It is perfect for the rope at the well of the woman of Samaria in my Bethany wall panels.

- I am told (inner voice) to leave the congregation of my birth, for another six miles down the road. To my amazement the move results in the completion of the biggest art work of my life, a testament of faith which took me six months, and many ten hour days to complete.

- I write situations and details into a book about Louhi, bronze age leader of Northern tribes, only to find research much after completing the writing which is specifically in agreement with my imagination. Some of it is new to discovery.

- "I must stop at Bud's house," I feel a strong message; a family friend has died.

- I make a phone call—the voice on the end of the line says "I need to talk with you." This happens many times.

FAR AWAY—CLOSE IN SPIRIT

"She spends so much time in the cemetery here—why would she want to waste time in them when she goes to Finland?" Because I had opportunity.

The huge cemetery in Helsinki which is devoted to war dead is amazing. Beautiful gold lettered stones mark hundreds of graves, each graced with a well-kept, blooming rose bush. Another cemetery we visited late one evening by the light of the 'midnight sun' was so like Lakeside that I felt if I closed my eyes I might be home at that very familiar place. It was in a rural location, evergreens, mountain ash and birch were close at hand. Almost all of the same names were there in stone. However, it was in another cemetery that I got a surprise that raised the hair on the back of my neck!

This story starts in 1994 when by some "coincidence" I became involved in a play produced by the KALEVALA

THEATER SOCIETY. I was cast as Louhi, Mistress of POHJALA, a clan leader from the north, (Sami —using the word "Laplander" is similar to using the word "Nigger") of Finland in ancient times. I was obligated, at that time, to play her as a forceful, yet hatefully powerful enemy. I began to study her story, as recorded in a collection of poetry (runos) from the epic legends of the Finns, the KALE-VALA. I began to realize that the runos contained both positive and negative stories about her, but emphasis from the southern point of view tend to obscure her good side and cast suspicion on POHJA (the north). At worst she was called a witch, Dame of Darkland or the old hag. At best she was called a sorcerer, Shaman, healer. The fact that women who have a gift of perception or other extra-ordinary talents is most likely considered by peers with suspicion or even fear may tie into the Biblical story of the garden of Eden, and of interpretations and emphasis of the Genesis story of the fall of Adam and Eve which forever place blame for sin directly on Eve. The extraordinary popularity of the HARRY POTTER books at the turn of the twenty first century reflects the acceptance, adulation, and involvement with a boy who realized at age eleven that he was a wizard. It would have been much more difficult to accept a girl as a witch, with some darker connotations, although we do accept some stories about witches. So in the KALEVALA Louhi, who possesses a good amount of "magic," is looked upon with much suspicion, in spite of some positive things she does, even for the enemy. Whether myth or reality I began to identify strongly with her. My life is lived close to the earth, I experience many extrasensory perceptions, I found myself very much at home among the Sami (or northern) people I "chanced" to meet. I found deep spiritual satisfaction from learning to Joik (an ancient Sami prayer chant).

The opportunity to visit Finland was a wonderful surprise, both for Margaret Webster and the MISTRESS OF POHJALA! I had longed to visit the country of my maternal grandparents for a lifetime. We were lucky enough to be welcomed to stay at friend Dan Reed's relative's farm in central Finland. Finland's farms have charm—and the most charming place I found on our host farm was a large, two story log house which had been well built in the early 1900s. Although it contained very little furniture (two over stuffed chairs and a table), it had a good feeling, a place I

should inhabit. Yes, there were good vibes in the Herculy house. The skilled, famous blacksmith who built it named it, as is a customary in Finland. I thought of my skilled smithy son, Paul, who had named his first child Auror which is POHJAN PALO (northern flame in Finnish). thought also of Illmarinen, the blacksmith hero of the KALEVALA who was a master of creativity, who designed "magic" when it was required. To the southerners he was hero, to the northerners a stealer and killer of women.

"Oh, I would really like to sleep here in Herculy house Could I please?"

A surprised frown crossed our hostess's usually jovial face. "Oh, NO, no. Definitely not!" She paused for moment, then continued. "It is not ready for a guest—w would not hear of it!" She left no doubt that the issue was closed.

That night I struggled to sleep in a comparatively airless room, worsened by a negative reaction to travel. I took remedy, stumbled out to Herculy house, made a nest of the two overstuffed chairs and did not wake up until they came searching for me at ten A.M. They had noticed my absence at once upon arising. Dan Reed tried to allay their fears "Oh, she's probably out painting."

"No. Her brushes and paints are here!"

"Then she probably went for a walk."

"And she's lost in the woods, we've got to go looking."

"No, she's not lost, she knows her way around the trees but I'll go looking for her."

Dan found me comfortably curled up in my nest, still asleep, but wakened at his presence. That afternoon they brought in a single bed, and I became the mistress of Herculy house. That seemed to be appropriate for the Mistress of POHJALA. I longed to bake bread in the beautiful floor-to-ceiling built-in baking oven which graced the room. Cast iron and tile were used to construct this wonderful old stove.

I enjoyed getting to know the Finnish family, especially eleven-year-old Matti. We shared many interests: art, dog stories and humor. So it seemed natural that while the rest of the large extended family were in one part of the local church cemetery laying a memorial wreath Matti and I were walking among other graves.

"This is part of the killing that happened in the upstairs of Herculy house!"

I had heard a murmuring about a shooting by a traveling woodworker. I had also found no passage to the upstairs of Herculy house accept an unaccessible second story door.

"What killing?"

"A boy shot his father."

"Why?"

"Because the mother was very sick for ten years and could not go to a doctor because the father drank the money."

"Was that a reason for murder?"

"The father also took the son's motorcycle and drank it up, too. A lawman was also shot, then the boy killed himself."

I looked down at the stone which bore the names of both the father and the son.

Arvid and Antti POHJA!

So the "Mistress of Pohja" had lived for a short time in the house of Pohja! My friends do not even shake their heads anymore. They expect the unexpected, know that events often mesh in some unbelievable ways in my life. Some label it E.S.P. Some say, "What a coincidence." I'm sure that a few individuals feel that it is a manifestation of evil. I only say that because I have been mistaken for a witch, in all seriousness. My feeling is that it is a positive, ingrained spirituality which is very evident in the Sami people. It is an ancient quality, one that is mentioned in the KALEVELA. It may have been called magic, but I prefer to call it spirituality. There are Sami people buried in Lakeside, although some of them may not have been aware of that part of their heritage. They may have foretold events, had an amazing healing power, been able to "read nature," or have spoken to animals. I believe that all cultures had these skills, but most humans have been too far removed from the use of them for too long. Our culture might be more positive, peaceful, respectful and insightful if we each took the time to cultivate these qualities, and valued those who exhibit them. It would be wonderful to respect the rights of the indigenous people who still value these qualities in their daily life. How many activities of our children encourage sensitivity and respect? Our lives could be so much richer. It is evident from my story that evil or misguided persons in the Sami culture are exceptions to prove

the rule, but I believe these are rare, not reflective of the culture in general. So rest in peace, Sam mi neighbors and relatives.

IT IS SUCH A SAD THING TO LOOK
FOR UNDERSTANDING AND FIND PREJUDICE.

IMMORTALITY?

Names on cemetery stones are certainly designed to remain for several generations at very least. It is a way to assure that one's sojourn on this earth will be noted, at least by those who visit that particular cemetery. Additional words or representations may further define a person. In most local cemeteries the words "MOTHER, FATHER, MOM, DAD" are the most common words used to describe and capsulize time spent in the community. "UNCLE" is also used to denote the relationship of the dead to the living. "OUR BABY" represents a world of dashed hopes and dreams. Teacher, storekeeper or even a picture of a turkey serve to credit a person's main occupation (I hope). Outdoor themes are an oft used art topic, to remember strong ties to nature, creation. Many flags are carved into stone, representing service to country. Lakeside has one photograph, embedded in granite around the turn of the century. I note that the photo bears a strong resemblance to a living relative. A trend, new to the area, is to list children on the stone. Many stones carry meaningful messages.

THE LAND, THE LIFE, THE MEMORY

Another type of memorial is the "home place." This place is the home/farm site on an individual or family and is usually called by the previous owner's name until the current owner "moves on." For instance, our farm was first called "The Old Luoma Place" when Neubauers owned it. It became "The Old Neubauer Place" when we bought it, and in all probability will become "The Old Webster Place" when we pass on. A new name on the mailbox may identify the new resident, but tradition honors the old. As I walked one day I noticed a newly painted mail box. The homesteader had died, and the new resident wanted to proclaim ownership on the metal box standing ready by the roadside to receive mail. Ironically, the letters of the old name came through the new paint job, in a rather ghostly fashion.

THE ULTIMATE QUESTION IS:
WHAT MAKES US HUMAN?

THE ULTIMATE ANSWER IS:
AS LONG AS SOMEONE REMEMBERS US AS
SUCH, AND HAS AN AWARENESS OF
WHAT WE HAVE DONE TO ESTABLISH
OUR HUMANITY LIVES IN MEMORY.

Do spirits establish humanity? Overwhelmingly I hear positive stories about sightings or dreams of those who no longer live in our realm. A dead mother appears to a woman who is perplexed by a knitting pattern. She awakens the next morning and can complete the intricate stitch. A man is puzzled about a woodworking technique, a friend appears to tell him how to do the job, and he then does it easily. A spirit comes to reassure a loved one that death is a positive step to another life: "Not to worry." (This one has been repeated to me by many people.) I know there are negative sightings or experiences, but all of the stories which I have heard first hand are positive.

I believe the best way to keep someone alive is to honor their memory, and to relate to the next generation the meaning (as well as can be established) of that person's life. Some people can do this best while visiting the cemetery.

GHOST POST SCRIPT

We have said that we continue to be human as long our activities establish us as such, or we live in memory.. Lakeside community (wider area) has a good number of "Ghost Houses." Does a house continue to be a home as long as someone considers it as such, as long as it lives in someone's memory? Our children visited two such "ghost houses" within a quarter of a mile of our property. We explored houses abandoned as a result of mine operations in Houghton Michigan. I have viewed several in this area, the last one having to do with stories in this book. Many of the houses give the impression that a family struggled to maintain life in the house, cupboards full of dishes, precious photos, closets and trunks full of clothing, appliances and other stuff of everyday life remain in testament to the fact that the house was at one time a home. Unrepaired windows, worn, torn flooring, collected garbage and unclassified chaos indicates that the family had made a valiant, but failing effort to live in this building, to continue to make it

TO THE PREVIOUS RESIDENT:
RURAL INDELIBILITY

Your name remains in ghostly letters
on the newly painted mailbox!
Materializing, getting the better
of metallic paint.

You outfox
For years, decades, whatever the case,
you have lived on that farm claim,
yet your well lived and loved place
bore the previous owner's name.

Your turn has come to "pass away,"
exchange the farm for life anew.
Wouldn't you know— only today
it bears the same name as you.

a home. Bulging wallpapered wallboard, rusted metal items, rodent residue, broken windows and the musty indication of a failing roof gave proof that the building no longer served a life purpose. Weakened floors make entry risky, as do an old building's leaning position.

The first story in this chapter deals with a man who went AWOL (absent without leave) in 1944. The story was based on reports by several local persons. I have said that the community protected the man—I now know this included a filtering of the story, so that it has been difficult to sift fact from legend. This ambiguity was a way of insuring the successful evasion by Steven of the searching F.B.I agents, who "were out for blood." I will leave the first story as written, but I will account here the rest of the story.

"That interview was a miracle," said Jasper, shaking his head in disbelief.

We had just visited Steven in a Duluth nursing home, and he had given us much information, being very open, and showing a remarkable memory for details.

"Is there anyone living at the old home place now?" I asked.

"No, everyone is dead, that's why Steven had to move into the nursing home."

"Whew. I'd really like to go out there sometime," I said, thinking of how a person can see much about the life of the former residents of these ghost houses from a thoughtful, observant visit to such an abandoned place of lifestyle.

"Let's go right now," said Jasper, as he, Dan and I finished our Sunday lunch at Nancy's café.

"No time like the present," I laughed, thinking of my best Sunday go to meeting suit, fragile hosiery and high heeled shoes. After I ditched the shoes and hosiery we began the drive out, with Jasper pointing out the location of long gone lumber mills, family farms, and local history. As we turned into the yard I noted that it was typical of many abandoned place. Four pick-ups from as many decades were scattered in the long hay/grass. Several old cars completed the transportation aspect, the oldest one being a thirty seven chevy. Nature, quite effective, was well on the way to reclaiming what had once been the yard area. Trees were closing in on collapsed buildings, undergrowth replaced lawn, moss covered much of anything wooden. The major house had been quite grand in its day, large, with many windows. The foundation buckled out, causing the entire

house to heave, sag and lose shape of an interior stair which led to the main floor. We congratulated each other for having the courage and agility to make it up and into the house. Buckled wallboard, nail ridden boards and a haunting array of the props of living seemed to fill the place. An eclectic mixture of what once had been elegant, and in direct opposition what had always been junk was strewn round, as if escape from the house had been accomplished hurriedly. This was not the case, however, as a newer dwelling place, a primitive "trailer," stood among long grass and trees across the drive. Jasper explained that old age was probably a factor in the inability to give the old house a decent burial. We left the virtual tomb, passing a well stocked garbage dump, located within twenty feet of the house. A collapsed outhouse and garage were strewn nearby. We carefully avoided the open (dug) well. A gaping hole is easier to fall into than a pipe.

One could see the once grand barn, also leaning into the ground. Beyond it were the spruce swamps and forests which could provide cover for one needing protection. It was a melancholy time, a time for introspection on the meaning of everyday life, especially as we live it close to the land in this area. I understood so much better now the venture of Steven.

"The house is kind of like Steven," mused Jasper, "hanging in there, existing, but in a far different condition than once was, early in the century." It hadn't changed much in essence.

Our first visit to Steven in the nursing home had been an uncertain venture, neither Jasper nor I knew if the man, who neared one-hundred years old, would or could even speak to us. Stepping into the living room, approaching Steven was very difficult for Jasper. The muscles of his jaw tightened, and he hesitated, standing still for a time, before approaching the man with the walker. Age had changed the man he had not seen for decades .

As we introduced ourselves I mentioned my father's name, thinking that Steven might remember, and make a connection. It was remarkable to see brown eyes light up, with amazing responsiveness. The eyes so dominated his face that the toothless condition of the man's mouth was hardly noticed. One long tusk seemed to be the only tooth remaining. I had direct contact with his family farm only once in my lifetime, and I believed that Steven might

remember that incident, which might also have been cause for the positive reaction to our visit.

In the 'seventies food commodities were being distributed from a Wright church. Steven's brother (really a nephew) Tony had come in to receive some butter, cheese, flour and such. The shy, quiet man was turned away. Our friend Lenny Carlson was present to witness that rebuff and had come to our house, steaming mad at the injustice of that situation. "Well, we'll just have to make a special requisition," I said, motioning Lenny to the car. We found a nice supply of commodities left in the church kitchen, selected a good amount, and delivered them to the farm home. Although I waited in the car while she made the delivery, (like most in the community, I had no wish to intrude upon the man) I have no doubt that Steven knew who delivered the food, and still remembered in the year of 2000 (story is not public knowledge).

"Your father died while he was loading a sack of oats," said the old man, looking me in the eye. (Correct–1964)

We talked for a time of mutual friends, the great fire, his family coming to Wright in 1908. "Living to the age of 88, your health must have been very good?"

"I had trouble with my legs, had to have surgery on the vessels. Had gangrene."

"When was that—just recently?" I wondered if he had sought surgery when in hiding.

"No, that was thirty years ago. I went to Dr. Marshall in Brainerd, but he was too busy to do my surgery."

"Yes, I've heard of Dr. Marshall, he is good!"

"But they said I would have to have it done by a student, who was studying under Marshall. So I said I would—but Marshall ended up doing most of it anyway" (he flashed a satisfied smile). "There were times when I wasn't among people." (So he opened the subject.)

"Did you know, could you feel that the entire community was behind you, supporting you?" *(One person, out for blood, could have brought about the death of this man. Regardless of politics, patriotism, or personal gain not one member of this community wished this man dead for his views. His views were his business. The community lost many men in the war, either for a time, or for an eternity. Still, not one of them betrayed the man in hiding. His presence in the area was not a universally known fact, but neither was it a complete secret.)*

Steven studied my face. "I didn't know, but the agents were out to kill me. Had they found me I'd have been dead."

"Did you ever feel exonerated?"

"No, I didn't trust them, not after what they did."

"Oh?"

"They tried to kill me. A two-hundred and fifty-pound sergeant named Mac threw me around, broke my ribs, right over my heart. They said they couldn't bring me to the hospital, they would throw me in the brig instead. They aren't angels in there either. I had already had my discharge as an objector, but they wouldn't let me go. Threatened to shoot me unless I changed my mind. So I escaped, by the skin of my teeth, I got away!"

"How did you get back to Wright?" (thinking of the story that he just did not return from a furlough).

"I said I'd work in the kitchen, rather than go to the brig. That's where they put me. They took my bed, then the officer-in-charge waited for me to try to escape so he could nail me.

"Then one day some guys were standing on the street, and a big car drove up. They said they were going to town, so I said, 'that's where I'm going,' so we all piled into the car. When we got up to the guard gate they didn't even come out and check us. I guess those guys were used to going out. Anyway, I slept that night under a sycamore tree, the next morning planes were flying low, overhead. I knew they were looking for me. I ran by the railroad tracks, ended up going the wrong way, to _____, Tennessee. I got turned around. Bought a sheepskin vest, and a civilian hat. I had my fatigues on otherwise. At _____, Tennessee I caught a Cherokee Bus, a small orange one, and rode to Illinois. From there I went to Minneapolis on the train. I didn't want to go through Duluth or Cloquet. Took a bus from Brainerd, got off by Cole Lake, someone else got off there too. Walked the tracks for a while, then cut across country (to the wild country around the home farm)."

"Did the FBI come out looking?"

"Yes, one time they told Tony: 'If you hear shots, you take your mother someplace so she doesn't have to see what's going on.' They intended to shoot me on sight!"

"Were you in trouble for something you did—or what you said or believed?"

"I said the war was started by the U.S. as a ploy to get rid of the extras, cut down the population. It was at one-hundred and thirty-six million before the depression, and at one-hundred and thirty-two after it, so they only got rid of four million. Then they needed something to get the economy going again. We were just going overseas to die."

"Did you ever feel that you could come out of hiding?"

"My case was brought up before Congress, someone (he named) said I had a pardon, but I couldn't trust them. I couldn't believe that they were willing to drop the matter."

Steven brought up many facts, and some opinions concerning action by our government. I do not doubt some things as fact, and they do little to instill confidence in our government. I have, however, the leveling experience of seeing many good things also, and of comparison with other political systems. I have struggled since childhood to understand pure evil in the nature of some human beings. Government is human, thus some of these people infiltrate it. The very intelligent man before me could not compromise his opinion of events.

"I say to you again, that most community people backed you, were glad you made it, that you are still living."

He was quiet for a moment, then looked at me with great intensity and said very deliberately: "IT'S A MATTER OF SURVIVAL." Steven is now at rest.

WAR IS HELL

Indeed survival becomes the center of all thoughts and actions. Many Finnish settlers came to this country to escape that exercise in death. It seems as if the comparatively small country has, historically, had it's share and more of war. During the migration at the turn of the century many young men wanted to escape the violent internal conflict between the "reds and the whites." Many others came (Sam Johnson, and John Oja Sr., for instance) to avoid conscription into the Russian army. The country did lose part of a region, Karalia, to Russia in the course of war, but did manage to remain a sovereign nation, and paid its war debt. It was only in 1917 that Finland had attained independence from a long history of domination by various countries.

Mr. Walimaa was of draft age in World War One. He had made the statement that he would "hop all the way home from the mailbox if I don't have to go to war!" At least one neighbor rejoiced to see him hopping along the two-mile way from the mailbox.

Many neighbors did serve in the life-altering duty. One young man, John, left a sweetheart at home, only to return and find that she was pregnant by another John. "Which John do you want?" He accepted her decision and did raise the child.

Others came to America to escape more personal wars. Dan Reed tells of his grandfathers forced move because of an accidental, misfortunate death of a wrestling ring opponent

The words from a popular Finnish song were recently translated for me. "Andrew from the Big House" had fought and killed Big Lake (Ranta Jarvie) in a knife fight. Their sister had to live down the shame of this episode in nearby Tamarack. Personal conflicts come to bad ends in every culture, knives are very much a part of Finnish culture in many ways.

8 Birth-Life-Death-Birth-Life-Death

Birth was (is) a miracle, but closely related to death for many reasons. Many area women bore double digit numbers of children. They bore many of them at home. This worked nicely, providing no problems occurred. Prenatal care was not an issue. Little or no provision was in place for caring for an infant with problems. At times there seemed to be a callousness in a patriarchal system toward these concerns. I was lucky enough to be born in a woman doctor's clinic (rare in any U.S. location circa 1939). My mother had suffered one stillborn birth and later lost a child at nine months from a digestive problem. I am told that "they" nearly removed me from mother's care because she was so distraught at the loss of two babies. Although these deaths were not mentioned in conversation, they were not unusual. Six of the first ten persons buried in Lakeside Cemetery were under two years old. Three others under thirty.

Risking Death

Births were often as traumatic as deaths in the early part of the century. Sometime (all too often) birth and death intermingled, with either the mother or child not surviving. Sometimes both died. There was a hardness in attitude toward these risks. One woman, after giving birth to eleven children wanted to prevent another conception. She was told, in no uncertain terms, by her husband: "It's alright for you to keep having babies, as long as I know that they are MY babies."

Gravedigger Sukie's children numbered in double digits when a well-meaning welfare worker took him aside to advise him that this new pregnancy should probably be the last one.

"It's not my fault," said Sukie defensively. "I was gone for three days!"

YOU DO WHAT YOU "HAVE TO DO"

A friend told me about his grandmother. "She couldn't deliver her fourth baby—it was too big—so they cut it out of her."

"At home?… In a hospital?… Did she have anything for the pain?"

"I don't know…They didn't tell me those details."

"Then that was the last baby she had?" I asked, thinking of the damage to important body structures and psychological concern. "No, She had thirteen babies that lived—one born dead," he said.

"It was a gruesome affair," said another neighbor in hushed seriousness. "It was either the mother or the baby, so they cut the baby out of her." Coincidentally, this sad event took place within a mile or two of the first one. Both mothers survived. It is not known if a doctor was available or not, as he would have had to take the train out from Duluth during that time period.

There was a hardness, or sometimes a stony silence about these deaths. I did not know, had never been told, about a stillborn uncle buried in 1909. I found his death certificate when I began working with the cemetery. Our family plot, dating back to that very year, is full now, and we never encountered the little boy. On the other hand, community men enjoy telling of the legendary mothers who gave birth, then finished the field work they had been doing, after which they made supper for the family. I don't doubt that this was true, but I do know that "milk fever," "summer complaint," or a "hard birth" took the lives of many mothers. A common course was for the men, then, to hire a young woman to care for the children and, with any luck at all, to marry her. Many grandmothers were also pressed into service to care for these motherless children. Infant mortality was high, so we have many babies buried in Lakeside, their pink granite gravestones marked with lambs, hearts, or lilies. At times the man of the household gave the impression of callous unconcern about the birth of a baby. A friend tells me of a perspective father at the time he was informed of his wife's labor proceeding, to the point of motoring to the hospital, some fifty miles away, for the delivery.

"Well, I'm not going into Cloquet for nothing. You wait while I load up a load of logs, then we'll go."

I wonder how that ride was for a laboring woman—in a loaded logging truck over a very rough highway.

She was not the only mother who arrived at the hospital via a pulpwood truck! A perspective mother from Floodwood hitched a ride into Cloquet with her neighbor who was on his way to deliver a load of wood. She delivered the baby, caught a wood truck home the next week. This took place in the late 1950s. It was her ninth child, and her husband was at home, seemingly uninvolved.

It was wonderful that my second cousin had an attentive and effective medical staff in attendance when she delivered, by cesarean section. The baby weighed nearly thirteen pounds, and went home in size nine-month clothing!

**FIFTH GENERATION AT
HOME FARM/CEMETERY**
*Isak, Jacob, Carl, Tadd, and now
Caitlyn, only she did not have a chance
to live on this farm, or anywhere. Her
mother Nancy, with the help of Karen
Atkinson (Northland Funeral Home),
found this wonderful teddy bear to
mark her presence, however brief, in
this world.*

"In 1930 one of every sixteen babies did not live to the first birthday." The American Red Cross Text Book on HOME HYGIENE and CARE OF THE SICK (Delano) makes note that this was a reduction, yet many were "needless." I would venture to say that many, if not most, stillbirths were not recorded, and even some infant deaths were considered the business of the family, and quietly buried, thus not statistically important.

I was born in the private home of the local Doctor/midwife in 1939. My one-hundred-pound mother gave birth to six large (one at over eleven pounds) babies. One died at birth, one as an infant, leaving four to grow to adulthood. Our family was "normal" or "average" in that respect. Roughly one-fourth of those buried at Lakeside are infants or small children. It amazes me, though, to hear stories of what those families and Katios (midwives) went through to keep infants alive. The oven was used as an incubator, a kettle of boiling water on the stove with a blanket formed a steamer, kerosene and other common plants or household products were used to medicate. A trip to the doctor, at any age, was not to be taken lightly (for both economic constraints and keeping up appearances). "We should be able to take care of that baby without a doctor sticking his nose into our business." And so it went.

OUR BABY—IN GOD'S CARE

CURIOSITY IS GOOD (SOMETIMES)

Dan's uncle Archie was gregarious, caring, funny and talented. He was very active in his community and did more than a share to make the world a better place. He enjoyed telling this story:

"Mother had her favorite midwife there when she was about to deliver her tenth baby. After the birth the midwife was cleaning up. Then there was this funny looking little sack! She had never seen anything like that before. So she thought, 'I'll open that up and see what it looks like inside.' And there was another baby inside that sack—and that baby was ME! Always, after that the midwife said that I was HER baby, because she found me! If she had not opened that sack I wouldn't be here! Well, anyway, they put me into a cigar box, then into the oven."

At this point in the story Archie's eyes would sparkle as he looked around the room, to enjoy his listener's reaction, and he would continue. "THAT'S WHY I'VE ALWAYS BEEN HALF BAKED!"

MOST PRECIOUS

She bent down and kissed the head of her father as he polished off his pizza in the school cafeteria. She moved her hand quickly as she scrubbed his buzz cut, smiling. I was struck by the obvious show of affection by this mid teen girl, who had come to our school to take part in a contest. The George Gobel type father offered her assurance about her performance as he finished his pizza and began munching on his cookie. He tried hard to conceal, (from her and us) his slight discomfort at being a judge at the event. I wondered if he realized how extraordinary this open show of love from daughter to father was in this present teen culture. As she turned and left he followed her with a warm gaze.

"I had to be the catcher when she was born." He spoke as if he relived the experience, as if it had just happened, so indelibly real it was in his mind. "Wife wouldn't go to the hospital—wanted to have that baby at home! So I was the catcher. I was petrified; didn't know what to do. That baby came out all blue and still… and there was the cord, pulsating, blue… seemed alive. I didn't know what to do."

"So you were not instructed in delivering a baby?"

"Oh, I had read all the books—but then there I was, holding that stiff, blue baby. I was so scared!" Fear was, even now, reflected on his face.

"Then that little baby opened her eyes, looked around. Her eyes focused on me… Then she gave a laugh, a deep happy belly laugh! Her color suddenly changed to a peachy pink. She never did cry, only cooed and laughed."

He smiled, I knew that he had just shared one of the most precious of his life's experiences.

ANOMALY

"She didn't have a marble in her head," said Jasper in his matter-of-fact/philosophical way. He took another bite of potato salad as we sat under the "Big Top" during what is known as "graduation party season" in our community. It was late in party time, so that we had the picnic table on the roofed cement slab all to ourselves.

We had been discussing earlier times, much earlier times, slightly after the turn of the century. I knew Jasper well enough to know that a statement so strong would certainly be founded in fact and or experience. I waited.

"I don't know why Matt married her. Maybe he felt sorry for her... Maybe he got desperate, or didn't realize how it was with her. I don't know. Anyway, they moved onto a farm not too far from my folks, and he was farming pretty heavy there." He paused in the narrative, as if to gather the facts of the story as it had been recounted to him.

"My mother hadn't seen the new neighbors for some time. She packed some garden vegetables up and made the walk over. As she stood at the door, enjoying the brisk fall air and sunny blue sky, the door opened slowly/ slowly an unbelievably sickening odor caused her to wretch. She tried to get into control of her revulsion before she went into the darkened hovel...She knew something was drastically wrong."

Jasper looked into space and time, as if attempting to find the words to continue.

"You know. That baby had been dead for six months!? There it was, wrapped in a blanket. In the living room."

"You mean they kept it in the house...for six months? Dead for six months?"

Yes, I know that Mrs. Swenson might not have known to bury it, but I don't understand Matt not seeing to that! Maybe he was trying to take care of his wife? Placate her. I don't know! Maybe they were both overcome... Maybe they didn't want anyone to find out. But six months...living day to day with that tiny corpse?"

Many questions will never be answered. Was the baby dead when the midwife brought it into this world? Did the inept couple struggle in vain to keep this baby alive?

Jasper attempted to put some closure on the story. "Mother saw to it that the remains of the baby were buried in the town cemetery in a little casket she had encouraged Matt to make from cedar boards."

And a lot of answers to unexplored questions were buried with that simple cedar "rough box."

GOD LENT YOU TO US FOR A TIME

BIRTH OF PAIN AND PROBLEM

(Circa 1951) Delivery room lights are ablaze—Mother has labored long enough—nurses run to make ready for the new life which is about to leave the dark safety of the womb. Time is running out, as nurses scurry, the mother struggles to complete her labor.

2:00 A.M. At last the doctor arrives. Nurses soon know why he is late. Several senses speak of an all-night party—alcohol, but the baby is coming! Help the doctor scrub and get into position to deliver the child.

2:15 A.M. Suddenly that baby comes—party or not. It's then that a most horrifying happening plays out. A fumble may be made in football, but not in life/death birth situations. The impact of the baby's fall to the cold delivery floor would be felt for over forty years.

(Circa 1998) The man had visited the site of construction several times. He seemed interested in the progress of the church building. On this day he asked, "Can I help?"

Seeing that the men who were working on jobs around the building were not entertaining the question, I said "Sure, we could use a hand." Bud and I were working on the installation of our huge bas relief panels along the walls of the sanctuary. We got to know the helpful man as he returned day after day to work with us. I admired his spunk, as he had several visible infirmities which should have prohibited such active participation in the building project. Basic breathing seemed to be difficult. Though he looked in some ways like he could/should have been tall he was only about five feet, with form that could probably cause him some serious health problems, or be the result of them. It was obvious that the man was doing everything in his power to prevent the infirmities from slowing him down.

Don joined our church, did so many service projects to further its mission. He served as chairman of the Called to Care committee (to co-ordinate volunteers with those needing service), as Sunday School Superintendent (along with his wife), on the facility committee, sang in the choir, and much more. Sometimes he needed oxygen to keep functioning, sometimes he needed to stop to rest, but he never complained about his health problems. But I knew "the rest of the story," for Don was that baby dropped on the delivery room floor.

Circa 2001 Don has gone to the doctor, this time receiving his death sentence: failing lungs, kidney and heart. The man still shows no anger, no seething resentment as many of us would. He continues to work within the church, and to live life at his best possible.

> A man is dying
> he told me so today
> not as tearfully
>
> as had his wife,
> only the hour before
>
> A good man,
> With concern for others,
> Hopes, dreams and a
> busy life… Sad
> to think: "no more…"
>
> A blow to the gut,
> glancing, fleeting,
> because I can't face
> what he must…
> Morbid to the core.
>
> A man is dying, he told me so today

WE ALL ARE DYING, HOWEVER,
VERY FEW OF US KNOW WHEN

HOW MUCH IS HARDSHIP?

Aune's husband Tom urgently knocked on his wife's parent's door. "Here are the three kids, Toini has got to come with me. The baby is coming, Dr. Butler is on his way." It was the only thing to do for one's sister.

Toini, now a great grandmother, recalled that day when she, at age eighteen, assumed much responsibility in a life or death situation. "It was a difficult delivery, we massaged her, helped her as much as we could. The doctor had never seen her—was new to the whole business. She had no pre-natal care. Water had to be carried in from a shallow well outside. A small baby boy was finally delivered."

"Bring this one out to its father… I think there's another one here," ordered the concerned doctor. A wood stove served to warm the baby.

"We did some more massage, and sure enough, there was another little boy. We heated him near the stove also. She didn't have enough milk for two, so we went to the co-op and got canned milk and syrup, mixed it with water. I heated it by kerosene lamp. I had to put embroidered clothing on them, so I wouldn't feed the same one twice." (I never could, nor never will tell them apart, they are sixty-one years old at present.) It is another miracle of survival in conditions we would label third world.

A RAY OF HOPE

Nancy works from dawn until dusk keeping our important local restaurant humming. The eatery is important for the town of Wright, not only as a source of food when circumstances necessitate that an individual eat out, but to the life of the town itself. Only a Lumberyard, food coop, gas station, several churches, a bar and the restaurant are left to testify that it is or has been a town. Nancy does most of her own baking and cooking, but hires some of the many persons who would like to work locally. She is married to the great grandson of Isaac Walli, who donated the land for Lakeside. A poignant teddy bear of granite marks the spot in that family lot where her stillborn infant rests.

It was a difficult time for the couple, and those close to them, when they lost their baby girl. Nancy told me, though, of an extraordinary moment during the grave side service for her baby. "It was a typical day of gloom—dark, rainy, cloudy. Pastor got to the part about God welcoming that baby home, when suddenly the clouds opened up to reveal a beautiful blue sky. Sunshine streamed through, with it came warmth and cheer. We could just feel that baby rising through and being welcomed home. It was the best comfort we ever could have had. That baby was safe and happy, we experience that certainty."

I later heard from the Funeral Director that same story, only she added that just as the grieving survivors were leaving the cemetery a most extraordinary butterfly flitted around, then landed on the beautiful casket spray. It stayed a moment, then rose in flight, climbing up into the sky. Lives are touched by what some consider small signs. Hope, inspired by these events can give us peace. Nancy's mother, Mary Purcell, gave me her written account of the story, and lists it as one moment which will stand in memory as exceptional, life altering. A person standing behind her at the grave side cried out, "Did you see that?" Pastor Kleinke also vividly remembers the moment. A total of four people recounted the story when asked about memorable life/death experiences; independent of each other, or knowledge that the story had been important to another person. Theological consideration of the Christian emphasis on light (Christ as the light of the world), or the butterfly as a symbol of renewed or restored eternal life was not a conscious factor in these accounts. It was a very powerful, instinctive, internal experience by all four persons, as well as others present at the cemetery that day. Mary sums it up well in her written account: "This is a most precious and sacred memory for me, and while I still weep when thinking about it, I do feel that God was very real and very present at that time."

BIRTH ANEW

It amazes me to scan the books about babies my daughter-in-laws use to update information from conception to childhood. What a proliferation of knowledge! One book

outlines decades of history concerning childbirth. It bring back sad and scary memories of a time when it seemed as i we knew so very little (and I had the advantage of colleg Home Economics classes), much of what we were told wa incorrect in light of today's research. Much of what we experienced, especially during pregnancy and delivery was fo the convenience of the doctor. Little or nothing could be done to solve abnormalities. I am thinking of a local woman who, in the early decades of the last century, lost numerou babies to spontaneous abortion. I believe she did carry on of the many babies to full term life.

Bud's son Jay and his wife Penny had experienced simi lar heartbreak, even with modern technology on their side Unbeknownst to them a very good friend had dreamed tha they would have a child. They had given up hope, when i November of 2001 they were surprised, even shocked to realize Penny was pregnant. The doctor, after hearing thei history, was preparing to let them down gently, to tell them of the hopeless statistical chance that she might be able to carry a baby at all, much less to term. He looked at the ultra sound picture, and told them later that he felt that he wa looking at a miracle. Signs continued to be evident and positive. During one appointment they were counting fingers when the baby held up her left hand. "All the fingers are there, wonder about the other hand?" The baby obligingly held up its right hand. Then another time she held up her hand with her forefinger and pinkie projecting.

"She's telling you she loves you," said a nurse.

"That baby has a special purpose on this earth, there is a reason for her birth," said the doctor.

Jay has a good amount of perception which goes beyond "normal." He lives over one hundred miles from his father—they communicate regularly, and very specifically—then at times they even use the telephone or personal visits. He has many premonitional visions. Some time into Penny's pregnancy his long-deceased grandmother appeared to him, lifted him up into the air, twirling him as she did so. It was as if she celebrated the baby, and, or was assuring him about it.

BIRTH IS A MIRACLE—IS DEATH?

Time Flies—a Lifetime Jets

TOO SOON OLD
This picture captures my father and his friend striking a pose of youthful exuberance. I am able only to picture him as a post middle aged man with many worries and "set backs." Time slips past almost all of us, changing us as it races on. We must set our priorities over bits of time, segment by segment as we go. Does our world move at a faster pace than father's world, or does it just seem like it? Might time be our most important resource?

Existence—time—space

Time is, as Einstein said, such a relative thing!

When one ponders one of life's most relevant factors it is interesting to tie thoughts together with "sayings" a culture has amassed concerning the topic. The short statements tend to answer questions one might ask. So it is with time:

WHAT IS THE VALUE OF TIME?

"Time is money!"
"I'm going to spend some time."
"Time is precious."
"I've got more time than money" or "more money than time."
"Those were the golden years."

ARE WE IN CONTROL OF TIME?

YES

"Take your time."
"I wouldn't give him the time of day."
"Take time to smell the roses."

"Time out."
"I don't have the time" or "I won't take time."
"Not on my time."

NO

"Time waits for no man."
"Ain't it funny—how time slips away?"
"Time flies (when you're having a good time)."
"Time will tell."
"I must make up for lost time."
"Are you on time?"
"Where did the time go?"
"What time is it?"
"It's about time." (Inflection can change this meaning much.)
"I'm pressed for time."
"She was having a hard time."
"I know how a clock works, therefore I understand time."

IS TIME NEBULOUS?

"Moments seemed like hours."
"In the rush of time."
"Time goes by so slowly."

"Time slipped away."
"Have you time on your hands?"
"Here is a historic time line."
"You had time on your hands."
"Time marches on."

"Does anyone know where the love of God goes
When the waves turn the moments to hours."

These lines from Gordon Lightfoot's ballad THE WRECK OF THE EDMUND FITZGERALD seem to resonate as a description of time in many life/death situations, as well as the death of seventy-nine sailors as the great ore carrier went down in a storm with 80-mph winds on Lake Superior.

HOW DOES TIME AFFECT US?

"She was time worn."
"You've weathered the years well."
"He had a bad time."
"It was a good time."
"These are the times that try men's souls."
"The darkest hour has only 60 minutes."
"Time marches on."

SLOW DEATH OR A GULP

A neighbor told of her brother coming home from a nearby farm to say of the man: "Gulp— He's gone!" Now when anyone hears of a sudden death in that family's acquaintance they say, "He gulped." Houses, like people may slowly decompose, almost imperceptibly, or they may be taken suddenly by tornado, fire or demolition. This neighborhood "ghost house" went slowly down into the ground.

IS THERE A TIME TO DIE?

"It was his time to go."
"Her time was up."
"There's a time to be born and a time to die."
(Ecl 3: 2, Bible)
"Only the good die young."

We can only agree with Einstein:
TIME IS A RELATIVE THING

LOSS IS OFTEN UNTIMELY

Delbert Brekke was a woodsman. He was also a fine, caring, vital man. He was present at a Bible study at our home in 1972. He made the comment that one of his favorite scriptures was Psalms 116, "Precious in the sight of the Lord is the death of one of his saints." Within days a tree had fallen, killing him with a blow to the head. I will forever think of him when I read or hear that scripture. When someone is contributing something or some support to our lives we tend to believe their death untimely. Grief at a death is almost always more centered on ourselves or other survivors than it is centered on the one who died, and is often directly related to the size of the hole left in our existence in this realm.

INDEPENDENT OF TIME

There are some ways to be independent of time. We have one neighbor who never turns his clock to Daylight Saving Time. We have one who never goes off of it. It works for them.

A MOMENT OF TIME

Mom used to wear a somewhat bemused, somewhat martyred expression, when on rare occasions she spoke of the "fire and brimstone" ministers of her youthful church experience. We thought she was exaggerating the length and intensity of the encounters with these purveyors of "religion." Years of experience have led me to believe that the intensity of faith of individuals within the Finnish community and the sense of urgency exhibited in their "preachers" can not be overestimated.

"Oh well, it will only be two hours from out this lovely fall day—time to pay last respects to a ninety one year old lady who lies in state in the tiny, barren, Finnish church in Kalevala Township." Dull yellow/gray window shades covered the windows, which were separated with crumbling dark wallboard. I wondered if the church was log or frame. Stark, dark—the church cried out "stern/old time religion," even before I noticed the King James Bibles calling out to sinners from each couple of seating spaces "Pick me up before you sit down."

I had learned quite early in life that if a Finn is going to sing a hymn it will be mournful.

Moving, but very melancholy, like the tolling of a bell at dusk, the sound of taps at the cemetery. This soloist, being the preacher's daughter, began to display her talent in turning a potentially happy hymn into a commentary of the sadness, unworthy and joyless condition of "MAN." On occasion my thoughts had run in the same vein, but I had tended to keep these thoughts to myself.

The "message" began rather nicely, with thoughts on the positive aspects of the deceased. Then came a warning not to label her as a saintly person, or forget that she had faults. That said, the preacher began a long lesson on theology that wove in and out in long-droning sentences. His voice did not raise, lower, pause or inspire any emotion. It continued on and on…

At such times one must be able to call up mind games to give at least the impression of alert attention. I took pleasure in imagining what oldest son Paul would do in this situation. Paul has a very logical, practical mind and an "off-the-wall" sense of humor or decorum. Would he get a weird, wild look of puzzlement on his face—glancing around at others, rolling his eyes? Then would he look innocent as they tried to control their amusement? Or might he break into the droning discourse, earnestly standing to interrupt, "but the apostle Paul also said… or worse yet… Is this a viable theory when you consider…" Husband Dan, who later confessed to playing the same game, had visions of Paul walking swiftly to the little entryway and playing an Irish jig on his tin whistle.

I had also gone through, in my mind, accounts of the great 1918 fire which had ravaged the area, undoubtedly this very spot.…had compared the life span now spent with the life time of my mother who had been gone for nearly twenty years. At last an amen was said. It seemed as if a giant puppeteer brought the dazed wooden figures around me to life. Some blinked into alertness, some needed to be elbowed into awareness. The long monologue was over now. One last intrusion of the forced, high pitched wail of the singer, who finished each stanza by raising her eyebrows in a rather provocative way, while the organ wheezed a commentary.

The ritualistic removal of the casket began with the unified nod of respect given by the undertakers as they stood before the tightly surrounded casket. We stood at attention as it was rolled out on it's collapsible metal lathe stand, and were warned not to line up for lunch in the basement until the family had done so.

At lunch in the white-washed cement basement a woman talked of the joyless service, but then philosophically said that it was better than the funeral of the deceased's mother. At that time the preacher had assured the family that their mother would go straight to hell because she had become "In a family way," when not properly married.

Before the service began an older woman had come in, sat in the back pew without going up for the token payment of respects at the open casket near the altar. She used her eyes and mouth in expressions I had seen many of the previous, or even grand parent's generations use. Her face expressed as much of life's difficult side as it did her Finnishness. She wore a nondescript long skirt and a worn black sweater. It was obvious that she had worked, or been worked very hard. Her coarse, bushy hair was mostly covered by an ill-matched "Huivi" (a piece of cloth tied under the hair at the nape of the neck). She wore her "huivi of submission" with the peak tucked into the knot, like the "old ones" did. Her skin was dried and wrinkled, ravaged by nature's forces. This lady was old enough to have "been there and back," but her face was one of the most interesting that I had seen lately, and a nagging little hint of familiarity crossed my thoughts.

My opportunity to find out who she was came as we stood out in the churchyard. I crossed over to where she was standing.

"Pardon me for being so brash, but I am wondering if I should know you? She looked at me expectantly, silently wondering who I was. Oh-oh, now I have offended this older lady," I thought.

"I'm Margaret Webster."

"Who were you?"

"Margaret Olson."

"Oh, yes, YES! I thought you looked familiar! I'm Jane Bakka," she said, smiling happily. "Do you remember those math classes?" While my voice talked of times spent long ago in the same high school classes, my mind raced to memories of that sparkly little girl—lively basketball player, lighthearted schoolmate. Does time play out differently for people, or do we only delude ourselves? Time is crazy, whether it is spent in listening to an overwrought sermon for what seems like an eternity, or living a hard life for a couple of decades.

When one has spent nearly all of a life of over six decades in one location it is easy to wake up one day and to have a very real sense of the passage of time. Maybe it is seeing a contemporary, gray haired, wrinkled, slightly hunched, limp over to greet you. Possibly to exchange small talk about events of decades ago. Maybe it is seeing the child of a former student rush into your classroom (incidentally, you muffle a laugh—they look so much alike at that age that you need not ask the child's name). It might come with the realization that the "old timers" are not around anymore. The thing that most gives me recognition that "time flies" is to see the astounding changes in nature and other surroundings. "I used to jump over that tree!" I'd tell our small children as they size-up the forty-foot fir. Now the pine seedlings that our young son watered are forty-feet high. An open field is forest. Entire farmsteads are gone. No cows grace the farmland. Many new homes dot lake shores. It's alright to remember, but one must not, can not live in that past. Time has passed, and we must live in its present, or think about the future. I admire most those persons who are able to deal with change gracefully, who are able to see the positives.

A fellow in an organization to which I belong was decrying the need to make a small change in the building. "Change is trouble—in is not a good thing," he snorted.

"Where did you park your horse and buggy," I asked. "Or have you a model 'T' now?"

It was one time when I was happy with a response, not thinking of the perfect thing to say at a much later time.

DID YOU EVER THINK THAT SPENDING TIME MIGHT BE MORE IMPORTANT THAN SPENDING MONEY?

IN THE WINK OF AN EYE

Alyce E Kangas was in my graduating class at Cromwell. Now I sat in our church, waiting for her funeral to start, wondering how time had slipped away. I expressed this feeling of fleeting time to an elderly (remember, this definition continually moves back in age) woman. She mentioned the Finnish descriptive words for this experience; silman vilaus. Translated it means "wink of an eye." Sometimes it seems as if early experiences happened only last week, and that one is not so different now then when in the teens and twenties. Sometime an event or discussion, or piece of music, causes a rush of memories to flood consciousness it seems as if that time was spent in another world, another existence. Maybe it was!? I know that as it becomes more and more obvious that the days I have to remain here are numbered I become more conscious of spending the time in ways which seem important to me and that give me pleasure. I have a strong desire for completion of my many projects.

I look into the future, especially when I am working on the cemetery, in terms of how can someone else pick up the pieces of my work here? In regard to the cemetery, I attempt to record as many "reservations" as possible, organizing family plots to reflect the desires of the still-alive.

Markers must be constantly uncovered, replaced and checked. Notes must be made of some variances which have occurred. I want to identify and correct mistakes in the map. The trick is to move at a pace which will not speed the need for it to be completed. I can remember oldsters telling me when I was an awkward sub-teenager: "Make good use of life's moments, because you'll be old before you know it!" It took me nearly fifty years to really assimilate that advice.

THE TIME LINE

The topic of my writing had turned to commentary on life's ironies, and to recounting some stories about deaths. Andrew had read the chapter and we were discussing heroic and classic ways to die a good death, and the fine line between life and death. My youngest son had just completed high school, and had begun to notice that realities in life were often stranger than fiction, and that strange "coincidences" were often the norm (at least in our family).

"Are you ready to go out for that fighter northern?" called Dan from the step of the house, fishing gear in hand.

"Sure." They were off, the canoe carrying them out into the lake that dominated our property while I remained, writing at the dining room table. The vista of budding trees, and wild spring flowers surrounding the lake was a wonderful tribute to life. Suddenly something did not look right. It couldn't be, but it was! Dan and Andrew were both in the frigid spring icy lake water! Dan has an artificial limb which extends to his hip, and could fill with water quickly. I considered launching a second canoe as I ran toward the lake. Thinking better of that, I returned to the house to call for help from Paul at his house, which also overlooked the lake. Thanks to three men's strength, no harm or death came to the two fishermen as a result of the capsizing canoe. Thank God. But it did emphasize the thought that there is nothing certain in life. There is nothing like an unexpected dunking in a cold Minnesota lake with big waves to help one visualize what a fine line exists between this world and the next, and how life's ironies bring us all in need of help now and then. A second of time can represent eternity.

Sometimes, as I lurch and glide through life, it frightens me how little I am aware of the lives of others. I seem isolated in the cocoon of my own existence, with little awareness of those individuals who live in such close proximity. Life and death goes on all around me, would it be to burdensome to perceive more about those who live near me?

Today I came home from work, enjoyed a snack, did some pleasure reading, light cooking and housework. I was oblivious to the fact that within one half mile Arvie Suhonen was fighting for his life, lying pinned under a tree which had fallen on him. Had been lying there for hours, suffering excruciating pain—alone in the ice and snow.

My head tells me that we can not know of these twists and tears in life's fabric of all those around us, but my heart still asks: Why? Why couldn't someone have received a perceptive message warning of this dire emergency? Couldn't someone have shortened this man's suffering? This is late in the twentieth century, yet this "mid-evil" thing has happened so close to us!

Could I have endured eight hours of solitary cold, fear, and pain without asking: "Where is my God?" We have the promise of seeing, someday, all things with clarity, but the dimness which exists in the spiritual, physical, and emotional realm of this world depresses and confuses me. Only when I learn more about God's "master plan" can I rest from asking WHY?

THIS MAN, AT THIS TIME, HAD WON HIS BATTLE WITH DEATH

Note: In 2001 the same man was haying alone. The eighty plus aged man fell off of his tractor, breaking a hip. In shock, he was able to remount the tractor and drive it home and into his barn. He got down (fell) from the tractor, but was unable to move further. Arvie spent three days lying on the floor, racked with pain, no food and water. Due to circumstances beyond her control, our regular mail lady who had called for a check on the man many times previously was not on duty. She asks herself, "Why wasn't I able to help?" The question is unanswerable, just that many of us believe that things happen for a reason, even if we do not know it. She had done her best.

AT THIS TIME THIS MAN AGAIN WON HIS BATTLE WITH DEATH

Within one hundred yards of that incident, but years earlier, a man was lying under his car which was up on a jack. For what ever reason, the car slipped, and fell on the man, trapping him underneath the crushing weight.

At that precise moment Perry and Andrew were on our township road, which runs between our farm and the trapped man's location.

"Did you hear that?"

"What?"

"Sounds like someone calling—calling for help?"

They established that it was, indeed, a barely audible cry for help. Our track runners sped towards the sound, spinning out gravel as they went.

They lifted the car, the man crawled out. Clockwork. The man credited them with the fact that:

IT LOOKS AS IF AT THIS TIME THIS MAN WON HIS BATTLE WITH DEATH

IT TAKES TIME TO GET YOUR 'STUFF' TOGETHER

George Carlin, popular comic, has a very funny routine about collecting "stuff." I am, myself, aghast at the amount of unclassified materials I have amassed in this house, the shed and the cabin. I am in the process of attempting to thin out the volume, in hopes that my children do not just throw up their hands and burn it all. Jasper Beseman and I were discussing the merits and demerits of being "junk savers" one day, when he came up with his solution to the problem. "My funeral procession will have the hearse in the lead, closely followed by a Brink's truck, then a line of twenty-five U-Haul trucks. I might be able to 'take it with me' after all!"

Jennie Hanson, also famed for her "collection" imagined that she would be at the pearly gates.

"WHERE'S YOUR STUFF?" St. Peter would ask.

"What stuff?" she would ask.

"YOUR STUFF, YOU WERE SUPPOSED TO BRING IT WITH YOU!" the saint would reply.

"I heard we couldn't bring it with us?"

"WELL, YOU HEARD WRONG."

Only we junk savers can appreciate that one. We might use it someday, in the next life.

TIME IS A MIRACLE!

People may call them "coincidences." I recognize them as signs that a higher power is at work in my life. I am talking about events which are amazing, without explanation, and often have to do with time. If I had journaled these events they could be a short book in themselves. One incident is fresh in my mind, and could not just have happened in the natural course of things.

Somehow, through a series of guided and orchestrated events beyond my control, I was commissioned to donate my time and talent to design and execute bas relief, white-on-white panels which cover two long walls of our new sanctuary at Bethany church (not for reimbursement in a monetary sense). Answers about the execution of them came to me, many times in the middle of the night. It was more difficult for those people working on the carpentry, electrification and other aspects to get a clear vision of what the ten-foot-high panels would look like when finished. This led to a series of proposed actions which ran counter to the effective completion and installation of the panels. "If you had any creativity you could figure out how to have a cord coming out, maybe cover an outlet with a rabbit or mouse?"

Brother Bud agreed to help me to saw out the more intricate pieces, to help me fasten it together, and to let me make it in his garage, and his well equipped wood shop. We agreed to work in solitude. As we worked many things seemed to fall into place, materials which we needed appeared. I noticed that Bud would leave the project, seemingly for no reason. He told me, much later, "Sometimes I had to leave, I didn't want you to see me cry." He was so moved by what he perceived as a spiritual presence. Every once in a while, during the course of construction, I would say: "Bud, we've got to get over to the church, RIGHT NOW." On one such trip we got there just in time to prevent what would have been an unfortunate and difficult to correct, application of dark stain to the window casings between the panels. We got to the church just in time to stop the fellow with brush in hand, ready to begin. It was difficult at times to convince the workers that outlets should not be placed where they would emerge from the figure of Christ, cords should not cross the sky and the finished panels should not be "trimmed, or cut off" to accommodate dark, heavy window trim.

The project was nearly done, in fact I had drawn and submitted plans for lighting the panels. On one particular day I was busy preparing a party for the confirmation class. I was rushing around, getting pizza, and preparing games, for our gathering at the "old" church building. A nagging thought kept creeping into my mind. I must stop at the new church at three o'clock. And so it was three when I walked into the building, just as the electrician was removing a lighting fixture from it's box. He looked up at me with what I noted as somewhat of a quizzical, surprised expression and said, "You're just the lady I wanted to see. Did your brother call you?"

"No, he left the state early this morning to get our other wood." My comment left him with an even more incredulous look on his face.

"Well, I needed you right now to check details of the installation of the light fixtures." We conferred; put the first lights up. He didn't have to wait for me, and I made it to the student activity in time.

I stopped at Bud's later in the early evening to see how his trip to Wisconsin had gone.

"That electrician asked me a strange question, he asked if you had called me?"

Bud looked at me and laughed. "I stopped at church this morning on my way through the electrician asked me if you were going to be around, he had some questions for you. I told him that if he needed you, you would be there."

"Should I call her?" he had asked.

"No, if you need her she'll be there, I told him," Bud said, grinning broadly."

It became clear now, the surprised and incredulous look that he had given me when I walked in at the precise moment when he needed me was a reaction to that time sequence.

THE SPIRIT HAS GOOD TIMING.

IS IT TIME YET?

My friend Jo Schneider has spent many hours at funerals in her capacity as a favored musician.

She recalls one funeral, held before the new funeral facilities were in use. The old parlor was quite primitive, with its potbellied central stove, walls which told many stress stories, lack of adequate space. She and the soloist were confined, out of sight, in a small 'casket room' off to the side.

"How will we know when it is safe to leave?" Jo asked her singer friend.

"We will hear the creak of the casket rolling down the isle and out, headed for the cemetery," answered her musical partner.

Again, let it be noted, time goes a little more slowly when one is waiting…waiting. 'We began to think that this was a very long funeral, but we didn't want to intrude on the solemnity of the occasion. So we waited, anxious to hear the squeak of the retreating casket.'

"This is just getting to be too much," whispered Jo. So they quietly got up from their bench, peeked out the door. Not a soul was left in the mortuary! They began to laugh uproariously.

CREMATION WAS A LOT MORE RARE
IN THOSE DAYS

TIME TO "GO"

Many of us have established, in our own minds at least, a proper time for death to be "logical" and "easier to understand." This time, I have noted in my own reasoning and from the comments of many people, moves back as one gets older. At sixteen a person might be ready to "kick the bucket" at forty or fifty. When one has attained the age of thirty death is sad but accepted when a sixty- or seventy-year-old passes on. But now at sixty it seems that a person should at least reach eighty or ninety. It is most difficult to accept death when it comes to a baby or small child, or even a young person. Death is a loss of fulfillment, of potential, and thus does not make sense to us. In each death we ask "What if," and think of what might have been, but more so with an untimely demise.

I lived for forty-five years, giving little thought to the beating fist of muscle in my heart which kept me engaged in the affairs of this world. Then, as we all do when something we have taken for granted is in question, I began to think seriously about the importance of my heart, and what were my time priorities in case time would be limited. A snag in the status quo really changes one's thinking. I went on a walking program and one of the things that I noticed is that all things seem to change in almost imperceptible ways, and if one doesn't pay attention these minute changes turn to huge differences. I walked by the Hunuri Ghost House. Suddenly it went from a fairly respectable building to a heap of old boards. Time.

Jo Schneider has also commented that of all the funerals at which she plays, the ones that involve children are the most difficult. It is especially difficult for siblings. My first experience with a body came when I was in second grade at a small four room school. A community family had lost a pregnant mother and her twelve-year-old son as a result of an auto accident. We students were lined up, and room by room we trudged slowly past the open caskets. I shall never forget the image. For six hours we were obligated to quench our thirst from a fountain located between the two caskets. I can't remember much being said at home or at school about death, or the family, or coping with the stark reality of the waxen figures which had invaded our school building, but the image is still very strong. If we are going to expose children to part of the death experience it is timely to offer them a more total discussion. We need to hear their views, which incidentally might not be as dogmatic or jaded as ours. We need to answer questions without transmitting our fear, without evading issues.

AT TIMES KIDS PERCEIVE MORE
THAN ADULTS DO

TED

Paul Webster— at age 12

I write these words so soft and subtle
that none can throw a heavy rebuttal.
These words I write with firm command
for on this couch I do not stand.
I sit this way to read my books,
Ted just smiles and on he looks
to read the books that no one reads—
he reads the ant hills, trees and sweetpea seeds.
He'll see the track that he spots with a peek
and follow them while reading between the lines, so to speak.
If you should come to meet him, by fate or chance
you won't know what you are seeing at first glance.
You see an old wise looking man
who is busily turning fish in his pan,
or picking a worm from his trusty worm can.
But take off the gray (if that's all you see)
and you'll wind up with a boy, just like me.
A much wiser, quieter boy you should know,
because this boy goes fishing or hunting to run off energy from high to low.
When you see him back with some fish or a buck
you know he's had some jolly good luck
and his energy has slowed so he can rest once again.
Mainly you see that glowing old face
that blends into Nature, and has it's own place.
He's picked up an aura that comes with those years
when they hustled and bustled with hopes and fears, smiles and tears,
and time has run on, with that clock's awful gears.
If you ask him how he feels
he will say he is glad and is happy, cause that's how he feels.
I know that he is, for it seems that he's Mom Nature's child,
it seems lots to me that he belongs to the wild.
When he's walking on pathways so tangled and thin
she's opened her arms and welcomed him in.
That's Ted

PERCEPTION OF TIME MATURES

"That's an interesting view of time, Paul, but I really don't understand it." Even before he was old enough to attend school Paul and I could stay up 'till midnight or later, talking about many subjects: attributes of certain animals, in depth discussion of interesting words, family events, the unpredictable nature of human behavior, or the words to a currently popular song. This time he had begun an explanation of his perception of time, which was far from the linear sequential understanding that I held. He tried to make me understand that time, like space, is not limited to a straight line experience. I dismissed it as the science fiction diversion of an exceptional third grade student. Now that I have seen some scientific thinkers who discuss time in similar ways, I wonder if we will actually see time in new ways in the future.

Paul had a very perceptive view of individuals at a very early age. It is interesting for me to see how, in the following poem, he combines his view of time and his great uncle Ted. He wrote this one at age twelve. The insights into Ted's character were amazing, some of them are enlightenments not seen by adults, or at least not vocalized.

In 1984 Ted survived several serious surgeries, but lost a battle to survive a heart by-pass procedure. His death was devastating to all of us, but especially to our children, and most especially to Paul. Ted was a hands-on mentor for many, he especially enjoyed teaching about his first loves, nature and woodworking. More than any of us realized at the time, he was an example of living life to it's fullest, and relating to other people in positive ways. Andrew was fifteen when he wrote this reflection for Ted's funeral:

REFLECTIONS OF TED

Andrew Webster (age 15)
Ecclesiastics 3

"For everything there is a season and a time for every purpose under heaven"

Ted Johnson, more than most, knew this for a fact. He had a familiarity with the turning of the seasons that few can claim. He knew that death and pain are natural—but so are life, beauty and joy. Ted had his finger on the pulse of that force that exists in the body one minute and not the next.

Now that spark is gone from him, but it is only natural—to be expected with the same sure acceptance as is the falling of the leaves or the snow.

All through his life Ted built, planted and made. The things he made will last a long time because of how well they were made. The trees he planted will continue growing. However, the most long-lasting, important thing he left behind is the sea of knowledge and values that demands respect and care for the environment from and for all who believe as he did. Without people like Ted the world would be a lot less green. He showed the same concern for the people in his life. Such details as how your garden grew and how many fish you caught were not too small for him to notice.

Ted can be with us no more in body, but every time those who knew him hear the echoes of duck hunters across the lake or see a child catch a fish or breathe clean autumn air—HE WILL BE THERE

My life is quite different than, say, an early Egyptian male's would have been, because of the time of existence and the perimeters in place during that span. Even a free falling drop of rain is defined by the dust, air pressure, and movement which surround it. The banks of a river define the direction it will move, the speed of movement, and the shape it will take. These perimeters vary with time and other factors. Our west bank of the Kettle River changed quite a bit when Don Huter got in there with his bulldozer. Not to say that water can not, especially when it unites and becomes powerful, change it's own surroundings.

God hath not promised skies always blue, Flower-strewn pathways all our lives through; God hath not promised sun without rain, Joy without sorrow, peace without pain.

But God hath promised strength for the day, Rest for the labor, light for the way, Grace for the trials, help from above, Unfailing sympathy, undying love . . .

IN LOVING MEMORY OF
Theodore Jacob Johnson
BORN
November 24, 1906 Tamarack, Minnesota
DIED
September 11, 1984 Duluth, Minnesota
AGE: 77 Years
FUNERAL SERVICES
1:00 P.M., Friday, September 14, 1984
Bethlehem Lutheran Church
Wright, Minnesota
OFFICIANTS
Rev. James Gronbeck
Rev. Gene Taplin
CASKET BEARERS
Kenneth Peterson   George Peterson
David Peterson   Michael Peterson
Daniel Webster   Rodney Olson
INTERMENT
Lakeside Cemetery, Carlton Co., Minnesota
+
Arrangements By
NORTHLAND FUNERAL HOME
Jeffrey A. Borgos, Mgr., Mortician
Tamarack, Minnesota

Uncle Ted's funeral program and cover.

TIME IS RELATED TO OTHER FACTORS

Kaija and I had discussed some heavy topics, I do not remember much of our conversation, but do have a letter with some thoughts on time:

Some thoughts stimulated by our discussion last night. On water:

The water I drink today might have existed in ancient Egypt three thousand years ago. It was then, and is now, shaped by the time in which it existed, and the place and conditions which were present. A molecule of water will take on a far different form here. It may freeze, it may be forced to mix with other substances which change it's very form. These forces are determined outside of it, and water has no control. So it is, more or less, with humans.

It is when there is more water than is practical for surroundings that these powers seem not able to be positive. There is only so much room in a cup, or within the bed of a lake. Then water is forced into another mode (spillage or flood). These changes are time controlled, they may happen in a second, or it may take a thousand years, but they are sequential also. In other words I believe that time is another of the ordered and beautifully orchestrated systems which we find in nature. I believe that our actions can modify those systems to a certain degree. We can modify them more in positive ways if we band together—and by modify I mean to put them back into the place that nature can at least live with, but that nature, time, space, conditions, resources will modify us much more.

My life is quite unique at this moment because of the time span during which I am operating. I can not control some of the factors which are in place at this particular moment in time, some I may be able to form in some small way, and learn to do the best I can in this particular situation and time.

Hope your time today is satisfying, and that you have a good sense of control over it. Love, Mom

THE PERCEPTION OF TIME VARIES

Terry Mejdrich, Swatara, Minnesota, writes about the perception of time in the AITKIN INDEPENDENT AGE.

WHEN TIME SLOWS DOWN

She remembers the accident like it was yesterday. She was with her husband, driving along Hwy 65 when suddenly an oncoming motorist crossed the center line and hit them head on.

Both she and her husband sustained life-threatening injuries. But she doesn't remember the pain. She does recall that time seemed to nearly stop. She can clearly remember seeing their car hood and the oncoming car hood slowly merge and buckle as they collided at a combined speed of over 90 miles per hour. She can see the sluggish movements of the people in the other car as they were tossed about. She can see the windshield crack and then slowly disintegrate. For her, events unfolded in crystal clarity, and in slow motion, when in real time it was all over in a fraction of a second.

He was blasting stubborn oak stumps in the pasture and was using three-minute fuses which gave him plenty of time to get behind a large pine tree 50 yards away. Then one set failed to explode. He waited five minutes and decided that a bad blasting cap had aborted the detonation. However, as he approached the stump, it suddenly erupted, drenching the area with a thousand deadly wooden daggers. At that moment, time shifted into super slow motion. A jagged piece of stump slowly rotating in midair held a collision course with his head. As if he had all the time in the world, he tilted his head a few inches to the left as the deadly missile went hurdling by, and time went back to normal as debris landed all around him.

Some might insist that these were "near death" experiences or in the man's case just plain stupidity because of the bizarre way time seemed to fluctuate. However, the explanation is not mystical. The sensation of time slowing down is common to life

threatening incidents. Of course, it doesn't really low down, but something in the brain makes it seem that way. Scientists suspect a sudden surge of adrenaline is a contributing factor. Some dangerous and illegal mind-altering drugs produce a similar effect.

It would be interesting if one could control (without the near death or the drugs) this ability to perceive the world in slow motion, and yet react in real time. One can imagine all kinds of situations where this ability would be advantageous.

The prize fighter fending off with ease the sluggish punches of his opponent. The batter patiently watching a fast ball moving slowly toward home plate. A surgeon might control his movements more steadily. The rapid-fire and sometimes unintelligible words of the auctioneer would become clear.

One could stretch enjoyable moments into what might seem like hours.

"Course it would be my luck to discover the technique while sitting in a dentist chair, having a root canal."

A FAMOUS EVALUATION OF TIME

I have, since I read the words in High School, been fascinated by William Shakespeare's comments on the meaning of time, and our human relationship to it. I learned these lines from his MERCHANT OF VENICE:

Tomorrow, and tomorrow, and tomorrow
    creeps at this petty pace, from day to day,
to the last syllable of recorded time.
And all our yesterdays have lighted fools
    the way to dusty death.
Out, out brief candle,
life is but a walking shadow,
a poor player who struts and frets his hour
    upon the stage
and then is heard no more.
It's a tale told by an idiot
full of sound and fury
signifying nothing.

I find a strange sense of comfort from these words when I am hassled, harried, and pressured. I am reminded not to take my self and my agenda quite so seriously. Having been active in drama helps me to relate to the "poor player" image. The play always ends, no matter who is performing,

or what is said. I am reminded that basically, I do not have all the right answers, nor does anyone else. We are all idiots in a manner of speaking. I imagine that our creator looks down on our earthly performances and wishes we would ask for help more often. Maybe I should strut and fret less. My time here is limited, however, when time seems to move from day to day in a perpetual way I am reminded there is a limit to those days here in this life, but that eternity, or that last syllable of recorded time, is difficult for me to visualize, with my limited understanding. The Bible book of ECCLESIASTICS 1:2–9 says nearly the same thing.

"Meaningless! Meaningless!"
Says the Teacher.
"Utterly meaningless!
Everything is meaningless."

What does a man gain from all his labor
at which he toils under the sun?
Generations come, and generations go,
but the earth remains forever.
The sun rises and the sun sets,
and hurries back to where it rises.

The wind blows to the south
round and round it goes,
ever returning to its course.
all streams flow into the sea,
yet the sea is never full.

To the place the streams come from,
there they return again.

All things are wearisome,
more than one can say,
The eye never has enough of seeing,
nor the ear its fill of hearing.
What has been will be again,
What has been done will be done again:
There is nothing new under the sun.[16]
Like the fool, the wise man too must die!"

Another quote from ECCLESIASTICS (3:1–8) gives me great comfort, no matter what my view of time: The teacher tells us that we are subjected to times and changes over which we have little or no control. Since we were made for eternity, the things of time cannot fully and permanently satisfy[8].

There is a time for everything,
and a season for every activity under heaven
a time to be born and a time to die,
a time to plant and a time to uproot,
a time to kill and a time to heal,
a time to tear down and a time to build,
a time to weep and a time to laugh,
a time to mourn and a time to dance
a time to scatter stones and a time to gather them,
a time to embrace and a time to refrain,
a time to search and a time to give up,
a time to keep and a time to throw away,
a time to tear and a time to mend,
a time to be silent and a time to speak,
a time to love and a time to hate,
a time for war and a time for peace.
The Bible

Time, like an ever-rolling stream,
soon bears us all away:
We fly forgotten, as a dream
Dies at the op'ning day.

ISAAC WATTS, 1678–1748

Celebrating Death

10

REALITY

Recognition and reaction to death will reveal much about a person, and even more importantly an entire culture. Let us look at one small facet—looking at the body—reviewal—visitation. It is a time to feel close for one last time? to imprint memory? Or— is it an answer to morbid curiosity, an attempt to move our emotions to a higher level, a primitive practice? I vote for the former, as it helps me to establish the reality of death, and remember the deceased in a very vivid way, say a prayer.

The Funeral

*A*re you going to John's funeral?"
"No, he won't be coming to mine anyway." (Account of a conversation heard at a meeting.)

Attitude and practices connected with local funerals have changed considerably, even during my lifetime. Even having or wanting a funeral has become a decision that people are thinking seriously about.

SOME CHANGES MIGHT BE:

Less fear/superstition
A more positive, happy message of comfort
Less rigid procedure
More emphasis on the dead, lifelike embalming, memorabilia
More cremations
Photos and memorabilia often shown
Music more "upbeat"
Women pallbearers
More casual dress and ceremony

A wider geographic representation in attendance
More people choosing non-traditional or no ceremony

Traditionally death ceremonies are as basic to life as living is. When one separates sophistication from instinct (if that is possible), the old and new reasons for these ceremonies or funerals seem quite similar.

CULTURES AND INDIVIDUALS THROUGHOUT THE AGES HAVE SOUGHT TO:

1. Recognize and acknowledge that death has occurred (this is often a very difficult aspect. We want "clean" proceedings, removed from reality of death as far as possible.

2. Assure that the deceased will not disturb the living, (in spirit, soul, conscience, or in any other way)

3. Memorialize the dead (propagate, idealize, imprint in the memory of individuals and groups)

4. Consider the meaning of life, both of the deceased and one's own existence

5. Comfort the living (unify, reinforce and support the idea that "Life goes on"

6. Rectify relationships to the dead (often guilt or emotional separation is motivation for this)

7. Release emotion (permission is given in our culture, but does not extend indefinitely)

8. Unify the survivors, while maintaining social order and structures

9. Consign events to a Higher Power

10. Achieve closure

These needs and contributions concerning death ceremonies are undoubtedly quite universal, although different priorities and semantics are used. Fear, desire for propriety, need for recognition and need for unification of the tribe or family are all inherent in funerals, whether it involves a tribe eating parts of the dead, or a clean, neat ceremony during which the body is never seen.

"That part about eating body parts is kind of drastic… primitive, isn't it?" asked husband Dan, after proofing the material at the beginning of the topic of funerals.

"Well, I believe it might be going on in parts of the

world today, at least it has during our lifetime!"

"But it still is a jolt to hear it," he said thoughtfully, trying not to imagine the process.

"I wonder, if it had been mentioned 200 years ago to any culture on earth, that we would take several cups of blood from one person's body and put it into another person, either directly or after it had been stored for a while…what would they have thought? Or say that we announced that we would take a heart, kidney, or lung from one person and put it into someone else?"

"They would have said 'it couldn't be done!'" He thought for a moment, then said, "And they would have been afraid of anyone that said they could do it. But still… the thought of eating flesh?"

"What is our concept of Holy Communion?" I mused. "Isn't it eating the body and drinking the blood of Christ?" (I believe we are "advanced," know it is symbolic, not realistic.)

"Yes," he said, "but that's in the context of religion."

"I'm sure that it is also religious with the people who practice ceremonial consumption of a dead relative or community member. It must have spiritual connotation. I believe they feel that the practice enables the dead to live on in the living, which is our goal in receiving communion. I could never practice it, but how can I condemn those who do, without a total understanding of their culture and belief system?"

This is the way funerals are, and should be. Most of us feel that the way we have experienced ceremonies or lack of them is, and should be the "normal" way of dealing with death, as survivors. Yet behavior of concerned survivors at a death are as diverse as the nuances of the great number of cultures in our world. We in the Lakeside community believe that we do what is right at a time of death.

My daughter-in-law, Samantha, has attended only one funeral in the United States, but worked in Zimbabwe, Africa for several years. She shared with me some funeral practices from that area of the world, which I am sure the people there thought completely right. Information from Africa is incomplete, as the language of death is not commonly learned by someone serving in a country for a short time. I would like to compare them here, in light of the ten reasons or purposes for death ceremonies previously listed in

this chapter. It will be only a superficial comparison of ways in which two cultures fill these human purposes/needs.

1. ACCEPTANCE:

If "only two things are certain: Death and taxes" why do so many of us have difficulty accepting it? The very act of holding a ceremony will help all involved to recognize that there has been a death. Filling out death forms, seeing the body, noting missing activities and relationships, talking with other mourners, disposing of the body seem to bring the reality of death to people in this locale. These things are all usually done within the space of a week. There is, it seems, a period of time when numbness sets in, and with it comes a certain disassociation, which postpones our sense of reality. This may not leave us until be try to resume our "normal" lives.

Death ceremonies last longer in Zimbabwe, with the body being viewed and visited for at least a week. In this warm, sometimes hot climate, with no preservatives, decomposition of the body would tend to lend more than a bit of reality to death. Word of mouth communicates the news of death, while food, games, and chants seem to soften the harsher aspects of reality.

2. PEACE:

One of our favorite Christmas classic stories (Charles Dickens' CHRISTMAS CAROL) involves the intrusion of spirits or ghosts into a man's life. One of the goals of the funeral is to put to rest any fear that the memory, or spirit of the deceased would have a negative impact on our own succeeding existence. The time it took the deceased to die may affect our feeling of "making peace." If the death has been sudden it seems that the funeral might be even more important in providing a sense of peace, settling the spirit. Honor and completion are often communicated at our funerals. Christians believe that the spirit or soul is at rest with God, and reiterating this belief at the funeral provides spiritual closure. The need to "put the spirits to rest" exists in most cultures, although it is hidden in some of our practices. Masks and ornaments are worn by some cultures to placate the spirits, thus avoiding problems with them, or to confuse them. It is assumed in Zimbabwe that the spirit will live on, it may affect survivors in a positive way. Riches and living needs are often provided to appease these spirits. The

funeral might take longer, say a week, to accomplish this peacemaking task.

3. REMEMBRANCE:

Eulogizing and providing durable reminders of the dead serves both the living and the dead, give meaning to the life of the deceased. The living may ponder the meaning of their own lives. Cards are often given which summarize the deceased's life, accounts in the media, or between people. Speakers, often eloquent, summarize the life and character in glowing terms, especially if the dead one is "important" in politics, entertainment or sport. Stones are carved and placed to make a lasting testament to the life now ended.

Gender of the deceased is important in Zimbabwe in how the dead will be remembered. Oral stories, visitation by other men, and praise will be accorded the dead man, but only the most important women will be given this honor. Stones will often be placed in a pile over the grave.

4. EVALUATION:

One of the outcomes of eulogizing is to consider the meaning of life for both the dead and the living. Will one's lifelong activities and attitudes make a difference in the short or long term? What value can be made of life? (or death?) This is discussed, but tends to be a personal conclusion, based of course on the culture at hand.

5. COMFORT:

Supportive presence, comforting words, expressive cards, prayer help with arrangements or other tasks, providing food are all acts which contribute to the idea that "life can go on." These acts of kindness and consideration are well practiced in the community surrounding Lakeside. In Africa games, food, supportive presence, wailing and expressions of mourning all support the survivors most sincerely. The language of death was not understood fully by Samantha and her co-workers, but they did understand attitudes and actions, which were geared toward support.

6. RECTIFICATION:

Part of comfort, as often as not, includes assuring survivor(s) that they have done well by the deceased, that they need not agonize over the "if only I had" or the "I wish I had nots. Guilt seems to be a part of death, although sometimes a reversal is used, blaming the dead. One of the most difficult things about dealing with death is to minimize or remove any negative aspects which may have existed in relationships prior to death. Although this seems universal, we do not know how it was accomplished in Africa.

7. EMOTING:

Our general feeling is that suppression of emotion is not healthy. The mood at a death ceremony encourages hugs, tears, vocalizing, on the part of the bereaved and those attending the funeral, contributing to the process of healing. Tears, hugs, moving music, are all acceptable modes. A New Orleans jazz parade may release a very different emotion than would a violin group playing one of Wagner's pieces. Anger may well be an emotion, as well as grief. Spouses who survived were, at the early part of the twentieth century, required to wear black and to limit social engagements as an expression of grief. Now the expressive time seems to be more limited; "get on with life." The wailing of women is the first release of emotion at death in Zimbabwe. The wailing is continued for at least a week, although the mourning period is forty days. Men are not expected to express grief in such a direct way. (Also true to a lesser degree in our culture.)

8. SOLIDARITY:

"Laugh and the world laughs with you. Cry, and you cry alone." Death seems to impact even the most insensitive of humans and to touch even the hardest of hearts. It is more difficult to hold someone at arm's length after experiencing death or a funeral together. In previous times most concerned people where within walking distance of the death. Today a cohesive group of most concerned people may be gathered from around the country, or even world. Old differences are often set aside, temporarily at least. Men and women, local groups and families seem to remain more separated, even in death in Africa. Attitudes of varied worth of individuals seem to prevent crossing those lines to accomplish cohesiveness, although it is probably practiced within each segment of population.

9. FAITH:

I could get "preachy" here, because I have no understanding of how one would make sense of life or death outside of the concept of a higher power. I believe that whether a funeral takes place in Africa or the United States, many of the other purposes for a death ceremony reinforce, or are reinforced within the context of "religion," or more specifically: spirituality. Each individual and culture will find that peace and power for themselves, and express it in suitable ways, and receive strength to survive.

10. CLOSURE:

We have come full circle from number one, we recognize finality, restructure our lives and do the "best we can" to be survivors. At least most of us do. Religion, the arts, social mores, (and now big business), all contribute, whether it is in painting the body to ward off the spirits, or building a beautiful casket which reflects the interests of the deceased, whether it involves drums, flutes or organs, a moving chant or a harmonious choir. The body might be painted to look alive (as in our fairly recent embalming customs) or wrapped in preservatives to prepare for existence in the afterlife (as in ancient Egypt). Christianity is the only "religion" represented at Lakeside, officially at least, thus that religion is at the center of funerals held in churches, homes, Lakeside Clubhouse or graveside. In Africa "Shah Allah" (if God wills it) was a theme, and prayer continued on an intense schedule.

These ten consolations can also be very helpful when applied on a personal level, in what you do and say to help a friend or family member through a death experience:

Acknowledge death, don't hedge around, in conversation, writings (cards) the sooner reality is personally accepted the sooner healing might begin. One might begin: "It seems impossible, but we have lost…," or "I have trouble sensing the reality of this death."

Memorialize the dead: "I remember when…," "…was so good at…," "One of my best memories of…"

Consider the meaning of life: "She certainly made a difference by…," "It seems as if he was put on this earth to…"

Comfort the living: "I know your faith will give you strength," "You have friends, (family, coworkers) who would like to help you through this time of sorrow. Do not say "Buck up, you'll feel better soon." Be willing to give time and effort on this aspect, one can not just talk about it.

Rectify relationships: "I know you did so much for … in his life (or in the last)," "It was wonderful to know how much you two shared" or "Even if you had problems…"

THE NEWS IS NOT GOOD
One can only imagine how disconcerting it was to receive a black banded envelope in the mail. It meant only one thing: Death. Many times these letters came from an ocean away. Black was repeated in armbands worn by pallbearers, or even by all family adults. Black clothing was to be worn for a respectable time. Some widows never wore color again. Translation of letter: Dear Sister, With sorrow I notify you that our dear mother died on December 7, 1915, peacefully at home./ It is sad that you are so far removed from our sorrow, but I know that your sorrow is as heartfelt as ours. With Love, Sister Helvi

BREAKING TRADITION/JAZZING IT UP
*Christian traditional funeral hymns are the
norm in this area, but exceptions are heard.
When our sons Perry and Andrew were in High
School they were asked by a fairly young man to
play at his funeral, along with three friends from
the Schneider family. The terminally ill man
had heard them play a lively New Orleans
rendition of "When the Saints Go Marching In",
and it was his desire to have it played at his
conservative Lutheran Funeral. Three trumpets,
a tuba and a clarinet rocked the small church in
a joyful celebration of music from the soul,
reverberating for a long time.*

Release emotions: "Shout, cry, throw something, I feel like doing so myself," "I wouldn't blame you if you…," "I am angry, too."

Unify survivors: "I know your family is sharing in this sorrow," "Please do not shut out your friends." This is also one which must be lived and acted upon.

Consign to a higher power: "This death makes sense only when you think of (higher power). "Please communicate spiritually with (God)." Do not say "Oh, God must have taken him now, because…"

Achieve closure: Do not expect a moment, day, week, year, or longer on this one. It must be accomplished on the schedule of the bereaved. You must help in increments during the process, while understanding that it is a process, different for each person. Do not try to close off the death, keep doing activities which help to fill the void.

MUSIC HAS POWER

"Little Frank" Lungren sat, (well, no, rested fleetingly) on the old glass ball organ stool. His back was ramrod straight, elbows flared in and out, while his hands flew imposingly back and forth over the keyboard of the simple, small wooden organ. His eyes rolled upward under the tousled shock of unruly hair. His facial expression indicated that he was transfixed in another time and place. His entire body rocked back and forth, side to side as the sad, mournful, most somber of music poured from the man and instrument. It was another example of the intensity of music when interpreted by the Finns, one of my earliest exposures to that phenomenon. The funeral, at "the clubhouse" (Lakeside), was one of the first, if not the first, I had ever attended. I have forgotten who had died, what the "Papa" or preacher said (it may have been in Finn), but I shall never forget the image of Little Frank pouring out his soul at the organ, nor the music which cascaded out in moving, thundering volumes.

Little Frank's total and very emotional outpouring is just another proof, to me, that music is in us, just waiting to get out. The music that we have in our soul must come from so deep that it is not even traceable. Few of us can trace our ancestry beyond say a dozen generations, and this innate music stems from much farther back! If there is a time when the "buried" music resurfaces it is at the time of death ceremonies. I am aware that I have strong musical roots, even in

the previous two generations, but something much more ancient recently resurfaced. The discovery came as I began to portray a Northern Sami shaman, (*witch* in negative gender) in plays based on the Finnish epic, KALEVALA. Although the woman was portrayed as powerfully evil for the first three years, I found myself having more and more in common with her. Her "magic" became spirituality, her "evil" could certainly be defined as leadership in defense of the people she led. About the same time I heard the stunning joik, done by the Sami people at the winter Olympics held in Norway. To make a long story short, I suggested that we include a joik in our drama that year, and the director stunned me by looking straight in the eye and assigning me that job. I had never sung a solo, or considered myself particularly musical, yet I sang in the local productions, a production at Northern Michigan University, and before a crowd of over a thousand at the opening ceremonies of Finnfest that year. I was keyed up, but when I began the yoik, a calm assurance overwhelmed me, and I was again standing in a swamp in the moonlight, singing from my soul. The yoik moves many people, some have tears streaming down their cheeks. Some may be unaware, like I had been, that the music is buried deep within them, at their roots, for I am sure that I am a Sami . Historic study of immigration reveals that there are many more Sami in this country than it would seem. Many of these "Laplanders" are not aware of their heritage, partly because it was not seen as something to be proud of in those earlier times. "We are not Sami , but my grandfather did work with reindeer." I enjoy sharing the culture, and recently helped to send one person into eternity in Sami style.

The funeral had been held previously, but the burial was to be at 5:30 P.M. I had not made a commitment to be there, only to have marked the grave, but at 5:00 got the strong urge to motor to the cemetery.

"We've been waiting for you!" Selma said, from her place within the handful of relatives standing by the open grave. That statement only makes sense if one is using *Sami Time* and is aware of extrasensory communication.

I surveyed the situation with an inward awareness, not a physical evaluation or recognition. Then from somewhere inside of me I vocalized a question which shocked me. "Would you like me to do a yoik, an ancient Finnish prayer chant?"

"Yes," answered Selma, seemingly without hesitation or surprise. She had no awareness of what a joik is, or that I had any experience in doing it. Neither she nor I had planned this, or even had a wild thought of it, yet we seemed to be moved by forces beyond present or conscious thoughts.

Somehow, the haunting, primitive sounds of the chant seemed to connect the dead man's ancient roots with his space age belief in a higher power. It seemed to comfort the survivors on some very deep level.

During a recent trip to Finland, I visited a man, Rauno Nieminen, who has researched and recreated many ancient musical instruments and yoiks. He has opened a museum, featuring these instruments. I felt the spiritual strength of this man, and his integrity in keeping a musical heritage alive. I had heard a group (KARALIA) play his instruments in Duluth, Minnesota, and had been very moved by the music. I did a joik for him, so he would know that we Americans are also trying to keep our heritage alive. He instinctively knew which of his beautiful birch whistles I wanted to purchase for my son Paul, and had taken the time to play many of the instruments so that I could experience the tone and quality of each.

"Do you know who Elias Lonnrot was?" the creative man asked as we toured his museum.

"Oh, YES!" I said, remembering the impact that this great writer's collection of historic poems had on that nation, as well as individuals (even distant Americans such as I). Lonnrot had skied into remote areas to collect those "runos" and had translated them into a collection called the KALEVALA. They truly reflect the soul of the northern people, and it is said that resultant national pride has enabled Finns to regain their independence.

"Come with me," he said, motioning to a stairway which ascended to the second floor, off limits to regular museum visitors.

Upon reaching the top of the stairs we stood facing a huge emerald green Kuntala. The kuntala is a string (traditionally five strings) instrument which, according to the KALEVALA, epic hero Vainamoinen constructed from the head and spine bones of a Pike (fish) to revive the spirit of the Finnish people and give them joy. It is traditionally only two-feet in length and six-inches wide, of natural wood. This one was over five-feet long, and three-feet wide. It still

Sympathy cards from (first row) 1950s, 1960s, 1970s; (second row) 2000, 2001, 2002.

bore evidence of being covered by flowers at one time. I was awed by the size and design of the instrument, but not as awed as by Mr. Nieminen's next statement.

"This is the instrument which was at the funeral of Elias Lonnrot."

Following a respectful, yet primitive urge, I reached out and gently touched it.

A country-western band and soloists made another funeral meaningful, while a most memorable rendition of HOW GREAT THOU ART was done at a classmate's funeral to guitar accompaniment by a soul singer in the style of Hank Williams.

For some reason, being part of congregational singing at a funeral can move me deeply. It may be that it is an emotional release, or that it unites one with the larger body of grieving people. I can imagine sometimes that the communal chants done by other cultures can accomplish the same thing. Drums were used in the African death ceremonies my daughter-in-law Samantha tells about. I heard soul expressed deeply in a drum/piano duet in Duluth recently. Whatever the tradition, whatever the instrument or voice, music plays a big part in comforting, releasing emotion, unifying survivors, consigning to a higher power and settling the soul

THE ART OF DEATH

At the turn of the century a black banded letter arriving in the mail was enough to unsettle a person. I find it unsettling, even now, to hold one of the "death envelopes" in my hand. Black has been a color of death in our culture, as white or red is in other cultures. Black was predominant at

A small mark of sorrow—a cross inked above her head marks the passing of this young woman.

the turn of the century. Now our remembrance cards may be beautifully colored and/or have nature or animal pictures on them. My collection of local and family cards from mid-century features church windows, Bibles, Christ, or cemeteries. Caskets were often plain wooden boxes, or even cloth shrouds at the beginning of the century. Now they may be beautifully finished, often with small drawings or paintings which reflect the deceased's interest or avocations. Simple, available, wild or garden flowers have given way to ornate, sometimes exotic floral arrangements. The art of making a body look pleasant, if not even alive, is well appreciated. Photos are often displayed near the casket or the place of post funeral congregation. Visual art, while always playing a part in funerals, is much more employed and sophisticated at the end of the century than at the beginning of it. I wonder if videos are ever shown at funerals now, or how long it will be until they are. One wonders how important the individual will become in our culture, in relation to a higher power, or the entire community. Employed by individual or group, a variety of visual art will always be used as a reflection, sometimes unconscious, of the culture's innate beliefs and characteristics.

Photography was a fairly new art before and at the turn of the century, but death often left it's mark on the family

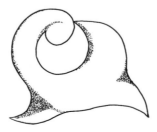

photo album. The practice seemed to have been abandoned by the 1930s or so. Photographs of the dead, especially babies was often done, sometimes with coins (usually fifty cent pieces) placed on the eyes.

The African death celebration is just that—games, communication, food, contests all contribute to a noisy, communal affair. We may say that it is "primitive" or "simple." I have a strong instinct that primitive is a word to put down others whose practices or beliefs we do not understand. Another put-down word is the word simple.

A funeral was held in our town recently for a man with simple tastes and a rather primitive life style. Country Western music rocked the huge cement and tin "Big Top" where the ceremony was held. Lyrics from a live country/western singer: "I'm so lonesome I could die," seemed to resonate and to be congruous with the occasion. But it was the Christian hymn which contains the words "Lay your trophies at His feet" which came to my mind when I viewed what was displayed to denote what was left of the man's life, what it had been all about. A couple of well-worn feed or baseball hats, soiled from activities close to the earth, basics, an award for his service with area firefighters, some symbols of his love for the outdoors were the "trophies" which graced a table at the front of the pavilion for reviewing. When we arrived at the grounds outside of the town's biggest roofed place, it was full, shoulder to shoulder, of "simple" people, milling around a "choker" or "bug" (a work vehicle converted from an old car chassis) and an aging riding lawn mower. Work clothing hung from the posts supporting the canopy of the bug. Everyone knew that these items were meant to sum up a life.

This young crowd, many of them the bar group had come in for the service. Some who had not in a lifetime attended a Christian service of any kind, came to pay homage to this "simple" man. All in all there were over 500 people, in a town of 169 residents! The primitive, simple man's life had touched many—many identified with him. It was almost as if they gathered for a silent demonstration of solidarity.

ISN'T THAT WHAT FUNERALS ARE ALL ABOUT?

11

The Auction

Farm Auctions have been and are an expression of the demise of the family farm. Loss of the family farm is an indication of a widespread change in ecology, agriculture, and human culture. It is the take-over of the production of food and clothing by less than a handful of very large corporations. It is not happening because the farmers are dumb or lazy. It is happening because big money controls much. This may be the upheaval which precipitates the most excessive, widespread change of life as we know it. Social, ecological, financial, and cultural responsibility and systems will be affected world wide. Where has this shift begun? Sixty-three dairy farms in Lakeside township have disappeared, leaving one remaining (2002). Normal—throughout the world.

Funeral For a Family Farm

Gloomy, gloppy, gray clouds containing potential for snow on this final day of April helped set an overwhelmingly melancholy mood for this day of scrutiny of a family farm. A farm which, as one of the first farms in the township, had been supporting the same family for nearly one hundred years. Couldn't this day be bright, sunny and cheery? Memorabilia, carefully cared for during much of the previous century had been removed from attics, sheds and living space to be exposed on large racks previously used to haul hay for cattle. The racks themselves would be sold from the farm when their last cargo had been distributed. Personal effects would, at the end of this auction day, be gone—scattered to incalculable places.

The major players in this service were arriving early in the day. As I drove north to do a few quick errands in Wright, I met them on their way south to the Suhonen farm. I noted auctioneer Carol Reinhardt sitting in the driver's seat of a large sound truck, easily recognizable by her blond hair and large western hat. Another sound truck, the registration trailer and a food-catering vehicle followed. I did my business, and hurriedly returned to the Lakeside area for the visitation. I signed in, presented my driver's license, named my bank to receive my bidding number. I walked among hay racks laden with stunning glass items, beautiful dish sets, cooking pots, sewing fabric, threads, knickknacks, jewelry, Christmas trim, paintings and photos… so many items which had defined life on this place for so many decades. I would walk through the large metal machine shed which held furniture from at least ninety years. I stopped to meditate at the maple kitchen table and chairs at which I had enjoyed a hospitable, neighborly sharing of food and drink. I looked carefully at the now empty hutch which had contained so many interesting and precious items. Familiar living room furniture and mirrors now stood in long rows, submitted already to many questioning eyes and prying fingers. Bedsteads, clothes racks, antique tables stretched out for all to see. I fell in love with a dark little rocker (sans the rockers) which was unmistakably old, and definitely Finnish with its carved symbolic birds on the back panel. I had never seen it before.

In the field at the rear of the furniture shed were tools, machines, and other objects which reflected such unrelentingly difficult farm work. Blacksmith son Paul identified and defined many of the metal items when he arrived. Hand forged planes, hammers, fire-tending objects, tree-peeling irons, hoes and knives, a tool to dress the hide of a pig after slaughter, a variety of saws witnessed the self sufficiency of inhabitants of this bit of land. It spoke of a struggle to clear the land, build structures, tend animals and raise

Heavy when full, ten-gallon milk cans made many trips to the creamery in Wright.

food. Twenty, heavy when full, ten-gallon milk cans made many trips to the creamery in Wright. But none since 1965 when that creamery closed. Plows, disks, hay rakes and other heavy equipment bore signs of wear and tear, acquired in a struggle to make this farm a sustainable operation. Newer equipment, a beautiful green pickup truck, and a "four wheeler" which reputedly had only twenty miles on it (at the time of Arvie Suhonen's death) were also carefully primped for this visitation. Sheds full of piping, metal, broken furniture stood ready to be sold as is, "clean out the shed—it's all yours."

My meditation was interrupted by an announcement that the service was about to begin. It was only then that I became aware that pre-estimates of an unusually large number of people in attendance had now been realized. Over seven hundred people were there to honor this farm, to realize personal closure, to acquire personal tangible remembrances, and some to realize financial gain. There were, of course, people who were strangers, but upon hearing of the day's activities wanted to take part or, maybe to buy things with which to restock their antique shops.

The unique music of the auctioneer began. Rising and falling in rhythmical patterns, the selling song was the basis for all activities for the next six to eight hours (more, had this not been a two-ring auction). Like some hymns the basic song was pleasant, yet induced a feeling of melancholy, probably because of past associations of its use at similar occasions. As a hymn intends to lead us to faith, the song of the auctioneer entices us to possess items now being lifted up.

Like human funerals the auction is a time to socialize. "I'm just here to see people," was said more than a few times. I had meaningful conversations with persons I had not seen for decades. Contact with some had been only a wave in passing. As at any memorial service the conversations range from a superficial discussion of the weather, to deep contemplation of the demise of the family farm or current trend of morality. Hugs were shared, hands shaken. People who did not necessarily like each other acted out on a pretense of social ability. Long-lost relatives were embraced. "What's new?" was a common greeting. I spoke with an eighty-year-old daughter of the farm. She told me of running through flames lapping from both sides of the road, to find refuge in a neighboring farm lake during the tragic, awesome 1918 fire. She recalled babysitting at a home in Kettle River when she was a young teen, where she saved a baby's life one day. Older siblings had given the child a piece of hard candy which had lodged in the throat. A cold, blue child was placed in Simie's lap by an anguished mother. She placed the baby face-down on her knees.

Top: The crowd gathers around the auctioneer. Bottom: A crowd builds checking out the goods; neighbors visit around the blue enamel canners; the small brick house and the yard are empty the day after the sale.

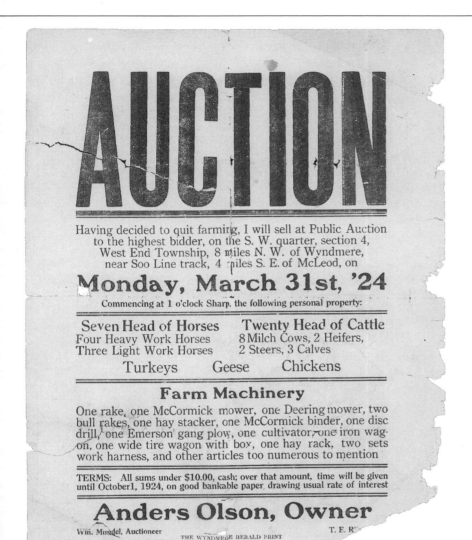

EARLY AUCTION BILL

Fact is, my grandfather sold his Dakota farm in 1924, died in 1928, at age fifty-two. It was at a time when farming was not a losing proposition, although the great depression took out many farms several years later. Speculation might tell us that grandfather was in poor health, could not pass the farm to any of his four sons (that is not even to consider his two daughters).

SUHONEN AUCTION BILL

Seventy-eight years later the situation is very different, both in the amount of equipment needed to operate the farm and in the volume of production necessary to support it. Skills needed to operate changed; marketing became a sore spot. Government policies supported large, rich, corporate farms. Bigger became better. Labor, thus production, is cheaper in other countries, without the bother of health or environmental regulations.

slapped the shoulders, and with surprise and pleasure still reflected in her voice years later, reported that the candy had popped out across the room. Simie was in a wheelchair, but had come a long way to attend this event.

Later in the day Leonard Aho zipped up on his four-wheeler, parked it near the food concession. He ambled over and was able to answer some of my questions about the farm. He has been married for over fifty years to a daughter of the farm across the road, where Siemi and her mother went for help the day of the big fire.

"Yes, I remember when that brick house was built," he eyed the house, small by today's standards. "It was 1926—Jack Wallies had one, and that same bricklayer made one on the Tony Heikkala place."

I was standing in a position to see Len's four-wheeler. A stranger was intently examining it—kicking the tires so to speak. The wheels in his head were turning out a highest bidding amount. He fiddled with the dials, examined the steering and stroked the metal cover. Noting my reaction Leonard turned around to see him, but said nothing, just watched him silently.

"I should have let it go," he said later.

Two persons gathered together in this area must invariably have a bite to eat, a little lunch, or coffee time. I dare

Arvie and Honey Jo are now at peace among family and friends.

say that this is true wherever Scandinavians meet others. This is especially true of major social gatherings, funerals and auctions included. Sociability is consistently centered around food. Food service in the large food trailer is most scientific in efficiency. Popular sandwiches including barbecues are pre-prepared and wrapped, can be heated in microwave. Beverage choices include a popular vegetable mixture, as well as the official transfusion drink: coffee. Soda choices can also satisfy thirst. Sweets include sweet rolls, doughnuts, and cookies. The volume held in the food unit must be great, as this auction has registered well over five hundred bidding numbers, and it would be reasonable to say at very least seven hundred people were on the farm. The line of people never ended, though the service was brisk. I bought hot-dogs for my young grandchildren, just to warm them on the cold, damp April day. We were set to return to the crowd.

People pushing, shoving into position around the remains must be watched carefully, as they have been known to rearrange boxes to get a better deal, to pocket

small items or to damage sale pieces. It is interesting t watch bidding styles. Some give a subtle nod, others shou out a current bid. The tall man in front will enter the bid ding immediately shouting out his "yep," while the wizene person in the corner will wait for the last "Going twice before giving the winning nod. I waited near the black bir rockerless rocker until one of the auctioneers reached i held it up and bidding progressed to twenty dollars. I the held up my registration card with its numbers in big blac letters. I waited tensely until "Going, going, gone for twen ty to number one-fifty-seven" was sung out. I wedged th rocker out through the tightly packed crowd and locate Dan to see if he saw it as a suitable remembrance of th Suhonens, past and present who have lived on this farm fo over a hundred years in an unbroken chain. Honey Jo an Arvie had no children, and even if they had heirs, the pos sibility of making a living on the farm is nebulous.

The farm may be resurrected, maybe by a younger niec or nephew working in Cloquet. It might have new life at th hands of a retired couple from the cities. Maybe someon will convert it to a tree farm. Whatever the case, it will neve again be the same. It is gone, along with Honey Jo an Arvie. Our children heard Arvie call her "honey," and I tol them she was called "Jo." So putting two and two togethe they devised the name which we all adopted—"Honey Jo. The name suited her perfectly; she had a big heart.

It is my seemingly futile hope that in this land our farm soil, fertility, family input can rise again, be resurrected kept viable, that it hasn't or won't all die and or go to hel Big food companies who now are in control of food seem t have no heart or conscience in this matter.

The auction is over: the reviewal, music, memories group support. The farm lies silent, poured out and empt at the end of the day.

1918–Fire–Flu–War

12

REAL SURVIVORS

Time in this area is often measured in terms of the year 1918. "Before the fire" and "After the fire." What is the effect of death occurring to large numbers of people at once? What effect does it have on the next generations, or the survivors? Two actors from The Kalevala Theater's 1998 portrayal of the fire in this photo help to bring that conflagration to life, as did the play. An unprecedented flu epidemic and World War One complicated life in the its own way.

Triple Terror

An unusually high number of death dates in Lakeside Cemetery fall within the year 1918.

Three terrible reasons account for this: fire, flu and war. These three catastrophic events took pre-natal babies, centurions, and a great number of people in between. The flu and the war affected people all over the nation, but the fire cursed Northern Minnesota only.

"Only" seems to be an inappropriate descriptive term for the devastation which this conflagration caused. Thousands of people lost home, farm, forest, livelihood, health, peace of mind. But worst of all—over five hundred and fifty people died in this fire, and many more from lung or other injuries from which they never recovered (see bibliography for further sources of information). It is beyond human comprehension, a nightmare reality which still affects the area. Time is still measured in terms of "before THE FIRE" and "after THE FIRE." Not one family living in the area at the time was unaffected. One person whose grave should be at Lakeside is Isak Walli. At the time of the fire he was working near a small town ten miles to the south (Automba). According to the survivors, he was battling the fire along

with other able-bodied men, trying to save some "saw logs" when the fire won the battle. "A log somehow rolled on him, broke his leg, and he became another casualty." The day after the fire his sons searched for him, but the National Guard had already gathered what remained and taken all to be buried in a huge mass grave at Moose Lake. A large monument is there today, to honor those fire victims buried in that place. It is ironic that Isaac could not be buried at Lakeside, as it was his family who donated the land for the cemetery.

Death came in a number of ways: people were suffocated as they took shelter in root cellars or wells, people were incinerated in sheets of fire, or large balls of fire which blew through the air or exploded in the 70 MPH firewind.

AN OVERSIGHT?

Most, but not all, of those relatives who survived the fire are now buried at Lakeside (except my grandfather—and that is another story). It is odd to me that by omitting my grandfather's name (Johnson, nee Moykke) from my grandmother's stone, the older Peterson sons make the four younger Johnson children, including my mother, illegitimate for eternity. Maria's first husband, Mr. Peterson was killed in a mining accident, leaving her with five small children. She took them back to Finland, then returned to America to marry Mr. Johnson. Grandmother's name was Johnson when she bore her last five children and when she died.

SERENITY AND SECURITY gave way to panic and fear, within the decade, as the holocaust known in this quadrant of the state as THE 1918 FIRE swept over this very same scene. The Johnson/Peterson family escaped harm huddled in a boat on Long Lake as the flames swept overhead, in all probability aboard this very same boat near this very same spot. The girls sat in the boat, the boys submerged in water, clinging to the sides of the boat. It is likely that they held wet clothes over face to facilitate breathing. Can you imagine the sound? This photo was taken several years before the fire.

People died from smoke inhalation, from the intense heat of the fire, which created its own tornado as it raced along. It took entire families, spared others, left many to die slowly, in agony. There is little understanding of what we commonly call "fate," for lack of a better definition. It must have been unbearable to try to understand why some lived, others died.

Those who were left alive were forced to deal with horrible memories. Many people remember stumbling over logs, only to find that the log was a body, in many cases a family member or friend. Some people came upon "normal looking" people, only to have them turn to ash as they were touched. Some parents had children sucked out of their arms and burned. Trucks rumbled by for days after, stacked with bodies: "like cordwood."

My friend, Dan Reed, writes in his book, "AUTOMBA"[7] "A gruesome, but funny story from Automba went something like this: On Thursday night at Automba, a tired and worn to the point of exhaustion, Sheriff I.E. Boekenoogen, chairman of the Aitkin county chapter of the American Red Cross, had worked all week at reconstruction

in the burned area at that place and Lawler, and could find no bed for the night. As a last resort, one of the rough boxes which were used for burial purposes was carried inside the cook shanty and the sheriff climbed in and slept soundly. Early the next morning, when the cook opened the door, expecting to begin preparing breakfast, he saw the form of the sheriff rising out of the burial box in the dim daylight. The cook took to his heels, and has not been seen since."

My family did not lose anyone directly from the fire storm, although my grandmother died in 1919 from what might have been complications. The family had survived the fire by rowing their boat out into the middle of Long Lake. The girls stayed in the boat, using wet clothing to moisten their heads and to filter breathing air. The boys spent the terrifying time in the water, clinging to the boat. The fire jumped overhead, across the lake (nearly 1/4 mile). It is possible to only begin to imagine the sights and sounds and smells of that force roaring above. The Johnson/Peterson family survived the 1918 fire!

In the seventies I painted a picture of people working to save a hay barn in the path of the fire. I presented the picture to my uncle Ted for consultation on its authenticity. "Can you see the ashes in the air?" I asked.

He stood quietly meditating for a time. "See them, I can feel them," he said.

My uncle Ted has written a short book about the fire and aftermath in which he tells about attempting to save the "precious" swamp hay, then walking home though a flaming forest to begin attempting to save the buildings (if you know anything about Ted, the use of the word "walk" is a misusage). My mother, sixteen-years old at the time, was left along the homeward trail, as she couldn't manage to go further without catching her breath. She eventually got back home, to board a boat to the middle of the lake. They were fortunate in that a dense spruce swamp deprived the fire of oxygen to burn, and a wind change then took the fire in a direction which spared them. He also tells that in the aftermath they were able to track deer in the thick layer of ashes. "Just like tracking in snow," said Ted.

Like many young men of the area, my uncle George was enrolled in the Army at the time of the fire. He had visited the farm on the night before the fire, to say farewell before going overseas. Many young men who were called to serve in World War 1 were given releases to come home to help family and community to survive. In some cases they were the only ones left of their entire family. Many veterans from that war, and other wars are buried at Lakeside.. It seems, from surviving records, that George was discharged from military service to come home after the fire. We know that he was hired to accompany, as interpreter, a man named Murphy who traveled to various families to see if their claims for fire loss were legitimate. He told of young Finnish children scampering under the bed, having no clothing to put on. Some families, then, did not even have the clothes on their backs. October is often a cold month in Minnesota

Today, a walk on the back forty of our farm will reveal remnants of huge pine trees which once stood, stately and tall on what is now the second most rocky pasture in Aitkin County (I have not seen the first). Stumps and burned knots are sometimes an almost grotesque reminder of the hell which burned here eighty years ago. Dan Reed wrote the play, THE MEETING PLACE to commemorate the fire on the eightieth anniversary of the tragedy. When discussing potential characters for the play I commented that one should be a person who had lost sanity. In almost any account which one reads there is mention of someone who either lived with mental illness, or could not tolerate life after the fire: suicide. Today we would call it "post traumatic shock syndrome."

It turned out that in the drama about the fire I played the part of an insane woman whose story was a composite of several. One of them had wool socks on at the time of the fire, and her feet and legs were burned and baked "like hams." A picture of this Jokimaki Daughter hangs in the Moose Lake fire museum. My character had also witnessed the death of her daughter and grandbabies. It was a very difficult role, as I felt after each performance as if I had endured that trauma and the resultant imbalance. I am amazed that most people dealt with the unspeakable truths, and most even stayed in the area, struggling to eke out a life from the desolate land. Historically, the Finnish people have endured…stoic, strong in spirit. They have witnessed horrible wars, occupation (by Denmark, Sweden, Russia), and difficult, if not harsh living conditions. It may be the reason for a minor key in their music, and a tragic thread running through their drama and art, even life in general. Although Finns have the highest suicide rate in the world many peo-

SOMETHING GOOD COMES FROM EVERYTHING

Surviving settlers needed to find something positive amidst the after-affects of 1918. One of the bright spots they found was the abundance of berries. Blueberries, raspberries,, and probably other native delights were much more available after the burn. Here we can see the huge buckets of blueberries harvested from near Long Lake. Mother, aunts Martha and Ruth, Uncles Ted and George are among well rewarded berry pickers. Note fire damage to trees in background.

ple set their sights on life. Survivors of THE FIRE concentrated on life, shifted from lumbering to farming and rebuilt this area of the country.

FLU

Late in the twentieth century one can turn on the television and hear: "Our coverage of the FLU EPIDEMIC will be important from early morning to the end of our broadcasting day."

In this year of 2000 the National Broadcasting Company (NBC) has seen fit to discuss how the disease is spread, how to treat it, HOW THE EPIDEMIC IS MOVING ACROSS THE COUNTRY, AND WHERE TO

GET FLU IMMUNIZATIONS." It is difficult for me to imagine, then, the panic when perfectly strong and health people began dropping dead from a mysterious cause. The flu seemed to come from no where, out of the blue, without a way of protecting against it, or knowing where it might strike. The confusion, panic, and incomprehensible fear must have made death a specter which gripped most people, in the entire country. At least in these days we can know the enemy, and immunization is available, as are some rather effective treatments.

In our area, in 1918, the flu followed the fire. Even on a national level it was one of the worst, if not the worst, flu epidemics ever recorded. In this area it was undoubtedly

Flu epidemic's culprit might have been a pig

By Robert S. Boyd
Knight Ridder Newspapers

Swine-infecting virus mixed with human gene to create 1918 strain, report says

WASHINGTON — Like voices from a tomb, snippets of genetic material recovered from victims of the great influenza epidemic of 1918 may explain one of history's most horrific medical disasters.

The villain could have been a pig.

According to a new report from a team of Australian scientists, a gene in a strain of flu virus that normally infects pigs somehow got mixed up with a gene from a human flu virus.

The combination was lethal. The so-called "Spanish flu" overwhelmed people's natural immune systems. No vaccine could contain it. Between 20 and 40 million people perished — 620,000 of them in the United States. That's more Americans than died in all 20th century wars.

"It wiped out entire villages at opposite ends of the Earth and depressed world population growth for 10 years," said Robert Webster, an expert on viruses at St. Jude Children's Research Hospital in Memphis, Tenn.

To avoid another such disaster, researchers are eager to learn all they can about how deadly new strains of flu virus develop.

Most common flu epidemics are caused by viruses that infect birds, notably Asian chickens. The viruses spread to humans and then travel around the world aboard ships and airplanes. Fatalities are limited mainly to sick or elderly people.

Significant Asian flu outbreaks occurred in 1957, 1968 and 1997.

Other pure swine flu viruses also have caused trouble, notably in 1976 when President Gerald Ford ordered every citizen be vaccinated against it.

The possible pig-human connection to the Spanish flu is reported by Mark Gibbs, a biologist at Australian National University, Canberra, in today's editions of the journal Science.

Gibbs and his colleagues analyzed the RNA — a simpler form of DNA found in viruses — recovered from the body of a 21-year-old South Carolina soldier who died in the 1918 epidemic. His tissue had been preserved in paraffin at the Armed Forces Institute of Pathology in Washington.

Gibbs said he found a chunk of RNA from a pig virus stuck between two pieces of human virus RNA in a gene known as HA (for hemagglutinin), an important gene in the flu virus.

"The virulence of influenza viruses is largely determined by their HA," he wrote in his Science paper.

The mixing of genes from two different species is called "recombination."

Gibbs theorized that the pig-human virus recombination event occurred a year or two before 1918 and infected soldiers in Europe during World War I.

Some victims died in a single day. Survivors brought the virus home with them after the war.

"The widely distributed coincidental outbreaks of the Spanish flu in different parts of the world seem to correspond with the return of soldiers from Europe to their home countries at the end of World War I," Webster said.

However, Webster said Gibbs' theory that a pig is to blame for the mass deaths, while possible, is unproven.

In another paper in the journal, a University of Wisconsin-Madison scientist found that a tiny change in a single gene caused the 1997 "bird flu" in Hong Kong to be so deadly.

That virus has been detected twice this year in Hong Kong, despite the government's killing of millions of chickens in 1997 and in May in efforts to wipe it out.

"What this tells us is, essentially, this can happen any moment," the University of Wisconsin scientist, Yoshihiro Kawaoka, said.

In a typical year, the flu kills 500,000 to 1 million worldwide. The Hong Kong flu of 1968 killed 33,800 in the United States, and the Asian flu of 1957 killed 69,800 Americans.

The Milwaukee Journal Sentinel contributed to this report.

Duluth
News
Tribune
Friday
Sept. 7
2001

WE KNOW NOW —From DULUTH NEWS TRIBUNE

much worse because people were already injured, ill, or distraught from the fire. People lived in makeshift homes, wells were contaminated, food and income sources gone. Many graves in all of the local cemeteries were dug as a result of the 1918 flu epidemic.

SISU

It is a tribute to the strength, internal fortitude (sisu), and persistence of the people of this entire section of the state of Minnesota that people stayed, continued to wrest a living and survive in this "burned over" area when also coping with war and epidemic fatal illness.

I recently attended the funeral of a man from Duluth who, at age nine, had lost his father as a result of the flu epidemic. The pastor said that the loss had been a life altering experience, especially since the family had recently immigrated from Scotland. "Scotty" became "the man of the house," as was dictated in the early 1900s. He held jobs at a very young age, and tempered his life decisions with his responsibility in mind.

Lincoln School in Wright was the sight of a makeshift hospital for the community. Women took the personal risk and sacrifice to see that the ill were tended to. The American Red Cross also helped with this effort.

Four persons in Lakeside are listed as having died from influenza from October to December of 1918, three of them under a year old, one at forty three. The fast spreading epidemic did not victimize only the very old or very young, it took healthy, strong persons. Just as in the case of massive fire, the systems set in place to deal with the flu did not begin to deal with the intensity and ferocity of the epidemic. Loss of control almost always leads to maximum tension and fear of a situation. Since the percentage of those becoming ill succumbing was relatively high (we will never know exactly how high) we can only begin to imagine the terror which was justifiably experienced. So, today, one must only mention the year 1918 to elicit strong feelings of empathy for both the victim and survivors of this nightmarish time.

In memory of the early pioneers who settled this area. Many later perished or suffered in the 1918 forest fire which started 3 miles west of here and burned Lawler, Automba, Kettle River, Moose Lake, and surrounding communities, including the area south of Tamarack.

From a memorial, Salo township, Aitkin County, Minnesota

Every blade
   in the field
Every leaf
   in the forest
Lays down
   its life
In its season
   as beautifully
As it was taken up

Thoreau

13   Elements of Life and Death

If all is said and done it could reported that the weather is a very powerful control of life here, or anywhere in the world. Our very life depends upon it, as does our peace of mind and quality of life. Breathtaking beauty or backbreaking work are brought to us as a result of the variance of temperature, precipitation, wind, and yes, even our care of the environment.

Weather—we like it or…not

We Minnesotans, especially those of us from the far north, have a conscious or sub-conscious awareness that many people on this continent wonder why we have chosen to live in this "God-forsaken climate." Many of us hope they never find out, because we like it the way it is. Many early settlers come from similar climates in Northern Europe. It was fortunate that they brought with them innate temperament and skill to deal with a climate which can and has had temperature fluctuations of at least fifty degrees, where winds have been known to reach eighty miles per hour (to say nothing of tornadoes). Both mosquitoes, which some people jokingly refer to as our "state bird," and ticks, some which carry serious diseases, abound in our climate. The land, heavily wooded when settlers arrived, presented a challenge to prepare for farming. Removing the forest was a primary project for lumberjacks and fires for nearly a century.

Into this land came people who were ready to deal with its particular mixture of elements which Webster's dictionary describes as (atmospheric forces) earth, air, fire and water, formerly regarded as the basic constituents of the material universe, the natural habitat of an organism (water, dry land, etc.). During an interview Toini Kari Aho gave several very pertinent comments: "The early settlers survived because they respected the weather. They weren't foolhardy. They had the attitude that 'you do what you have to do'—we coped with the weather."

To be accepted as any kind of a communicator at all here you must be able to talk weather. Anything from a conversation starter to an in-depth expression of serious philosophical leanings is acceptable. When we had wimpy, no-snow winters in 2000 and 2001, one could hear far more complaints about the fact that "We never had a winter" than one ever hears complaints about a bad blizzard.

Speaking of bad blizzards, a group of friends came up with a list of HOW TO TELL IF YOU ARE IN A BAD BLIZZARD:

- You are slogging through deep snow, decide to sit down and rest and discover you already are.
- Your house is dark, can't see through the windows and the power is out.
- You're turning a little blue (couple of ways to take that one).
- All your machinery gives you guff.
- The best way to negotiate a drift is to roll over it.
- You are driving down a road and somebody has dropped a barn down on it.
- Your air cleaner is so filled with ice that your car won't run.
- The man of the house has an urgent errand he must get "out" to do.

Some helpful statements you might wish to inject:

- In our area it is documented that it has snowed during each and every month of the year.
- If you don't like our weather—wait an hour—it will change.
- Grass isn't going to grow unless we have rain.
- Little chilly this morning (25° below).
- Those clouds don't look good.
- On a sunny day in April: Well, there went our summer.

General consensus has it that much more snow fell each winter in the earlier half of the twentieth century than the

EARLY MAIL SLED
To keep moving mail uncle Vic built a snow machine in 1936. It was built from a Model "T" with chains on wheels in back and runners in front. It worked!

HORSE VERSION
This horse sleigh proceeded the mechanical version, hitched to "Fanny, the fast, white, western horse."

last half. Bud tells about tunneling under the snow to carry wood into the house. The tunnel was so deep that he as a ten-year-old had no trouble standing up in it. "No one fell through the top of it either." The same year my sister slid down a hill, fell into softer snow where she couldn't be reached. Father had to dig her out ten feet from the side. Bud tells that during another blizzard, out of fourteen trucks to deliver Minneapolis Star and Tribune papers he was the only one to make it back after delivering his load. They sent him out again and he didn't make it back for three days; kept the truck running all the time.

A railroad engineer told Walter Johnson about pulling a train through a blizzard so blinding that even the signal lights at the side of the track were invisible. He suddenly stopped the train, knowing that he could not go further. As he debarked to check the tracks he discovered he was within ten feet of an oncoming train which had also stopped. "Thank you God," he spoke in amazement.

Traveling during a blizzard is, by far, a major cause of death during a blizzard, although we have had two fairly local deaths from becoming disoriented on foot in blinding snow and freezing to death. Ice can make it very difficult to control a vehicle and many local deaths can be attributed to that fact.

Today we have large, winged plows, snow blowers, off-line communication, and well-built houses to deal with the Minnesota blizzard. Toini tells of her father-in-law hitching a car to his team of horses, sitting on the hood with the reins while young Toini steered the car as they struggled out nearly a mile to a plowed road. She remembers at a later

time the Finnish children were excited that there was to be a rare appearance of a 'kissa' or cat coming to clean out roads drifted high with snow. Some of them had visions of a large tom cat, so were surprised at the appearance of a large, yellow caterpillar tractor. One Easter found Toini and her children walking over two miles through drifted snow in their Easter finery to go to Easter church services. "It was uphill both ways," comments her now adult daughter. Toini shares the following account of the birth of her first baby:

"Leonard was working at Deer River during my entire pregnancy. I lived at home with my parents. Letters were my only means of communication with Leonard. His brother, Art Aho, was the first local young man to be drafted, but a farewell party was canceled because of a bad blizzard. I knew at about four in the afternoon that something was about to happen because I did not feel well at all. I went upstairs and tried to sleep, not wanting to worry my parents. My water broke and I was miserable but I stuck it out until morning, not wanting to spoil my parents' sleep. Then as soon as I heard mother moving in the kitchen, I went down and told her that I had not slept well, that the baby was coming.

"How long have you been sick?" asked mother.

"All night," was the only reply I could honestly give.

She ran over to John Walli's to use the nearest phone. She called to see where the roads might have been opened. A widower who lived in the near-by former teacherage threw some hay on his sleigh and we began the trip on what is now called Finn Road. We stopped at Tuomi's but because it was so cold, their car would not start. We continued to your parent's place. Your dad had his schoolbus ready, and Kulmala asked him

"Can you take the Kari girl into town in your schoolbus—she's sick?"

"What's the matter?"

"She's going to have a baby!"

We got to Wright in the bus, and as Cliff had to deliver the school children, Carl Nylond offered to take me to Cloquet, to the maternity home there. His wife and Hanna Walli went along. Hanna had the foresight to bring a scissors and cord along. We got to the home, and forty-five minutes later I had delivered a bouncing eight-pound baby boy. (Named Marvin Clifford—dad was always proud about that.)

I wrote to Leonard and in a week he arrived to take us home. Again—you did what you had to do—even if weather was making it difficult.

After several days at my parents' home, Leonard decided that it was time to move to the home farm which we had been readying for the move.

"That's enough of that," said the determined patriarch. "We're moving home."

"Is the road open enough to bring the baby in," asked a worried mother-in-law?

"Ya, it's open."

"That stubborn Finlander just wanted his wife at home."

It was a tough walk in, with Leonard crashing through the snow with the baby, me floundering close behind.

"My mother had to send brother Raino to fetch Father when she was ready to deliver Eino. 'Tell him the baby is coming!' she had instructed. Father was working on Suhonen's house—on July 12, 1926 (see chapter 11). The little red brick houses are starting to take on a life of their own.

IT'S NOT JUST A SAYING— THE MAIL MUST GO THROUGH.

Rural mail delivery was as important to farm families during challenging weather conditions as it was on any other day. Uncle Victor Peterson constructed several versions of what we would now call now machines or snow mobiles to get the mail into the boxes. "He always got the mail through." Sometimes he even had to ski parts of his route. Water and mud in the spring were also hazards which he overcame. He bought a Jeep in the fifties to negotiate on "bad days."

School students walked, even on bad days early in the century. When vehicles became available, cars may have been the first transportation. Later my father fashioned a schoolbus from a truck chassis and sheet metal. Bill Wanous helped him with the project, and the bus became our family car also. My brother tells of "going courting" in the boxy bus. One time in the nineteen-forties my father got the children home, but had to walk home for several miles. Blasted by pelting snow and wind he wrapped his hand around the telephone line (yes, snow was that deep) for guidance home. He had a four-inch icicle coming down from his eyebrow. It was nip and tuck for him to make it home that day. Spring brought flood and mud. Bud was sixteen when he drove the bus through the water that always

BUS NO FURTHER
In 1951 father's bus stalled, forcing him to walk home in the blizzard. He held onto telephone lines for guidance. (Yes, snow was that deep!).

collected on the end of Tamarack Lake in the spring. The water was high enough to begin coming up the step, almost to the floor of the bus. He lost the brakes when they were soaked with water and took a harrowing ride for the rest of the route. He slowed the bus by shifting down. As he neared the end of the route he noticed that his elbows felt funny. It was the nervous sweat which had run down his neck and arms and collected in large pockets in the elbows of his shirt. He had obtained a chauffeur's license when only fifteen. "Paid fifty cents for it." Where was dad? Fishing in Canada.

I think I enjoyed "snow" and "mud" days off from school as a teacher more than as a student. Often driving bus through mud, snow and water was a very real challenge, and school was not called off on a whim.

Cold weather made hard work on the farms even more difficult. Watering cows in the winter was at best a real chore, but really a trial when water could freeze in a few minutes. Some opened watering holes in lakes, some carried from hand pumps. When electric pumps, pipes and cow controlled drinking cups became available it was a blessing, but pipes burst when they freeze, and no machinery liked to work when it was cold. Electricity often went off for long periods during a storm. After the advent of milking machines in the 50s, it was not pleasant to go back to hand milking a good-sized herd for the duration of the outage. One man went off the road in the and walked across a mile of swamp toward my parents house lights. He slept under our wood stove that night. Houses were certainly not built and insulated well. I remember even in the late forties going to bed after sweeping the snow which had drifted through the cracks between logs and sifted onto the quilts. Log structures were fairly warm while chinking lasted, and cool in summers, but much heat was lost if it was windy. Wood heat was exclusive until the fifties. It is still quite common in the area.

No one ever worried about starving during a storm in the early days. Dairy products, garden produce canned or stored, meat (domestic and wild) was available, most farms

SKIES AT NIGHT

SOMETHING'S BREWING

LOOK FOR PICTURES

SKY OF HOPE

Some people in the area have positive images as forecasters of weather.
Many signs are used — aching joints, plant and animal behavior and appearance.
Many read the sky for information.

had chickens and had set in flour, sugar and the all important coffee. Berries had been canned, as well as some commercial fruit.

DEPENDING ON RAIN

Animal and human food were extremely dependent on the correct amount of precipitation. Walt Johnson, local weather guru, says that we need thirty-two inches of precipitation per year to replace that lost, mostly to evaporation, to "break even." During the dust bowl years this area survived because farmers were able to harvest the "swamp hay" which although, not as nutritious, did carry the cows through the winters. Jasper says seed from "Reed Canary" grass came from Russian Siberia, was sown by people and later by nature.

Amount of rain before and during the hay harvest was always directly related to production, thus farm survival and profit. If it was too dry during a growing season or too wet during a harvesting season, the amount of milk produced was directly affected. My father was very nervous during haying season, and of course, that is when the rain would come at the wrong time, or machinery would break down.

With the blessing of rain came the dangers of lightning. Although it supplies essential nitrogen for the plants, it has placed one person in our cemetery, and scared a few others nearly there. Sometimes it comes without warning. A man up on a ladder, was struck and received injuries from which

Putting up winter food for cows and horses depended on weather; survival and profit depended on the hay. Rope slings are built into this hayload, but one needed to be careful not to string them around wagon boards. It wouldn't be a happy sight to see the wagon go up into the hay mow.

he never healed. Another bolt from the blue came to a man using a metal hand pump. Sunshine can be deceiving as the storm, according to Walt, can strike from as far as five miles away. "Fuzz" Strom from this community has been struck four times, and survives.

Is our weather all negative? Winter recreation is enjoyable to most of us in one way or another. Several area eighty-year-olds still ski. Maybe someone's idea of winter recreation is to curl up by a warm fire. If you think winter is an overwhelming cross to bear, a Minnesota spring will convince you otherwise. Everything seems to come alive with breathtaking newness. Hope and ambition are renewed. The strength and beauty of nature is incredible.

ESPECIALLY FITTED

Many people who live in this area believe they are Finnish, Swedish, Norwegian or Russian. A larger than previously thought percentage of them are actually from the northern parts of those countries and are Sami . That would explain why they chose to live here, and are geared to mak-

CEMETERY SEASONS—Seasonal change is eternal; so is the cycle of life.

ing the best of it. Many second and third generation people were not told of their Sami blood because people who have experienced oppression and discrimination seldom make choices for children which could involve more of it. First generation parents made the decision to assimilate. Persecution still persists in their homeland. For instance an investor from Minnesota is committing virtual genocide in order to obtain possession of Sami fishing waters. A culture holding onto ancient lifestyle and values longer than other cultures is not viewed positively in our own culture. Sami s in their homeland do, however, retain many gifts and understandings needed to deal with our northern environment, while preserving its integrity. Acculturation is resulting in loss of these skills, however.

Sami s are close enough to nature to forecast weather, understand animals, use natural cures, creatively fill needs from natural materials around them. They have perception which exceeds "normal." This was called "Magic" in the Finnish epic THE KALEVALA, all skills needed to survive well in this area. The climate probably seemed mild to Laplanders when compared with the Arctic circle.

BONDED THROUGH SUNSHINE AND STORM

Most of the people interviewed for this chapter make a point of saying that the weather, good or bad, brings people together. "Hardship builds close relationships," said Toini. "Neighbors were really good to us during the long blizzards," said Jasper. I would say that it is second only to death in bringing people together. Though not as strong as it once was, this feeling still exists.

IF WE ON THIS PLANET
DO NOT CONTROL
THE NUMBER OF HUMANS ON IT,
NATURE WILL

Leaders of a movement to give recognition and appreciation to Sami culture by Sami s themselves as well as the general population, Rudolph and Solvig Johnson of Duluth are patriarch and matriarch of local Sami s. Rudy served as head librarian at the University of Minnesota Duluth for decades, and Solvig is an accomplished artist. Their son Arden publishes THE ARRON (along with Mel Olson), a Sami Publication.

Address of the Sami newsletter, THE ARRON, is 712 West Franklin Dr. 1, Minneapolis MN 55405. The North American Journal, BAIKI, is available at 1430 32nd street, #2, West Oakland, CA 94608.

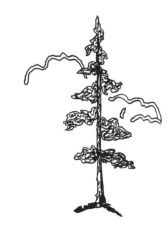

14 Characters in Life and Death

HEADED FOR TOWN
What is behind these expressive faces? What is the occasion for this photo? What will the future bring for these young bachelors? What will the rest of the day bring for them? Do I only imagine that they are fun-loving individualistic, devil-may-care? If they are, will they remain as such? For a lifetime? What legends will these individuals generate in a lifetime?

Put the Bachelors Over There

Many bachelors rest in Lakeside and surrounding cemeteries. Several people have spoken about the "special" areas in some local cemeteries for these bachelors, although our unmarried men are buried within the family which attempted to nurture them. These often neglected bachelor areas were sometimes buried off to one side, or the rear of the regular cemetery, and the graves were many times left unmarked. Many of these graves will never be located or identified. Some unwritten assumptions about the never-been married men in our community were communicated, unintentionally, to me quite early in life. Never directly, never in so many words…maybe a slight smile when discussing one of them, maybe in overhearing a plot to "find a woman for _____, maybe in some gentle "ribbing."

The bachelors certainly did not meet the social norm of the day, and thus were to be looked on as objects of pity, jokes, and maybe even a little mistrust. Single women were even more maligned, as it took a very special woman to dare to strike out on her own in those times., when most women were very dependent on marriage for All needs. My aunt Martha, however had made the statement early on : "Being married would be like being dead, and I'm not ready to die yet!" We have had, in the early, mid and even late nineteenth century, very few unmarried women. Even other women could not tolerate this lifestyle by a woman.

I suspect that some bachelors do even equate marriage with death. In one case this was a very literal connection. Evert had lived alone since his divorce and, while still under forty, had adopted many of the old bachelor ways. Many times the seeming inability to find a suitable home inspires a well meaning neighbor women to "help." Such was the case with Evert. He had lived in a small, converted motel room. So on that Sunday morning our helpful neighbor lady was eagerly awaiting Evert's appearance so she could share her good news.

"Evert…I've found a great trailer (mobile home) for you, bought it for a song! It's yours, only one requirement…You must marry that young woman

She never finished the sentence, for, as you might have guessed, at that instant Evert fell over dead. He took peaceful residency in our cemetery that week.

LUCKY OR UNLUCKY IN LOVE.

It is fair to say that many of the lonely situations resulted from the pain of unrequited love. Choice of a solitary lifestyle is, many times, a result of dashed romantic hopes. Rejection by a woman, an object of desire and pursuit (is that where the word suitor came from?) more than once resulted in withdrawal from family and society in general. Alice Graff tells us of an uncle who was in his early twenties when the girl of his dreams said "good-bye." Thereafter, he would communicate with only a few people of his choosing, never left his property, grew his own limited food supply (including coffee and tobacco substitutes) and accepted only small favors. Salt and flour were among those things he accepted from others. He wore the same "overalls" continually. One ritual which gave Alice a glimpse of his life once a year was the scrubbing of his floor on Christmas eve.

"How long was this his lifestyle?" I asked, wondering how many years Alice carried on the holiday tradition.

"As it turned out, he lived to be eighty-six," smiled Alice.

"Was he ever happy?" I asked, wondering if one could make some sense of that long, lonely life.

"Happy…HAPPY?" Alice smiled again. "NO, he was a Norwegian…wasn't he?"

Existence of a number of bachelors in the community seems to bear out the claims that Finnish character exhibits a high degree of quiet mistrust and withdrawal from overt relationships with the opposite sex. Many of the bachelors were, and are, very independent and sensitive to any "wrongs" which may have been committed against them.

The ground impression, or indentation indicating human habitation is, to my knowledge, the only trace that remains of the bachelor who lived across our lake in the early 1900s. My mother remembers that the socially cautious woodsman had struck up an unprecedented, deliberate relationship with a local young woman, but that the involvement had taken a bad turn when she traveled to a distant town. She sent a valentine to him which featured a large, green leafy head with the caption: "LETTUCE BE FRIENDS." Unable to read, he thought she was calling him a CABBAGE HEAD. No one ever saw him again, although his rifle, tools, and those things he needed for survival were found in his humble "dug out" (semi-submerged sod shelter).

MISTRUST

I think it fair to say that many, if not most , of the bachelors have a deep and abiding mistrust of women. If I am driving a family vehicle and Raino is out along the road fixing fence he will wave if he thinks Dan is driving. Several times he has taken back the wave when he sees that it is me at the wheel. His hand will dive down from mid air and huddle close to him. This is not because I am a "newcomer" or "stranger." I have lived next to this person for a lifetime (excluding about six years). He will not speak to me at any time, though he did give his orders when I worked in the local café during my high school years. He speaks to other people (mostly men) once in a while, if there is a pressing need or a deer hunt or other urgent activity on going.

This mistrust may stem from the local lore of the male. One day my father was attempting to make small talk while waiting for ten-gallon cream cans to appear on the conveyer which emerged from the local creamery.

"How are you doing, Antti?"

"Preddy goot, but wife…hell, hell, hell."

Dad really enjoyed telling that story.

THEY LOOK AT THINGS IN DIFFERENT WAYS:

That might be just another way of saying that sometimes they seemed eccentric. Two brothers, John and Eli, farmed a small acreage in the area. No one seems to remember what the quarrel was about, but the result was that the men split their small house down the center with a wall, lived in that house for years, never speaking to each other. It was said by some that one of them moved his horse inside, but that is one of the wild rumors that intensify small behavior anomalies. One thing for certain: they now lie side by side in our cemetery. How much hardship they imposed upon themselves in life!

One of our more reclusive, non-communicative bachelors had made a rare appearance at a community event. (maybe at his father's funeral). Anyway, he was standing near a woman with an infant in her arms. The infant suddenly lurched and would have landed on the floor if Raino had not caught him.

Slowly, metering each word, Raino said, "You almost lost your rockpicker!"

AGREE TO DISAGREE

Sam Johnson, at age ninety, and Henry Carlson, at age ninety-two, each engaged to live in house and enjoy the cooking of Mrs. Jack Walli, age eighty. It was an uneasy arrangement at best. Henry felt it was an insult that Sam could not speak to him in English. Sam felt that Henry ate too much, but when he began to deride the Swede for that weakness in character he was frustrated because Henry could, or would not respond to his words.

"You'll have to remember that Henry can not speak or understand Finnish," said Sophy, as she tried to make peace.

"WELL, HE CAN LEARN…CAN'T HE?" shouted an indignant Henry.

NATIONAL PRIDE

Bill drove up to the post office in his new white truck with blue stripe. Knowing that his "P CUP" is one of the most important things in a bachelor's life, I wanted to make a positive comment.

"That new pick-up reminds me of the Finnish flag, with it's blue stripe on white, Bill!"

"Well, someone's got to keep up the patriotism."

A HUNTING FATALITY

Dan has come home, as I write, with a new bachelor story. I must preface this short account with the explanation that we are in the middle of a harried, surreal three-week holiday known as hunting season. Normally staid, steady people become obsessed with buck fever. Even our more non-communicative, solitary individuals are caught up in the frenzy of attempting to bag a white tailed deer, or at least enter the discussion of why they missed that important shot. I could fill a book with deer hunting stories, but will relate only this one:

Chuck Hanson had taken a little midday break from hunting, and was just coming out of his house, rifle riding on the crook of his arm, when he spotted a huge buck, within good shooting range, behind his parked pickup (a new Dodge Ram). He stealthily used the vehicle as cover to creep up closer, and to remain hidden while he raised his gun. He got the point buck in the cross hairs of his sights, fired, and wondered why the buck leaped off, and the shot sounded a little weird. He had shot his pickup. The shot went through the hood, knocked off a wiring cable and lodged in the innards of his hapless truck. The truck was indeed dead, as the bullet had hit a vital spot. Thinking of the dead Ram sitting in his yard as testament to his mistake, I commented: "Bet he felt sheepish about that."

For all the mistakes, wild shots and lost hunting parties we have no deer hunting fatalities on our cemetery, to my knowledge. That is amazing!

THIS FOR THAT

It is difficult to explain the importance of the hunt to local culture. I recently became aware, again, that it sometimes seems more important than life itself. Art, our neighbor has always been a great good neighbor. So when I happened to see him during hunting season recently I invited him and his son in law over the line which divides our property. I called them when I spotted a deer close in to our house, then watched with some trepidation, as Art painfully put one foot ahead of the next to set out on a drive. I was really concerned that he was in no condition to walk easily on a level floor, to say nothing of the tangled grass and brush he was encountering in the swale now. The term 'dead man walking' could describe my impression of his dogged struggle to drive that deer. It soon became apparent that the thousand drives Art had made before would guide him in this one. I heard some whistles, strange noises, then saw the deer crash out exactly in the place it should have, where his son-in-law was ready. One deer, bagged and tagged.

As I was recounting the hunt to Perry, and speculating on the importance of it He said, "Well, you've got to remember that we aren't so removed from a time when ' the hunt' was life itself.

Karen Atkins tells of a fellow who was an avid goose hunter. He never missed a chance to get out into a blind (a well camouflaged shooting station), wait in the cold wetness of a fall dawn in anticipation of shooting a big bird. She recalls that when he died (of causes unrelated to hunting) his earthly support group was gathered around the casket at the cemetery. At that very moment the traditional "V" formation of geese flew over—very low, and making a very loud noise.

"Those geese certainly got the last laugh!" commented Karen.

"And so did the mourners," I thought. Karen had told me that after all his effort, the man had never shot a goose!?

IN SOLITARY

Bachelors are sometimes mysterious people. Especially during the early to mid-1900s when the norm was more commonly and closely adhered to. Jasper remembers one stand-out.

"A Mr. Jenson (Larson or Hanson) lived way up north. He had long hair (somewhat shocking in the twenties). It took him all day to ride in to town on his sway-back horse to buy groceries. His dog always walked in his shadow."

Later another neighbor confirmed that there was , indeed, a "Prairie River Hanson" who had been a teacher at Yale, and had an entire shed full of books. "They went into the ground though." The man had, for reasons unknown, left the academic world to dwell in an obscure settlement, whose inhabitants looked upon him as an abnormality. As such as he was not to be considered a full member of the community, and was not quite to be trusted. One of his claims to fame was his practice of dancing with the broom at local dances, rather than trusting or wanting association with any of the young ladies present.

It was not uncommon for a man to have come to the United States with thoughts of sending for his wife. A friend tells of an uncle who had that intention. "He would save money, even buy her ticket, but then when his need for alcohol overwhelmed good intentions, spent the money or sold the tickets. Finally, after twenty-six years he went back to Finland. 'It would have been better if you had stayed in America,' they said."

These men were essentially bachelors.

NON-VERBAL

We carefully placed rabbit tracks across the floor of a roomful of tables at Lakeside clubhouse when we set up for our 'SCANDINAVIAN DINNER THEATER.' The plan was to begin the play with two bachelor lumberjacks entering at the back of the room, striding through to the rabbit tracks, stopping to look at them. One of the men would say

"Rabbit," then they both would continue walking out the front (stage) exit. When the show was over they would come back through (as if on their way home from a day in the woods) and the other man would say, "Yep." Then they would continue out the back door. We rehearsed many times, yet I wasn't sure until the performance if that bit would go off without a hitch. I got the impression that they never really understood the purpose of the two words, although the local audience assuredly did!

To complicate the matter of communication, many of our bachelors are Finnish. In the ancient Finnish epic, THE KALEVALA, mastery of an entity (human or other/both have character) may be achieved simply by speaking words. It is my theory that this attitude towards words can manifest itself in two opposite ways. Either a Finnish person is very proficient, persuasive, colorful and poetic with words (which seems to be the case many times in women) or there is an innate feeling that words are too precious to "waste." That seems to be the case with many of our neighborhood bachelors. There is, though, the old joke in which the wife, on her deathbed asks her husband if he loves her. "I told you I did when we got married…if there is any change I will tell you."

On occasion a fear of not measuring up may inhibit relations with the opposite gender. I was told of a conversation with one of our local bachelors during which he was asked why he didn't marry.

"I'm lucky enough to be able to pee," he retorted.

Then there is the language transition. Many neighbors, living in these times, did not speak English until they started school. Even church services in this rural area might have been in Finnish, Swedish, or Norwegian until the twenties predominantly, even so occasionally today. Sometimes one can hear these languages spoken at local events, even now, especially among the bachelors. A friend recollects that the only time her father spoke English was to "holler" swear words and directions to an errant horse. The bachelors had even less motivation to learn English than the married men, as they didn't have any children to encourage them.

CHILDREN?

Though a certain caliber of single person may have produced children, knowingly or unknowingly, it wasn't unusual for bachelors to be concerned for children.

Many stories concerning bachelors relate to "helping" young people to experience activities and substances which are new to youngsters, and which may cause unpleasant or even dangerous reactions to the uninitiated. Snuff, smokes, home brew or whiskey were among favorites which might cause fainting, nausea, disorientation in the uninitiated. My first theory was that they enjoyed seeing young people suffer the consequences of participation in previously forbidden activities (vices). Dan brought it to my attention that the bachelors may not consider these things as vices at all,

but are merely attempting to share some simple joys, which for them may seem an important part of life. An educator friend surmised that the propensity to offer youth these experiences may be an attempt to set up a rite of passage, to say "now you are old enough to do these things—let's see how you handle the challenge." Other little tests might include putting a manure spreader into throwing gear when unsuspecting youth will be showered with unwelcome filth. Another favored trick might involve asking a youth to test an electric fence. This was done by touching the fence with a long stem of hay. Discovering that the "juice" was off they might confidently proceed through the fence, only to be quire shocked to discover that the fence had mysteriously come on.

Then there is the thought that actions speak louder than words. My brother-in-law, who is not native to the area, remembers coming to visit, courting. During one of his first local dance hall visits a burley bachelor approached him.

"Have a drink."

"No, thank you, not right now.

"HAVE A DRINK," repeated the local, picking Bill up by the scuff of the neck with one huge hand!

"I had the drink," says Bill, with a smile and raised eyebrows.

Which brings us to our next chapter, a battle with "The Bottle."

15 A Problem With Alcohol

LAUGH OR CRY?

One of the entertainments that this family friend sometimes engaged in was to pretend to be "drunk." He was never a heavy drinker, but in an age when people saw humor in intoxication he was a master at humor. We now may realize that to show the effects of alcohol should be no more funny than showing the affects of overdosing on drugs. Nevertheless, I remember laughing almost continually when he was around. It was a more simple age. Jimmy, who lost both parents in the sinking of the Titanic, was seldom seen without a big cigar in his mouth, except on his death bed (lung cancer).

A Community Situation

It's the old speculation of "which came first, the chicken or the egg? Did a "problem with alcohol" interfere with socialization and marriage, or was a problem with alcohol the result of having no friends or spouse? At any rate, in a culture which had, and has, many problems stemming from over consumption it was obvious that many, if not most bachelors, were troubled by "drink."

SAM JOHNSON

"Sam Johnson." A soft smile of remembrance crossed Rod's face. "Sam Johnson," he said again, as he scanned names on the newly printed computer list of those at home in the cemetery. As a Walli he had many relatives buried there.

"Sam Johnson?" I couldn't put a face on the name; remembered only that he was one of the semi-antisocial older gentlemen who lived out their lives in relative isolation and independence, and who had decided, for one reason or another to forgo the accepted norm of marriage and

family. Rod picked up on my curiosity, appeased it with this account:

"I was in High School the spring that dad arranged for me to cut and peel popple on the 40 next to Sam's place. I rode my horse over each day. It was hot, hard work. No chainsaws…just an ax, handsaw and a handmade peeling iron. One hot day I forgot to bring my water jug. I felt that I knew Sam well enough to ride over and ask him for a drink of water, having seen him walk past our farm on his way to and from town. I remembered marveling at the frequency of large sacks of sugar going by on Sam's back. I knew, too, that Sam grew a good potato crop each year.

"Does Sam sell potatoes?" I had asked.

"No…No, he doesn't sell potatoes." dad had said, with typical Finnish taciturn.

"So I asked Sam for a drink of water."

"No water…BEER," said Sam, after recovering from the surprise interruption of his solitude.

"Thirst is thirst I thought, as I accepted the tall glass of amber drink. Sam removed one of the hard, flat, round loaves of Finnish rye bread which he had baked and hung on the rafters to dry. We dunked the bread as we finished the second tall glass of beer.

"Well, thanks," I said as I moved out the door. BOOM! I fell flat. Out cold, not too far from the doorstep."

"What happened?" I asked, as Rod had already turned his attention to some details on the computer printout.

"When I came to it was chore time"

HE LIVED LIFE HIS WAY

OH SUGAR!

In the "early days" roads were very primitive, often just tracks through open fields, or narrow trails on high spots. Jasper and a friend who he describes as "half crocked" were attempting to drive to a nearby town for a dance one night. They had stopped for drinks then continued to drive on the narrow, clogged road with less than good visibility. Suddenly, they lurched off the road, took a scenic tour through the semi-frozen swamp, over stumps and rocks, through hazel brush, then miraculously returned to the road. Later, on their way back they saw their tracks, and on the other side someone had made an almost identical "detour." Our mailbox seemed to be an attraction for drivers who veered toward, instead of away from objects in their path. Did prohibition make a difference? I venture to say that it created an opportunity for many business ventures in

SAM JOHNSON AND JACK WALLI

Jacob (Jack) Walli became the patriarch of the Isaac Walli farm when father Isaac died in the 1918 fire. He and his wife Maria are the parents of Sulo, Jenny, Alma and Carl (who have contributed to this book) and eight others. His grandson Tad now operates the homestead, along with his wife Nancy.

Sam Johnson remained unmarried, but seemed to enjoy neighborhood children. He was very colorful—loved by some adults, while he irritated others.

the community. Potatoes, beets, dandelions, and rhubarb often became a beverage for which many would walk quite a way to purchase or barter.

The business was not without hazard, of course, as one could be concerned about detection and detention if apprehended. Moonshiners were often identified because of their need for sugar. During those years people were limited to one hundred pounds of sugar per household. The illegal producers of "liquor" would get it from various towns, in various names, but STILL (no pun) were sometimes caught because of this purchase. Jasper mentioned that his mother used a lot of sugar in canning. She put up eight or nine hundred quarts of preserves during each fall season. I have heard from another source that another family confused the "revenuers" by putting a pear in each jar of hard liquor. My computer has difficulty with all of the antiquated words. In this paragraph it wanted to change "moonshiners" to Monsignors. It might have been attempted, but no doubt failed.

Local moonshiner, Moses King, was known for concocting the most "impure gut rot." He was allegedly not clean in the process and for a "kicker" he added lye. "He couldn't even keep his face clean," said one detractor. I remember Moses as an old man, coming into the restaurant each afternoon and ordering a hot pork sandwich, paying for it in gold pieces.

A BACHELOR'S BRIDE

Bruno's eyes sparkled, as he recalled Teimo. "We were all at Teimo's shack. Not too fancy a place! Bachelor's tar paper shack, rats, stinking underwear. We were all sitting around, shooting the breeze. Except Teimo; he was sleeping in the other room. Passed out. "He drank a little too much." (Drank a little too much was, and is, a local euphemism for an alcoholic.)

Bruno continued, "We heard a shot; ran in there. He was sitting on the edge of his bed with his twenty-gage (shotgun). Dazed; he looked at us, still fondling his gun."

Bruno paused at this point, and I could tell it was to prepare us for the punch line. "MY BRIDE BURPED."

"He walked straight, you know. He had been in the Finnish army—had some injuries. Thin as a rail, could hardly notice him if he stood sideways. Well, on this day he was on his way to the outhouse. It had iced during the night—slippery as heck! Well, he walked straight as an arrow—up the hill. Then he took his tumble. Bad; rolled him right over and over. Well, we watched as he got himself up, brushed off." At this point the story teller could not rely simply on words. He stood up, patted and prodded his body, in a harried, panicked fashion. He looked around, took an imaginary bottle from out of an inner pocket and took a deep swig.

COMMUNICATION WAS AND IS A PROBLEM

Gust was attracted to the forested, untamed land he had heard was available to homesteaders in northern Minnesota. To make it even better the land was similar, by all accounts, to his homeland in Finland. He told his wife that he would send for her and their two small children when he had made enough money in the new country to do that. We do not know what his intentions were at that time, but the single life in America seemed more and more attractive. He worked for many years as a lumberjack. We do not know if he communicated with his family in Finland, but he made a decision. He faked his death, somehow got relatives from out of state to send notice of his "death" back to Finland, and proceeded to live as a bachelor.

Years passed. Suddenly a glitch in Gust's plan ended with relatives revealing to the Finland family that he really was alive. The children's mother had

STAY TRUE TO ME DARLIN'

Every culture has it's own rituals, and orderly ways of structuring itself. This is a useful item for keeping husbands in line (Zimbabwe). A woman would wear it on her upper arm, use it at her discretion to make up for his indiscretion. It could make a nasty, if not fatal wound.

died, but the oldest child decided that at sixteen she was old enough to take her fourteen-year-old brother in search of father. When they did find him he was less than happy. He told them that they must support themselves, and that he wanted little to do with them. Helmi became a cook in the same lumber camp where Aro worked as a lumberjack. It was grueling, difficult. All three survived. Both children married and had children of their own. Father married twice more also, but never seemed to achieve true happiness. Some graves related to this story remain unmarked by design.

Some of the bachelors were far from reclusive. Charming and debonair, they charmed their way through life, complicating the lives of many unsuspecting women. They seemed the direct opposite of the reclusive men, with an abundance of well-used social skills and appealing attributes. They seemed to need a bevy of admirers to be totally happy. They accepted no responsibility , and couldn't understand a man who did. Did men of the middle ground exist? Yes. Usually they were called "husbands." If a married man proceeded to adopt "bachelor" behavior there was not much "the wife" could do about it. The option of a woman being self supporting was often complicated by the birth of children. Women were subject to a lop-sided value system which judged women harshly for behavior not "normal," but at the same time allowed a "boys will be boys" mentality. There remain whispers of a particularly harsh husband (or six) being found dead in "unusual" circumstances. These men might have been better off had they stayed unmarried. Few people realize that this was a frontier, with a living pattern often attributed only to the "wild west." It was a man's world, but the women were so very strong, out of necessity. Daughter-in-law, Samantha, returned from her work in Africa with an item made and worn by married women specifically designed to deal with husbands who were caught "screwing around" (to use our own vernacular). It consists of a leather holster for a very imposing knife, with a band to slip it onto the woman's arm.

My grandfather adopted a bachelor's (or more correctly 'monks') life after the death of his wife. He left to join a religious group in Ohio. His stepchildren were happy that he had left, as they did not like him. His own children showed little emotion. His departure is recorded in my thirteen-year-old aunt's diary, this way:

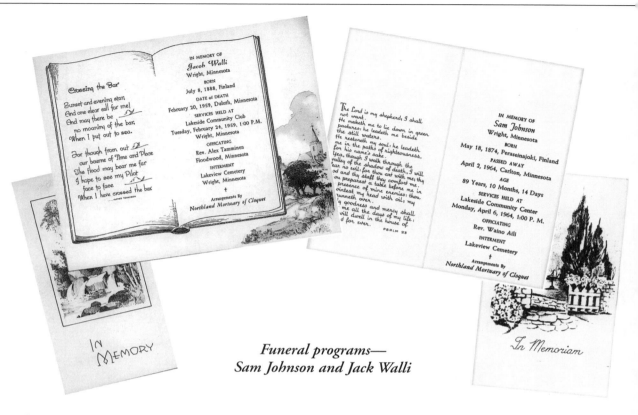

Funeral programs—
Sam Johnson and Jack Walli

"Pa came to school today. Gave Teddy and me both chocolate bars and five dollars each."

They never saw him again, and heard where he was only after his death, when some things were found in his effects to indicate that he had been a father. I observe the effects of

abandonment on his family. True trust is difficult, as are good marriage relationships.

DICTIONARY DEFINITION: MORTIFY—
TO CAUSE SOMEONE TO LOSE DIGNITY

16 Are They Buried or Not?

TO ANSWER THE QUESTION

The purpose of digging up bodies and or records is similar. To find out more about them, to research, draw conclusions. I do not know much about the murder trial which necessitated the opening of a grave at Lakeside. It was not a matter of concern for many locals. Conversely, the records of the Lakeside cemetery board were very important. Buried in another language for over fifty years, the records said much, some of it by what they left unsaid.

Not In Any Cemetery

Olla, the father of the family had come to the United States at an earlier time. Then his son came to settle in the area also. A neighbor from the same area in Finland reported that this adult son had murdered his mother to get money to come here. His father was apparently never aware of his wife's fate, or chose not to acknowledge it. The son was a "rowdy"—loud and abusive. He was drunk much of the time, speculation is that he was attempting to forget what he had done to his mother. They lived up on the Balsam Road. Young Olla married and had a daughter. He was wild and abusive according to reports.

In about 1924 Albert Beseman intended to visit the family, but something told him not to go. It was discovered shortly thereafter that the mentally unbalanced man had, "in cold blood," shot his wife, his five-year-old daughter, the man who was going to help them to escape, and his father. His last act was to take his own life.

The neighbors buried them out in the woods, and may have held a memorial service for them at a later time.

Another man got a mental message not to visit neighbors and probably lived to see another day because of that for-

bearance. The couple was found later, buried in the manure pile (usually a buildup of cow and horse manure over months or years, directly out the back door of the barn). Exactly how they ended life was and is somewhat of a mystery.

Many families, although they did not suffer physical violence, suffered much mental anguish because of alcohol. Money spent for "drink" was not available for food, clothing, doctor's care, to say nothing of other niceties. Behavior was often cause for embarrassment: "Pa knocked over the neighbor's mailbox again, on his way home Saturday night." "It was a bad fight, and we don't know if they'll ever act like neighbors again." "I could have crawled under the bench when uncle John caused such a scene." The ultimate embarrassment caused by overindulgence was endured by a wonderful, large family. Some drunks give away prized possessions in an effort to gain approval. Some grow spirited, even violent when intoxicated (sometimes, the family suffers more loss of face than any negativity the community might feel, and I am sure this is the case in this instance). I am also sure that it was hard to accept that a father dropped dead on the steps of the local bar, even though the community as a whole struggles very hard with the problem of alcohol, and over-consumption of it.

A friend told me that in tracing family history he had located an uncle. As he told about the search, and eventual location I asked, "Was he married?"

"Yes, but she's in Finland, he came alone." (To the United States.)

"Do you then have cousins in Finland?"

"No, she starved to death."

EXHUMATION

To my knowledge we have had only one grave reopened in Lakeside. It was the body of the only third generation son of the local Lundgren family. He had been the victim of murder. The exhumation was done to resolve a court case involving the crime. It brought violence, or the realization of it, back again to the consciousness of locals, even though it had happened in a far-away city.

DIGGING UP RECORDS

So if that is the solitary example of digging up a grave, what is the meaning of the chapter title? I have been digging up the history of the cemetery, and in this chapter I relate specifically the history of its organization. Some of the facts are quite surprising to me. For instance, it was a real mind

BUILDING A CEMETERY
Lakeside's book of minutes dates back to 1907, and was first written in English in 1963. Sacrifices were made to establish a place to honor and remember the dead.

blower to discover how recently the minutes of the cemetery board were written in Finnish.

Historic language first became a barrier when we were approached about the purchase of specific lots. We had absolutely no record of which lots were available for sale. At that time I requested that those current members of the cemetery board who still spoke Finnish translate the minutes to see if we could piece together a picture of lot ownership. They did, at the time, do some work on the translation. I did not realize this until 1999 because the reported that "they could not make any sense of the lot numbering

systems, so that the translation would be useless." I was ready, at the time, to accept that evaluation, as I had four young children and much work to do. Now, I have discovered the translation, have learned so much from it, I have cracked the code, and it follows the order we have now, with a very different numbering system. One of the most surprising discoveries was that the minutes were written in Finnish until 1964. The language was a bit more "Finn/English" in 1964 than it was in 1907. That is there were more English words interspersed with Finnish, or with Finnish word endings added (la, a, ouri).

I understand that many Finns, often men, do not "waste" words, especially in writing. The brief, almost terse, accounts of cemetery board meetings should not have come as a surprise. However, I can not help but read into those minutes some of the information I know would have had to have been discussed, or some of the situations which had to have had an affect of that board. Some minutes "spooked" me to read, as I know the "rest of the story." For instance, I can hardly read the minutes for April 1918 without thinking of the tragic fact that within six months these men would be in an unimaginably heroic battle to save family, home, and livelihood in the tragic 1918 fire. Isak Walli would lose his life in the conflagration, and it would forever change the world of other board members. When I read that my father purchased two grave sites on April 4th, 1964, I must wonder if he had a premonition of his death in two weeks. He had lived one mile north of the cemetery for thirty-two years previous to that time. I had deduced some name changes, for instance Holsopakka to Bakka (in Finnish the P and B are interchangeable) but the minutes confirmed some of my guesses. Maybe Bill Haro never intended to be a bachelor, as he bought two lots at organization time. My grandfather's name suddenly appears in the minutes but I cannot find record of his election, or his departure as he left the area. There is recorded replacements of others, but not in his case. I found that the preferred method of clearing stumps, leveling, or whatever they were trying to accomplish was done with twenty five pounds of dynamite and some fuse. The cost was recorded in expenditures, but the explosive purpose was not mentioned, nor was the names) of the stalwart individuals who employed it for whatever end.

FOOD FOR THOUGHT
One Sunday morning in May Sulo Walli approached me at coffee hour.

"Hey, We've got a cemetery meeting on Tuesday evening. What are we going to have for lunch?"

"I don't know, I hadn't given it much thought"

"Well, I was thinkin' of Tombstone Pizza!"

"I guess that would be great."

"Ya, people would really shovel that down!"

On the drive home I decided to call Sulo's bluff—so I got him on the phone. "I've been thinking about our lunch those Tombstone Pizzas for our cemetery meeting sound good. Let's do it. I'll bring two and you bring a couple."

"Oh, I thought that was a dead issue."

We served pizza at the meeting.

EXHUMING THE RECORDS
The board minutes were finally in my temporary possession in 1999. It was an uncanny experience to hold them in my hands, and remember some of the board members familiar to me (alive in my lifetime). The board minutes would be interesting to print in their entirety, but then they were rather repetitious. I will include the minutes of some of the first cemetery meetings and will also summarize board membership, concerns, and action for the first fifty years of Lakeside, also the first "official" map (which includes plans for graves where the land drops of so steeply that graves there are not to be possible).

FOR THE RECORD
POYTAKIRJA
(Table Book or minutes of the Lakeside Cemetery)

8th day of April, 1907
Held at Henry Lund place first meeting.

1st ORDER OF BUSINESS Election of trustees: for three years Isaac Walli, Henry Lund,

2nd ORDER OF BUSINESS Association would buy 5 rolls of barb wire fence (Isaac W. to buy)

3rd ORDER OF BUSINESS Suggested the group have a committee to clear (cleaning bee). Day selected 10 day of October, 1907

4th ORDER OF BUSINESS Suggested to add additional members into organization and decided to take into membership at .50 C Jacob Holsopakka (Bakka).

5th ORDER OF BUSINESS Suggested to collect money for fence wire and staples $1.00 for each man until it totals $15.00.

6th ORDER OF BUSINESS Suggested/considered to buy 25# dynamite, 50 feet of fuse, 25 staples

7th ORDER OF BUSINESS Considered where they would hold the next annual meeting, and when. Decided to hold first Monday of April, 1908 at Isaac Walli home.

They saw the need for a meeting in October, 1907. To "call in" a county surveyor and clear cemetery property—in the fall before freeze up. Four men helped. Nels Walli, John Oja, Sr., Henry Lund, Eric Nelson. Set 24 by 24 as family lot size (it must have been changed to 16 by 32 quite quickly, but this is not mentioned in the minutes).

Another meeting was held the 8th day of December 1907

At the meeting agreed one family lot to Jacob Panttila, cost $6.10 (Arvottiin?) The following men received the following lots:

John Oja	5, 6
Mike Salo	21, 28
Robert Martin	1, 2
Isak Walli	3, 4
Eric Nelson	19, 30
Gust Makela	11, 1 4
Mutti Latvala	8, 7
William Haro	10, 15
Victor Ranta	22, 27
Jacob Panttila	12, 13
Hiskias Johnson	24, 25
Leander Oja	23, 26
Henry Lund	31, 32
Jacob Bakka	20, 29
John Walli	7–18
John Lehtinen	9–16

These lot numbers bear no relationship to the layout of family plots which contain graves from the very earliest years.

Paid Isaak Walli for dynamite caps and fuse: $2.31

The recorder has sold to Frank Lundgren a lot for $6.10 which I have paid to the Secretary. (Treasurer)

I did, after some study, break the code and relate it to the ownership of lots to our knowledge and practice.

POYTAKIRJA

LAKESIDE YEARLY MEETING, APRIL 9th 1911, JOHN OJA HOME

FIRST ORDER OF BUSINESS: Election of officers: President John Walli, Vice President Isaac Walli, Sec. Mutti Latvala, Treasurer Jacob Holspakka, Sergeant of Arms; Isaac Walli

SECOND ORDER OF BUSINESS: Trustees for three years: Mutti Latvala, Leander Oja (previously elected), and 4 named: John Walli, 1 year; John Oja, 1 year; Henry Lund, 2 years; Isaac Walli, 2 years.

Treasure's report on hand $1.96.

Previous balance $4.00.

Receipt for $5.96 on hand.*

*ANNUAL MEETING, AT HOME OF JOHN WALLI, APRIL 11th, 1915

FIRST ORDER OF BUSINESS: Meeting opened

SECOND ORDER OF BUSINESS: Minutes read and approved

THIRD ORDER OF BUSINESS: Treasure's report $6. 39

FOURTH ORDER OF BUSINESS: Discuss condition of fence, decided it was in good order.

FIFTH ORDER OF BUSINESS: Same officers were reelected

SIXTH ORDER OF BUSINESS: Next year's meeting at home of Jacob Bakka

The original cemetery workers are all at rest. A new generation has taken up their work.

*ANNUAL MEETING 2ND DAY OF APRIL, 1918, Hiskias Johnson home.

Meeting called to order-officers reelected, next annual meeting 1st Monday of April 1919. Adjourned, Mutti Latvala

*ANNUAL MEETING, MATT LATVALA, APRIL 6, 1919

Meeting called to order, treasure's report, on hand receipts $5.00

Balance $10.39.

Officers elected: Chairman—Isaac Walli will be replaced by Jacob Walli (son of Isaac, who had died in the 1918 fire); Secretary—Mutti Latvala.

It was unanimous vote that the sale of single graves were to be raised to $3.00.

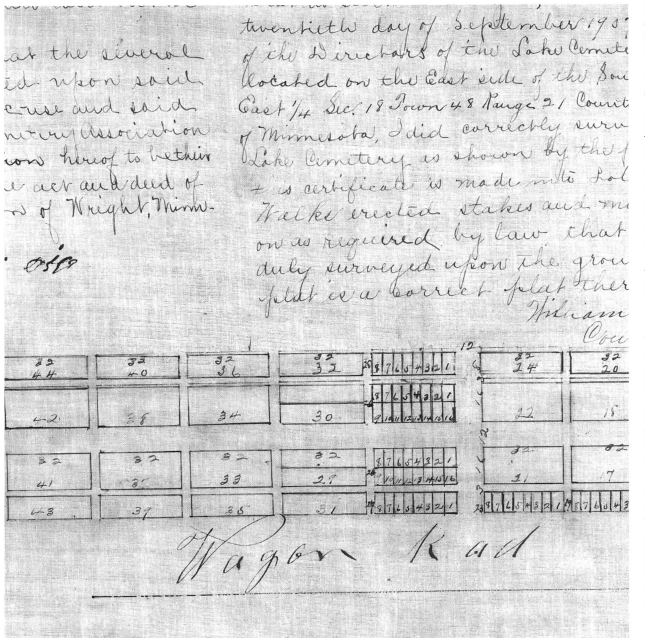

Portion of cemetery map showing groups of grave sites.

Decided to have each member bring 10 fence posts to the cemetery by 13 day of September, 1919. (This must have been a hardship for some, because of the 1918 fire destruction.)

Decided to meet at the cemetery the 13 day of April to give contract for fence repair to lowest bidder.

Decided to accept membership of Gust Makela in place of John Markanen, who gave his share to Makela.

Next meeting at the home of Gust Makela (I would guess a move made to make Makela feel welcome to the board— mw) 1st Monday of April, 1920.

Meeting Adjourned.

On January 5, 1920 Secretary received from Emil Walimaa $2.50 in payment of single grave.

WHY BECOME INVOLVED WITH THIS PLACE OF DEATH?

Because I see it as a place of life:

The most lively person around, Lenny Carlson, was working on the cemetery. I am interested in people, history and in posterity. I only knew the physical side of the cemetery, did not see the history of the board meetings until later. They added another dimension to the work.

The meeting reports are remarkably similar, until Lenny Carlson took over as Secretary in 1963. That was also the year that I became involved. Thirty-five years ago when I began working on the Lakeside cemetery I had a number of conceptions about the work.

1. I thought it would be a fairly short term piece of work. Measure and map the cemetery, make corner markers, straighten some stones. How long could that take. What about unmarked graves, unknown locations of known graves, keeping the map up to date, keeping graves located properly, reserving lots for people, or finding out individual and family wishes for plots, essentially telling the digger where to dig? The list goes on and on, and so does my work in the cemetery.

2. I thought it would be cut and dried, rather boring work. I didn't count on the friends and neighbors stopping by to tell me stories, share experiences, recount history of

the area. I didn't know death certificates could tell such stories: "summer complaint, gangrene, milk fever, lightning strike, old age." I am surprised, though I shouldn't be, at the intensely interesting conversations which happen when I keep appointments at the cemetery with people needing my help. Sons and daughters from this area have made interesting lives, are very knowledgeable, see life with much humor and philosophy. They come back from all over the state, country, and even the world with a wide range of experiences and viewpoints

3. I thought that people within the funeral industry would be difficult to relate to and work with.

What a surprise it was to realize the sensitive, down-to-earth jovial people who deal with death on a day-to-day basis. I appreciate that they are willing to share experiences for this book, and I recognize that they really are understanding, helpful, and positive people.

4. I didn't know that my personal outlook would change so much.

I thought of myself as quite mature at thirty; I thought my attitude toward life, death and faith was quite "jelled." So much has been given me in understanding what life is all about, how to accept death, and how faith can help in a person's daily walk. There is that word WALK again. When I was considering a name for this book, I had just had a heart flair-up. I had gone though the agony of not even being able to breathe to the bottom of my lungs, or walk over ten steps. Part of my recovery was accomplished through walking. I walked until I could take a deep breath, and walk two miles very fast. What a joy these things were to me! I had taken them for granted for nearly thirty years, and I suddenly realized how gifted we are by even the simple things in life. So for me the walk represented life. My walk took me through the neighborhood, and ended at Lakeside Cemetery. My goal in walking is to be able to visit that cemetery for some years, and yet find a place for my earthly remains there. My parents, grandmother, all maternal

aunts and uncles, most cousins are there, as well as two sisters. So while the cemetery is a short-term daily goal each day, I recognize that it will be, in one way, my long-term goal. I enjoy, learn from and want to share experiences from each journey.

Here is a poem I wrote for McGraw Hill book: Mid-America Walking Atlas. I called it my heritage walk, and wrote: "Walking is, among other positive things, a time to get in touch with ourselves, in body, mind, and soul. A walk which takes us back to the pathways followed by our hearty ancestors can open new paths to discovering more about ourselves and the people who came before us.

WALKING IS MY HERITAGE

Walking is my heritage
My route...one that has been well walked before me,
This unpaved narrow country lane
   has borne the weight
Of many moods and modes of errands.

The sweet pungent smoke
Which has curled up from the Walli sauna
Through dusk for nearly a hundred years
Puts me in touch with my world, now and then.

Yeasty, the smell of the earth
Is good as it rises after the rain, rich and real.
Birch, aspen, pine, maple and oak, Tamarack, sumac
Swamp grass, cattail and wild rose grow as if forever.

The Hunuri Ghost House
Home of the local Katilo,
Who handled births and medical needs
As she saw fit, flamboyant,
Not caring how others valued behavior.

Proud old white schoolhouse
Scene of a new language struggle, books and chalk,
funerals, parties, war projects, dances and talks
Whose large, long windows turn to gold
   in the setting sun.

Mother, were windows gold
as you sprightly hiked to dance or spelling bee?
Or hurried home with pails of berries,
   or turned the corner
In the flivver of your new suitor

Ted in his pickup
Saw more on this road than I hope to.
Numbered the trees,
Knew when one rabbit visited another.
Never before so still
In granite garden.
The end of his walk and mine.

Hunuri House Drawing

The wide gold band on my finger
Links me with his mother.
She traveled this road,
My grandmother, offering life and love and service,
Sharing her skills and her songs

Now I walk this road for my life.
What will it mean to others
that I've moved this gravel,
If ever so slightly in my daily journey?
Walking is my heritage.

    Margaret Olson Webster

17   A Glimpse of Lakeside's Future

A DIFFERENT DRUMMER

Whatever else may be said about the next generation, individuals will march to a very different drummer. Persons who react well to inevitable change in the drumbeat will best contribute and be rewarded in the future. Will Lakeside continue to be a living cemetery—or will it be a mark, a blip in history?

Which Future?

It would seem expedient to divide speculation of the "future" into two classifications: one on this side of death, one on this side of that great divide. I will relate only one story specifically from the other side of death.

BEEN THERE

"I died in 'eighty-seven," she said, as her bright blue eyes looked into mine. It was Memorial Day, 'ninety-four and we stood among the graves at Lakeside. She was not among those buried.

"I was mad—mad when I had to come back," she continued." I shut my eyes and turned my head when I came to on the kitchen floor. I pretended I was dead. But a voice, not from this world, had told me that it wasn't my time yet."

"You still had something to accomplish in this world?"

"I think the devil tries to have a hand in things."

"But you definitely had been in a good place? Can we understand at all?"

"No, I can't describe the peace and joy—I didn't want to lose it! Here we're just us—and there we are…" At this point she was at a loss for words, gesturing upward and outward with her hands and smiling a smile beyond description. "I was with God. I just didn't want to come back. I closed my eyes, but I had to stay here."

This is not the first personal account I've heard regarding the other side of death. The scientists may say what they want to about brain chemicals and hallucinations, but I am assured that I do not fear death, nor do I feel it is the end of the essence of what makes us what we are. I have respect for the remains of this earthly time, but I feel that the dust we are here has no significance in our next form of life. I do feel that we need to remember with some respect and try to learn from the lives of those proceeding us. We as a culture tend to become arrogant with our knowledge and fail to reach for wisdom. We can scientifically explain how many things happen—but do we know why they happen?

So I will continue, for as long as I am able, to measure, mark and trim, at the little cemetery, but most of all to listen and to learn, and to think once in a while about the transition made by those whose earthly remains are gathered in this granite garden.

IN GOD'S CARE

A GLIMPSE OF THE FUTURE ABOVE THE SOD

I remember vividly the night our first grandchild arrived. Many people of experience had commented to me that becoming a grandmother was a pinnacle of joys, one of the best experiences of this life. I took all of that with a grain of salt, thinking that maybe they had led sheltered lives. I had a family of four remarkable children, who gave me all the joy and satisfaction one woman could desire, or even expect. What could top this?

The call came early in the afternoon. A baby girl had been delivered to Kris and Paul in a Duluth hospital. My daughter-in-law had graciously offered to us the chance to be present at the delivery, but the memory of my own four arrivals was still too fresh in my mind for me to desire to witness the birth. However, we were in the car headed for Duluth in a matter of minutes after receiving the news of the birth of a baby girl, our first grandchild. Holding her in my arms brought back a flood of memories. I had not recalled how tiny (and she weighed well over eight pounds) and dependent a newborn is, how fragile and yet how strong. I loved her at that moment, and had not a clue as to how strong that bond might become.

I was surprised by the choice of a name for this precious new member of our family—Aurora. We stayed as long as we could, considering that the new family needed to rest and regroup. A warm glow stayed with Dan and me as we drove the sixty miles back to the "funny farm" (or home, to those who haven't heard our children speak of their origins). As we neared the farm we began to see one of the most spectacular displays of light and color in the sky that I have ever seen. The midnight sky danced with huge flashes of light, glints of neon green, red and blues added excitement to the display. The moving, pulsating light streaked over the entire sky, continuing for as long as we could watch it in the chill spring Minnesota night. At that moment I knew the name was meant to be. Full realization came later, as I realized the name in Finnish means Northern Flame. At this writing Aurora is four years old, and the light and joy she has brought into my life is immeasurable.

Aurora was three when she first became aware of Lakeside cemetery. We had been discussing my mother, her great grandmother Esther. She wanted to meet her relative. I explained only that the introduction was not possible, I was sorry. At a later time, Paul had apparently pointed out the cemetery and told Aurora that her great grandmother was there. It warmed my heart to hear that Aurora insisted that they stop at the cemetery. She was very disappointed when she could not visit or see her ancestor. Observing her as she grows I believe this might happen for her on some level. At three she insisted on spending much more time there than Paul had allowed, and she wanted a complete tour of the burial space. She has since asked me to bring her there, and has wanted a lengthy, very adult exploration of the cemetery.

Death is a subject I tried to avoid in discussions with Aurora, but she must have discussed it with her parents. One day, after a satisfying time together, she startled me, "Grandma, when you go to that place where you can't come back from I want to go with you."

I cleared the lump in my throat and attempted to tell her that she would have things to do and that she would live to do them long after I was gone. We talked of what she wanted to do, that she might have children of her own someday, and other potential aspects of her future. She enjoys hearing some of the stories told in this book, "even the adult ones," to quote her. This should not surprise me. One of the early

childhood educators spoke to me as she watched Aurora in a learning center. "She's been (on earth) before, she's just brushing up a little, here." Aurora went with her parents to visit my brother Bill and his wife Irene when their son had died. Irene told me later, "Aurora sure is interested in everything—she wanted to see every room, looked over everything really well—even wanted to tour the lawn outside. That's pretty unusual for a three-year-old!"

Later, when I told Aurora's mother about this exchange she laughed. "We had told her that we were going to see a family that had lost one of its men to a death," Kris remembered. "When we got home she looked disappointed, and complained, 'I looked all over that house, and didn't see a dead body anywhere.'" A second grandchild was on the way when I began to question my ability to love a second one with the depth and intensity I had for Aurora. I needn't have worried. Our grandson was born a charmer, a lover and an individual in his own right. He was named after my favorite uncle Ted, who had a great impact on my life, and the life of my four children. Sometimes I see the character similarities as uncanny. Ted was an avid fisherman. One of Teddy's first and most important words was fish. He loves to see fish in books, to play with fish toys, and especially to eat fish. He spots fish everywhere, and makes sure everyone else observes them also. Uncle Ted was the consummate outdoors man. One way to make the infant Teddy cry was to bring him in from outdoors. Ted was vitally interested in people. Teddy studies people, and shows much understanding of them at a year and a half. It will be interesting to see if further parallels develop. I know that he will be his own individual, but in this last year of the millennium I hear with interest the interesting new research on genetic make-up, DNA research and the discussion the impact of heredity versus environment. I do feel that Uncle Ted lives on in some ways.

LAKESIDE IS HOME TO THE GENERATIONS—OR NOT?

The records of Lakeside cemetery provide a very complete composite of the names and final resting place for most of those who lived in this area during the first half of the twentieth century. That would be the first and many of the second generation of immigrants. It is safe to say that all adults settling in this area before nineteen fifteen came from

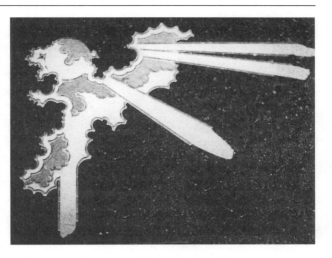

This stone design reflects hope and a new beginning even in death.

another country, some of whom brought children also born overseas. Over seventy adult immigrants from Finland lived in the township in nineteen fifteen. I can confirm that all but twelve of them are buried in an area cemetery. Our family is quite typical. Of the twenty members of the first and second generation, eighteen of twenty family members lived in the area and are buried at Lakeside. Only my grandfather, who left in grief, and one uncle by marriage and a game guide in Alaska, are not buried there. Many third-generation cousins are also buried there, and now some fourth-generation also (generations are calculated from immigration).

If community family life centered in the area through life and death for the first and second generations, this observation holds less true for the third and especially the fourth generation. Many third generation natives have moved and lived away, but return to the area for retirement, either in this world or in the cemetery. This out migration plus immigration to the area has had, and continues to have a profound impact on the profile and lifestyle of this community. The larger impact of media, television, electronic communication, and transportation, has worked to make the culture more homogenous with other populations. That fact is difficult for those who have roots in other backgrounds to realize. Rural, rather isolated populations have,

THEIR FUTURE IS PAST

My grandmother and her children from her first (L) and second (R) families, as a widow with five children plus oldest child Victor from first family. Her families all rest at Lakeside. Their futures in this realm have been determined, played out. First husband Leander (Feggerstrom) Peterson rests in Michigan where he died in a mine accident, second husband Hiskias (Moykke) Johnson is buried in Ohio, where he lived in a religious commune after the death of his wife. Mother Maria is surrounded by all of her children and many of her grandchildren (son Uno is under an oak tree about a mile away—see chapter one).

in the past, been correctly identified as unique, or "different." It is a disservice to rural people, in this new century, to paint them with the same outdated brush as was used in the previous century. Our school systems are more equal, rural occupations are being rapidly phased out, isolation is a thing of the past, but still the bias persists. It saddens me

in many ways to know that our township had, at one time, at least over sixty-five family farms, while one survives today (ironically Isak Walli's). Many of the stories I have related in this book may, at first glance, tend to reinforce these past differences and peculiarities. It is my belief that given a stable population, intimate and prolific knowledge of that

population in any city would yield as many interesting life and death stories.

Although rural naiveté and isolation may be a thing of the past, I cherish the truth that most people who choose to live close to the land have done so for a very significant reason. That is that they value the earth, water, and pure air. We look more directly to nature for sustenance, and therefore respect it and actively live within bounds of environmental preservation. We know where our food comes from and become troubled if control of that food seems to move into the hands of non-rural people, namely less than a handful of large corporations. The same holds true for soil, air, and water quality. Most of us hope that the same humanity which enabled us to solve the problems of living in the harsh conditions of the new frontier will persist to help us through the challenge of responsibly using, yet preserving our natural resources. We need to work together in cooperation, rather than allow power and control go to greedy, unscrupulous individuals or groups.

It is certain that the next generations will march to a different drummer. Information is distributed at an unbelievable pace, while expectations grow higher and higher for people wanting to be informed, with a high "standard of living." Some people may long for a time when life seemed to move at a slower, more stable pace. Some people may appreciate the rate at which we are now discovering solutions to our problems (health, social, communication). One of the most important questions could be: Are we, and will we in the future implement knowledge of sustainability? I know that all over this great country and world there are cemeteries full of people who, for the most part, lived and died to do their part to make this world a better place. I know this is true of those buried in Lakeside. I hope that we, who seem to have discovered so much information about our world, can continue to make decisions and take action based on intelligent concern for our environment. We owe that to future generations, as well as those past.

Social environment is also cause for consideration. The farms which existed in Lakeview township produced more than dairy, beef, and other crops. They produced several generations of people with great social conscience, outstanding work ethics, some ecological concern for the land they farmed, and sturdy values. One farm has survived in the township, ironically it is the farm which Isac Walli

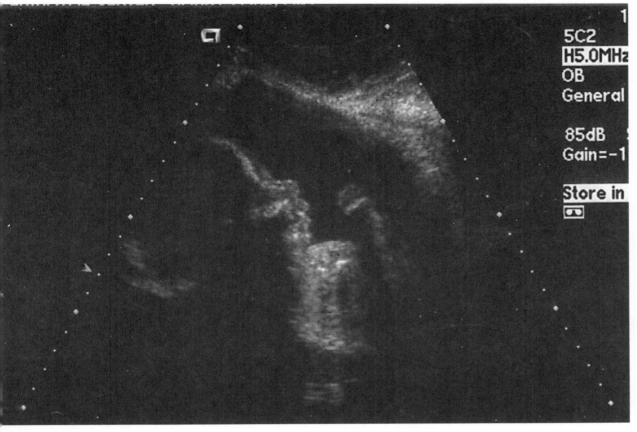

THE FUTURE

This pre-birth photo of a child of Jay and Penny Olson is in itself a sign of the future. Advances in technology, medicine, and other areas allow parents to see a bit of the future much earlier than previously possible. It is only one of the developments applied to this fifth generation baby which would have absolutely astounded first generation people. Wouldn't past (even our) generations have been amazed and amused to be able to look at the unborn child, see the chambers in its heart and the curve of its spine, the line of its nose? One must study with experience, with real live babies and a projection of educated speculation to make sense of the ultrasound image, to identify details and condition of the baby. So it is with projecting the future. We can make projections based on past experience, but the future will only be real when we hold it in our hand, see the reality of it.

homesteaded, now farmed by great grandson Tad. We have lost much sense of community and a way of life which contributed much to well-being in this part of the world. Big money interests (five or six big corporations) own most of the food production in this country. This will change us to the very core of our health, our financial stability, and our social structure. Will the township and wider area survive? Will political practice allow the township governing system survive? Not as we have known it. Change is a necessary part of life, but are sweeping changes out of our hands? What can each of us do? That is another book.

IS THE CUSTOM OF USING LAND TO BURY OUR DEAD DEAD ITSELF?

Some trend seems to be indicated in some locations the land has become too precious to use for burying the dead. Land usage policy, city planning, a system of land use, population planning which conscientiously looks at the future, does not give prime and immediate power to money and money mongers, might leave room enough for this ancient tradition of honoring those who have gone before us. Today there are many people who die, leaving instructions for ashes to be scattered. Many people believe that cemeteries are a thing of the past. I hope that our priority consideration would be of the living, especially the lower and middle classes. I hope that large corporate farms care for the land, so that food can be produced on viable soil. I hope that our demand for things and a style of life that uses water at an alarming rate leaves some water for our grandchildren. I hope our live bodies will adapt to the new quality of air. We all must learn to consider future generations in decisions and actions each of us take today. I also like the concept of remembering and honoring in cemeteries those who have gone before us.

LOOKING TO THE FUTURE IS ONLY HUMAN...
AND HUMAN ONLY

HUMAN VISION

Johan (John), Kajander dreamed that he would be an exceedingly rich and powerful gold mine owner, baron. He died from overexposure to the sun, after an overdose of alcohol caused him to go to sleep in his yard one hot, sunny day. He, his wife, his one child and son-in-law are all buried at Lakeside.

Bill Mattila had visions of flying. He made the dream come true. Consequently neighbors had nightmares of him crashing into their yards after "buzzing" buildings and silos, people on the ground or lake water, missing them by what seemed like inches. He had made an airstrip in a rare large flat field, and had built himself a hanger at his farmstead near the lake. He never had a crash!

Vivian Peterson's dream was to publish a book. The wonderful story teller had worked on the manuscript of a western. Experience living in Montana had given her an insight into the legends which could be told about the far west. We shall never read her work, as she lies now in Lakeside.

Cliff Olson dreamed of having a large, well-functioning acreage of cucumbers or rhubarb. It was never to be so, at least on the scale that he envisioned.

Gorden Bushnel fulfilled one dream—he became a Minnesota State Legislator. His attempt to legislate an additional road from Duluth to Fargo failed, so he took on the task of working daily, persistently to construct the road. He laboriously cut trees, cleared brush, leveled land. Traces of that work can still be detected, though all else that remains of his dream is the memory of it as it was featured on national television, and many more local news stories.

Most of the dreams and hopes of those buried in lakeside remain unknown to me, having died with the dreamer. It is very safe to say that the universally largest dream of area residents in the first, second, and most of third generation people was to live a peaceful, productive, healthy life. The dream was not so much to be indulgently rich, but to have enough to eat. It wasn't to be a land baron, but to own a bit of land. It wasn't to set a fashion standard, it was to be warm or cool enough, and not laughed at. It was not to laze in idleness, but to accomplish much through hard work. It was not to be extremely powerful, but to build a good community. It was not to have the constant care of an expensive doctor, but to be relatively healthy. It was not to form a dynasty, but to pass good values and in some cases the farm to one's children. It was not to be forced to fight wars constantly (as the Finnish were forced to do in their native land), but to be patriotic. It was not to separate themselve from the main culture of the United States, but to maintain their heritage. It was not to have doctorate degrees, but tha their children be well educated. Religious traditions varied but one thing was certain: They stood unmoved, and uncompromising. Fairly simple dreams.

As farms which made up a township fade, and are gone mostly as a result of the dreams of big business, area mean of livelihood, personal dreams, and population changes are occurring, and will continue to occur. What dreams wil these new generations have? Will they hold on to some o the old vision, or will they form their own "new world? Certainly it will be the vision of the people and how it fit into the immutable laws of nature which will determine th future of this, or any area in the world.

WORDS OF WISDOM NEVER PERISH,
THOUGH THE WISE MAN PASS AWAY
Kalevala: Runo #17, Line 25–26
Eino Friberg translation

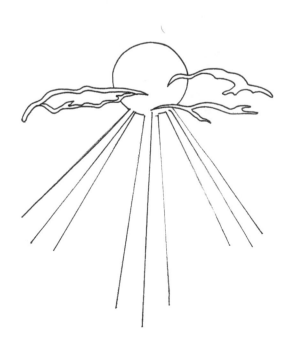

Photo Credits

Page	Title	Details	Photographer	Date
vi	Dance of Life	Family on Cole Lake	Martha Johnson	1945
vii	Death Registered	State of Minnesota form	Mn Department of Health	
viii	Ghost Forum	Cartoons	Margaret Olson Webster	2002
viii	Andrew's Fagen	Drama at McGregor School	Roland Olson	1983
1	The Dance of Life	Cole Lake People	Martha Johnson	1945
2	Cemetery Board Meets	Recreation of early board meeting by sons and grandsons	Andrew C. Webster	1999
3	Eternally Blooming	Artificial flowers at Lakeside	Margaret Olson Webster	1999
3	A Little Color	Grave site at Lakeside	Andrew Webster	1999
4-5	Air View Sixty-Two	Area of book action	Loma Peterson	1962
6	Lakeside Schoolhouse	Now used as a clubhouse	Andrew Webster	1994
7	In Remembrance			
8	Uncle Uno's Oak	Marking death at age thirteen, end of Long Lake	Margaret Olson Webster	1999
9	Fear Available	Montage from DULUTH NEWS TRIBUNE		
11	Granite Mass	Fort Snelling National Cemetery, St Paul Minnesota	Paul David Webster	1976
13	OOPS Cow in Trench		Esther Olson	1956
15	Maria Walli's Stone	Lakeside Cemetery grave marker	Andrew Webster	1999
17	Symbolic Life	Perry Webster with butterfly	Margaret Webster	1975
17	Mr. Snake's Funeral	Andrew, Perry Webster Junior Nelson	Margaret Webster	1976
18	Friends For Generations	Lauralee Peterson, M. Olson, A. Webster, Teddy Webster	Unknown/Margaret Olson Webster	
19	Horse Friend	Unknown	Unknown	Unknown
20	Cowboys	Long Lake children	Martha Johnson	
21	Long Lake Weekly	Cat family, dog	Johnson Children	
23	Children of Loss	Unknown	Unknown	Unknown
25	A Closer Look at Death	Esther Olson on crank phone.	Martha Johnson	1943
26	Two Generations of Partners	Isak and Marie; Jack and Sofija Walli	Unknown	
28	Annti's Funeral and Stone	At home, and Lakeside Cemetery	Unknown/Andrew Webster	1919/1999
31	Water, a Matter of Life and Death	Louma Lake (Websters)	Margaret Webster	1976
32	Peace of Water	Clifford Olson fishing	Martha Johnson	1942
32	Swimming	Friends and relatives swimming in Cole Lake	Martha Johnson	1943
33	Harvesting Ice	Peterson/Johnson brothers on Long Lake	Loma Peterson	1920
34	Aino	Actress Sara Wieditz	Kelly Photography-Moose Lake, Mn	1995
34	Vainamoinen	Actor Leonard Maki	Kelly Photography-Moose Lake, Mn	1995
37	Living Death and Death Living	Margaret Webster as Louhi, Mistress of the North	Kelly Photography-Moose Lake, Mn	1995
37	The Unknown Soldier	Memorial at Salo Township, Aitkin County	Margaret Webster	1999
38	Cannon Fodder (3)	Victor and George Peterson ready for action.	Unknown	1917
38	Mother and Two Sons	Victor Peterson, Maria Johnson, Ted Johnson	Unknown	1917
39	That's Monumental	Enough Said	Andrew Webster	
40	Another War Another Bro	Ted Johnson in France "Fisherman's Cot"	Unknown	1945
41	War News Clip	Uncle Ted	Duluth News Tribune	1945

Bibliography

1. OUR DIOCESAN CENTURY, Evans, Storch,Beck, Catholic Diocese of Duluth, 1989, Library of Congress 89–82571

2. DESCENDANTS OF MIKKO YLKANEN, Peterson, Gary, Self Published Family History, 1995

3. EUNUCHS FOR THE KINGDOM OF HEAVEN, Ranke-Heinemann, Penguin Books, 1990, L.CISBN O 14 01.6500 2

4. DULUTH NEWS TRIBUNE, Knight Ridder, Knight Ridder, 1999 October 23

5. KALEVALA, Eino Friberg Translation, Otava Publishing Co.Ltd, 1988, Finnish American Literature Society, Inc

6. AUTOMBA, Daniel Reed, Self Published, 1990

7. CORDUROY ROADS, Alma Lundeen, Self .Published, 1985, Republished 2000

I am also indebted to The Lakeside Cemetery Association, Lakeview Township Records, Long Lake Weekly, and a host of personal interviews.

OTHER FIRE REFERENCES

FIRES OF AUTUMN, Carlton County Historical Society, 1997

HISTORY STORIES, Kettle River, Automba, Kalevala Edwin E. Manni, Self Published, 1978

MEMORIES, T.J. Johnson, Self Published, 1976

FIRE COVERAGE, Moose Lake Gazette, 1918 Oct. 13–31

The Author

Margaret Olson Webster has served the University of Minnesota as a County Extension Agent, and as a classroom instructor. Junior and senior high school classroom teaching has, however, has been the most long-term aspect of her career. She has entered into many community activities in her lifetime home area in northern Minnesota. From Synod church leadership to 4H club leader, County Historical Society to charter member of ARTs (Advancement of Rural Talents), she has a wide-ranging record of community service which earned her a statewide Hubert Humphrey Leadership Award. Her play, THE AURORA AND THE RED MOON was performed at an national Finnfest. She has served as Lakeside cemetery sextant for over twenty-five years. The white-on-white bas relief panels which cover the walls of Bethany Lutheran Church in Cromwell have drawn regional attention. Her four adult children are the pride and joy of her busy life.